PEOPLE
NOT PATIENTS

TO

Helle, Paul, Steve and Martin
— the patient people

Peter Mittler

PEOPLE
NOT PATIENTS

Problems and Policies in Mental Handicap

Methuen & Co Ltd

First published in 1979 by Methuen & Co. Ltd
11 New Fetter Lane, London EC4P 4EE
Published in the USA by
Methuen & Co.
an associate company of Methuen, Inc.
733 Third Avenue, New York, NY 10017
© 1979 Peter Mittler

Typeset by Red Lion Setters
Printed in Great Britain by
The University Printing House, Cambridge

ISBN 0 416 72710 7 (hardbound)
ISBN 0 416 79450 5 (paperback)

British Library Cataloguing in Publication Data

Mittler, Peter Joseph
  People not patients.
  1. Mentally handicapped — Rehabilitation
  I. Title
  362.3   HV3004

ISBN 0-416-72710-7
ISBN 0-416-79450-5 Pbk

CONTENTS

Acknowledgements   vi

Preface   vii

1 From Rights to Resources   1

2 Defining Mental Handicap   19

3 Numbers   41

4 Early Help   57

5 Teaching Children   75

6 Leaving School   103

7 Teaching Adults   125

8 A Place To Live   152

9 Hospitals   175

10 Training Staff   199

References   221

Index   231

ACKNOWLEDGEMENTS

In writing this book, I have obviously been deeply influenced by my work with the National Development Group for the Mentally Handicapped and my ten years in the Hester Adrian Research Centre. But the book is essentially a personal statement and represents only my own views.

Among the many people who have helped me with comments I would like to thank Roger Blunden, Cliff Cunningham, David Felce, James Hogg, Bob Kedney, Mia Kellmer Pringle, Ken Leeming, Derek Legge, Alan Martindale, Brian Stratford, Stanley Segal, John Turner, Alan Tyne and Edward Whelan.

Very special thanks are due to Alyce Sandes for invaluable secretarial help.

Above all, I owe both thanks and apologies to my family who have supported me in writing this book and put up with many absences.

Manchester   Peter Mittler
September 1978

PREFACE

This book discusses what can be done by, with and for mentally handicapped people. It reports positive achievements of mentally handicapped people and the staff who work with them and it is based on the premise that a great deal more can be done if we apply what we already know.

The perspective from which the book is written is thus primarily educational; it emphasizes what can be done to help people to develop their skills and abilities, the kind of services which might be provided for them and how they can be helped to use the ordinary resources and services available to everyone else. But although the emphasis throughout is on helping mentally handicapped people to learn, the task calls not only for skilled teachers but for an educational approach in the widest sense, involving everyone who comes into contact with mentally handicapped people, whether they are full-time professional staff, families with a handicapped member or have relatively brief and superficial contacts.

This book is intended as a contribution to the attempt now being made on many sides to convey a sense of enthusiasm that much more can be done than was previously thought possible. But many people still believe that because mental handicap is an incurable condition, little or nothing can be done by way of teaching, and that enlightened care, and occupation, are the most that can be offered or afforded. Variations on this theme can be heard on many sides, unfortunately sometimes from people in positions of influence.

Decisions about the allocation of resources are nowadays largely made by people for whom mental handicap is only one of many competing priorities. Despite the fact that the Government has given the lead by repeatedly stressing the high priority which should be given to mental handicap services, decision-makers at local level have not always followed this lead, with the result that the quality and quantity of services vary greatly from one part of the country to another. The reasons for this are far from simple, but they undoubtedly include a serious lack of knowledge of what skilled staff can achieve, given resources and the support of ordinary people in the community.

Much also depends on those professional staff who come into only brief contact with mentally handicapped people but whose attitudes may exert an influence out of all proportion to their knowledge of modern developments. Included amongst these professionals are many doctors, health visitors, nurses, physiotherapists, speech therapists, occupational therapists, social workers, teachers, staffs of colleges of education, polytechnics and universities, and administrators of all kinds. Many of them may be aware in a general way of major changes in the field of mental handicap — publicity from the media and particularly from television has certainly helped to convey increasingly positive attitudes to what can be done — but they may still be uneasy and anxious about actually being with mentally handicapped people. One has only to watch a party of local or health authority members walking round a hospital or Adult Training Centre to realize that it is not always the mentally handicapped who are lacking in social skills. And no one who has listened to objections to a proposal for a hostel or group home can be complacent about public attitudes.

The problem is not only one of convincing influential professional colleagues and the general public but also one of helping people working full time in the field to bring their knowledge and skills up to date. The means must be found in the next few years of narrowing the gap between what we know and what we do. This is why staff training is the key to a better service, and why this book contains a number of suggestions for fresh approaches.

This book is therefore addressed not only to full-time practitioners (and this includes parents and families) but to the many people who come into only occasional contact with mentally handicapped people but whose attitudes may profoundly influence the quality of life they lead.

The book is written from several perspectives. The emphasis on learning and development will already be clear, though it should be stressed that this in no way undervalues the work of other disciplines. Furthermore, I have tried to show that if we take a broad view of education as everything which actively fosters growth and development, then it will be apparent that there is an educational component in the work of everyone who works with mentally handicapped people, whatever his training. This too is why parents should be helped to develop educational skills.

A second perspective comes from working in a university

research centre devoted largely to the study of learning and to attempts to develop and evaluate effective methods of teaching. Since its foundation in 1969, the Hester Adrian Research Centre has tried by various means to work closely with practitioners, to disseminate research knowledge and research attitudes to people working in the field and also to learn from them about the day-to-day problems of teaching mentally handicapped people. But however committed a research team may be to developing two-way communication with workers in the field, the obstacles to doing so effectively are substantial.

A third perspective comes from an opportunity to become involved in the development of mental handicap policies at government level through the National Development Group for the Mentally Handicapped (NDG). This Group was set up in 1975 by Barbara Castle, when she was Secretary of State for Social Services. Its terms of reference are to 'play an active role in the development of Departmental policy and the strategy for its implementation'. The Group is small and multidisciplinary, consisting of people with a known interest in mental handicap, many of whom however have wider responsibilities as well. The Group includes a parent (Alec Nutter), a consultant in mental handicap (Gerry Simon), a Director of Social Services (Malcolm Wren), an Area Nursing Officer (Bill Tamkin), an Area Administrator (Jim Cottam), an educationalist who is the head of a residential community (Stanley Segal), a social work officer (Alf Austin) and a member with experience of health and social service committees who is also Chairman of the Committee of Inquiry into Mental Handicap Nursing and Care (Peggy Jay). The Group is independent but has direct access to Ministers through its Chairman and works very closely with DHSS officials. The Group is complemented by a Development Team (directed by Gerry Simon, with three associate directors drawn from social work, nursing and educational administration), whose task it is to help field authorities to improve their services. The Group and Team thus represent yet another attempt to build bridges between theory and practice, between policy development on the one hand and service delivery on the other. The Group has published five pamphlets on various aspects of services — joint planning, services for children and for school leavers, short-term care and day services for adults — as well as a substantial report on hospitals. Although recommendations do not necessarily represent the official policy of the DHSS, the Secretary of State has encouraged local planning groups to use them as the basis for discussion, to implement those suggestions which seem to them 'of immediate relevance to their situation and to try them out as they think fit and without delay'. The pamphlets are also used by the Development Team in their visits to field authorities; the day services pamphlet is the subject of formal consultations at the time this book is going through the press.

But apart from its publications, the Group's work 'behind the scenes' has provided much food for thought about the evolution of public policy in general and about ways in which knowledge derived from research can influence policy. As a scientific adviser to DHSS, there have also been opportunities to try to understand the processes by which decisions are made about the determination of research strategies, to study the development of research programmes to meet agreed priorities and then to consider ways in which results might influence services and practitioners.

The aim of this book, then, is to consider how we can utilize what we know about mental handicap in order to provide better services. This is an ambitious aim, for a number of reasons. In the first place, it is difficult to secure agreement on what is 'known', because people will vary in the degree of confidence which they would place in any given piece of research. This is in the first instance a problem for the research worker who needs to be convinced that any conclusions drawn from research are reliable and valid. The degree of confidence which can be placed in research findings becomes a particularly important issue if the research has practical implications for the provision of services to clients.

Policy or services will only rarely be affected by a single piece of research, however well done or far reaching in its implications. Policy is usually influenced by a growing consensus from a variety of different studies, using a range of research techniques and involving the study of different populations. What is needed, therefore, is some means of establishing a communication system between research workers and policy makers; research trends in a given area need to be 'translated' and their possible implications for public policy set out, at least in the form of alternative courses of action which might be pursued. These might then be tried out and evaluated.

Policy makers will not wait passively for research workers to produce relevant information but will wish to stimulate and commission research in areas which they consider important. Recognition of the need for the establishment of a dialogue between research workers and government departments led to the Rothschild Report (*A Framework for Government Research and Development,* 1971). Although this report came under strong criticism from scientists, its main strength undoubtedly lay in its clear perception of the need to establish an effective system of communication between researchers and policy makers, not only for their mutual benefit but also for the sake of the general public to whom they are both ultimately accountable. This consideration is particularly relevant in the case of services for handicapped people who are not in a good position to express their own opinions on the value of what is being done for them.

Granted, then, the need to secure some measure of agreement on what we know about mental handicap, we are faced by a third problem; how do we translate what we know into services? Having duly reviewed, integrated and translated research, should scientists regard their work as finished and leave governments to accept or reject their findings or recommendations? Research workers who wish to see their ideas adopted may need to spend as much time and ingenuity in following their recommendations through to successful implementation as in pursuit of the actual research. This will not be acceptable to many workers whose main aim is to get on with the next piece of research. If this wish is to be respected, then the argument for some form of dissemination or translation machinery is strengthened. Too much material relating to mental handicap is already buried in learned journals and unpublished reports, inaccessible to all but the most persistent searcher. Some of this material may well be lacking in practical implications. Given that at least some research workers consider their work complete once it is committed to paper, it is going to fall to others to retrieve their conclusions from oblivion. But how many research workers are content to spend their time in this way?

A further problem concerns the mechanics of bridge building between research and practice. For example, there may be a general consensus derived from research findings that early education of the mentally handicapped is beneficial. Even assuming that the government of the day is not only persuaded of the wisdom of this policy, but also financially and administratively able to implement it by building schools and recruiting teachers, we are still left with the question of what is to go on inside the schools. What in fact are the children going to do? These are essentially questions of curriculum which can also be tackled by research and experiment. Governments are too easily satisfied with buildings; they reflect an obvious investment, and are assumed to be providing a service. But it is easier to erect buildings than to think about what is to go on inside them.

The task for the research worker is to ensure that research knowledge which has already been accumulated is made available to those planning and delivering services. He cannot expect planners and administrators to seek out the research literature on, say, the potential ability of adults to benefit from work or social training schemes; nor can architects design a 'purpose-built' training centre or school without detailed briefing on the educational aims and objectives of the staff. In fact, the two examples quoted imply a more radical commitment to the planning of services and curricula than most research workers have so far permitted themselves. It is more than a matter of merely passing on information; it involves the further step of being involved as a research worker in the planning and evaluation of services. The research worker must not only ensure that the services are designed in the light of the fullest utilization of existing knowledge but could go further than this by helping to evaluate the effectiveness of the intervention. His training should enable him to design an evaluation which is not only objective but which can be used by others as an ongoing system once the researcher himself is no longer involved. In this way, he will achieve one of the main aims of the research worker: to pass his skills to others through demonstrating that constant evaluation is an essential and integral part of any service that is provided. Research attitudes and methods are not the prerogative of the research worker alone but should be shared with all those involved in day-to-day work with clients. Research is far too important to be left to research workers.

1

FROM RIGHTS TO RESOURCES

There have been some fundamental changes in our knowledge of mental handicap in the last twenty years. Some kinds of handicap can be prevented altogether, others can be medically treated if they come to light early enough. We have also learned that mentally handicapped people are capable of learning to a far greater extent than we previously thought possible, provided they are given skilled help and time to learn. The limitations do not all lie with their inability to learn but with our inability to teach. Of course, there are limits to what can be achieved, but we can no longer confidently say what those limits are. We do know that the abilities of mentally handicapped people have been greatly underestimated and that we have only just begun to provide them with skilled and systematic teaching.

Although most mentally handicapped people begin life with severe limitations in their ability to learn from experience, this does not mean that they cannot be helped to do so. We now see that teaching is needed from the very beginning, and that education must be broader than that which is provided in school. It is a process which begins at birth, involves the family working in full partnership with professional staff and should continue after leaving school. Indeed, it is sometimes said that all who work with and for the mentally handicapped are educationalists, in the sense that the aim of all our services in this field is to help mentally handicapped people to learn and to develop new skills and abilities. All of them in their different ways are concerned with creating environments which will facilitate learning and development, even in the most profoundly handicapped.

Unfortunately, many people are unaware of these possibilities. The general public still has difficulty distinguishing between the mentally ill and the mentally handicapped — the word 'mental' hardly helps. It is widely assumed that mental handicap is largely a medical problem and that mentally handicapped people will all sooner or later need permanent hospital care. Even where the problem is seen as one of limited intellectual development rather than illness, people still have a very static view of the extent to which learning and development are possible. They assume that all the difficulties of mentally handicapped people can be attributed to low intelligence and that, because this in turn is often caused by brain damage, little or no progress can be expected.

It is also all too easy to talk about 'the' mentally handicapped as though they were a homogenous and easily identified group. In fact, they are composed of individuals who differ as much from one another as any other group and who all have individual needs, strengths and weaknesses. Professional staff now try to assess these needs in order to build a programme of training and activities designed to meet them.

Citizenship and civil rights

Mentally handicapped people are full citizens of local communities, with rights like everyone else. As citizens they have the right to education, the right to a place to live, the right to have work to do and the right to live their own lives. Although it is true that they are often not able to meet the responsibilities that go with rights, more could do so if they were given the opportunity. But these rights tend to be expressed in rather general terms. For example, the 1975 United Nations Declaration of the Rights of Disabled People states:

> Disabled persons have the inherent right to respect for human dignity. Whatever the origin, nature and seriousness of their handicaps and disabilities, they have the same fundamental rights of their fellow-citizens of the same age, which implies first and foremost the right to enjoy a decent life, as normal and full as possible (para.3).

The Declaration then lists specific rights, including:

(i) the same civil and political rights as others;
(ii) help to become as self-reliant as possible;
(iii) proper medical care and treatment;
(iv) education, training, rehabilitation and guidance;
(v) a decent level of living, including the right, according to individual abilities, to secure and retain employment;
(vi) a normal living environment, within a family where possible, including participation in all social, creative or recreational activities;
(vii) protection from exploitation, discrimination, abuse or degrading treatment.

The notion of civil rights is a useful one; it helps us to ask very concrete questions about the rights of access of mentally handicapped citizens to the ordinary resources and services of their local community.

This can be done at several levels. Families can be encouraged to ensure that their child has the right of access to all the resources and agencies of the community; no one should be debarred from health, education or other services on the ground of mental handicap alone. Anyone who tries to restrict right of access to a handicapped person needs to be able to justify his action, or he lays himself open to charges of discrimination. Indeed, it can be argued that mentally handicapped people should have the same rights of appeal against discriminatory procedures that have been won, rightly, by other groups. It is not only religion, sex or colour of skin that are discriminated against; perhaps we should add disability to the list.

We can also look at the way in which mentally handicapped people live, and ask whether the quality of life available to many of them is consistent with a civilized society, however impecunious that society may be. The drive to improve living conditions in our long-stay hospitals has been successful up to a point, but how many of us would want to live even in one of our above-average hospitals if we became mentally handicapped through severe brain injury? How many of us would accept such conditions for any of our relatives?

Advocacy

If we look across the Atlantic, we find an increasing use of the law courts on behalf of the mentally handicapped person. But legal cases have to be well chosen, since not even a judge's ruling can achieve the impossible. For example, courts in the USA have sometimes decreed that state hospitals be closed within months, but without making other provision for the residents who were to be discharged. Use of the law draws attention to unfair discrimination, and can also lay down the general principles indicating which services should be provided, but cannot of itself meet the needs of the people involved. Similarly, legislation within the USA and in Britain has established the principle of integrated education for handicapped children but has not yet been able to provide the full resources to ensure that their educational needs are met in ordinary schools or classes. It remains to be seen whether the educational needs of handicapped children will be met by the implementation of the 1976 Education Act, introduced as a political manoeuvre during the parliamentary debate on comprehensive education. Social justice and educational realities can be uneasy bedfellows.

Expressing accountability

The historical isolation of the mental handicap services has resulted
in a lack of accountability either to the clients served, their families,
the local community who support the service or the general public,
as represented by Parliament. Lines of accountability are also weak
in many other sectors of the service, partly due to the much vaunted
'clinical freedom' of doctors and the apparently unquestionable
'professional judgement' of teachers, social workers and other
staff.

Although the autonomy of professional staff clearly needs to be
respected, there is increasing recognition of the need for the mental
handicap services to be accountable. Successive governments are
pressing for certain minimum standards to be achieved and for
service targets to be reached by certain dates, and yet progress is
slow and uneven across the country. In 1969, following the publication of the Committee of Enquiry into Ely Hospital, Richard
Crossman set up, against considerable opposition, the Hospital
Advisory Service which visited all hospitals for the mentally handicapped and mentally ill and made detailed recommendations.
Many of these were accepted and implemented but regional variations remained and some hospitals were many years behind others.
In 1975 the Development Team for the Mentally Handicapped was
set up to help both health and social service authorities who sought
their advice to develop better services (see Development Team
(1978, 1979) for annual reports). Although the Team can only visit
by invitation, it has been asked to visit many areas and has been
able to have considerable impact on the planning and delivery of
better services particularly in relation to joint planning between
health and social service departments.

Accountability is being increasingly demanded not only by consumers but by professional staff themselves, many of whom would
welcome more professional guidance and some means of judging
the effectiveness of their work and comparing their own facilities
with those provided elsewhere.

An important initiative was taken by the National Society for
Mentally Handicapped Children (NSMHC) who have begun to
publish (1977) a series of short STAMINA documents incorporat-
ing minimum standards for specific services — e.g. Educationally
Subnormal-Severe (ESNS) schools and Adult Training (Social
Education) Centres. These documents are then used by local
branches to discuss the quality of service with staff and officers of
the authorities concerned. The Personal Social Services Council
have also published a document called *Residential Care Reviewed*

(1977). Although it makes only brief reference to the mentally handicapped, and discusses general principles and concrete practices of residential care, this document also recommends that every residential facility should provide a statement of its aims and objectives as well as a personal statement of objectives for each individual resident.

Accountability is expressed in North America and elsewhere by complex accreditation procedures. Accreditation is a form of programme or professional audit; as well as auditing the finance, you audit the work of the facility, its aims and objectives and the extent to which they are achieved. Attempts have also been made to link resource allocation to the extent to which the facility achieves its objectives.

Accreditation exercises involve meeting a wide range of objective criteria for residential and community facilities, agreed by all the leading government and professional organizations involved. The service objectives are highly specific — everything from the availability and use of a personal toothbrush to a written-down statement of treatment goals for each individual. Elaborate accreditation manuals are produced and agreed, and the facility is given ample time to go through the manual on its own, before it declares itself ready for the visit of an accreditation team. This team then stays in the facility for as long as is necessary to assure itself about each and every item in the manual (see Accreditation Council for Services for the Mentally Retarded (1978)).

How can accountability be improved in this country?

First, each treatment facility might write down an agreed statement of its aims and goals; one of these goals should include the specification of a programme of services for each individual person; there should also be a statement of how the effectiveness of the treatment programme is to be reviewed and evaluated.

Second, all treatment facilities could consider the preparation of an annual report; this report should contain detailed summaries of what has been achieved, the extent to which there has or has not been progress since the last report; and what it is hoped to achieve in the coming year. Such reports, if they are to be of any value, should be open documents; they should be sent to families, and shown or read to the clients themselves wherever possible; above all, they could be used as the basis for programme evaluation with the service providers and planners. Very few annual reports are published by hospitals, Adult Training Centres or residential hostels, though most special schools do prepare reports for meetings of their board of governors, which are then passed for action to the Education Committee and its officers.

Service targets

Another way of expressing accountability is to encourage much more open discussion of service targets. Although the field of mental handicap is one of the few that has service targets, people working in the field are distinctly hazy both about national targets and about the extent to which their own locality has achieved them.

The general principles of a good mental handicap service were very fully set out in the 1971 White Paper *Better Services for the Mentally Handicapped*. But the White Paper did not confine itself to statements of general intent, admirable though these were. It suggested targets and dates by which specific elements of the service could be provided for population units of 100,000 people. These planning targets are not equally relevant in every single part of the country but they have been found to be a fairly useful guide, and do at least provide minimal estimates of the kind of service that we need. Some of them, of course, have been called in question, particularly targets relating to the number of children who need to be in long-term hospital care. By suggesting specific targets for service delivery, the White Paper made it possible for each community to evaluate the extent to which its services have progressed, and how they compare with national targets. Parents of the mentally handicapped, citizens of the local community, Community Health Councils, voluntary organizations and other interested citizen groups are beginning to look very critically at the achievements of each community, and to enter into dialogue with authorities in order to discuss how services can be improved and targets attained.

But grand general aims have to be translated into specific objectives: it means little to talk about 'helping the mentally handicapped to achieve their maximum potential', 'to help them to adjust to the demands of the community' or even to 'help parents to adjust to having given birth to a handicapped child'. It is essential that we translate these global aspirations into specific objectives. Just as we need to identify what it is that the mentally handicapped person will be able to do that he was unable to do before, so we need to identify and define quite precisely what we mean by the planning terms that we use, to identify who is going to provide the service and which individual will be responsible for providing specific aspects of the service. We also need to know right at the outset how we are going to decide whether we have attained our objectives or not: in other words we need built-in evaluation — not as a luxury for research workers but as an essential tool in the process of accountability (Kushlick 1975).

Minimum standards — and more

The hospital minimum standards exercise launched in 1969 was a five-year plan for certain basic essentials, including the elimination of wards of over 50 adults and 30 children and the setting of specific objectives — at least 50 square feet of bed space and 48 square feet of day space per person; personal clothing and a locker; minimum ratios of medical, dental, nursing and domestic staff; the elimination of differential feeding costs between mentally ill and mentally handicapped residents; provision of adequate social work, psychological, occupational, speech therapy and chiropody services; training, recreational and play facilities for all residents; access to voluntary services; provision of staff training schemes and a number of other specific service targets.

The results of that exercise are published every year: most hospitals have attained some of these minimum standards, but there are still a number of hospitals that have met hardly any of these standards ten years later. And yet there are few signs of a dialogue or of local discussion about ways in which these hospitals can be helped even to reach the very basic minimum standards laid down nine years ago.

There are two main sources of information in this area. The first is the yearly Statistical and Research Series published by the DHSS, entitled *Facilities and Services of Mental Illness and Mental Handicap Hospitals in England and Wales* — these are always several years out-of-date but provide detailed information for each individual hospital on the number of residents without any form of occupation or training, and the reasons why; the numbers engaged in various forms of education and training in the different sectors of the hospital and figures for numbers and ratios of staff. These figures reflect alarming regional inequalities which are just as much a feature of the personal social services as they are of the NHS. The second source of information is local authority figures which are published by the DHSS and the Chartered Institute of Public Finance and Accountancy, and can also be deduced from the replies given to questions in the House of Commons.

These local variations show that however much the principles of the White Paper are accepted, their implementation depends on local priorities and local decisions. These in turn depend on an informed understanding of the needs of mentally handicapped people, of what can be achieved using knowledge and skills already available.

Principles

So what kind of services are we working for, what are the principles on which they are based, and what kind of targets have been set for the different local services?

The 1971 White Paper principles are worth quoting, since together with the service targets, they enable local people to evaluate the extent to which their own services reflect these principles as well as the national guidelines suggested for achieving specific service targets.

(i) A family with a handicapped member has the same needs for general social services as all other families. The family and the handicapped child or adult also need special additional help, which varies according to the severity of the handicap, whether there are associated physical handicaps or behaviour problems, the age of the handicapped person and his family situation.

(ii) Mentally handicapped children and adults should not be segregated unnecessarily from other people of similar age, or from the general life of the local community.

(iii) Full use should be made of available knowledge which can help to prevent mental handicap or to reduce the severity of its effects.

(iv) There should be a comprehensive initial assessment and periodic reassessment of the needs of each handicapped person and his family.

(v) Each handicapped person needs stimulation, social training and education and purposeful occupation or employment in order to develop to his maximum capacity and to exercise all the skills he acquires, however limited they may be.

(vi) Each handicapped person should live with his own family as long as this does not impose an undue burden on them or him, and he and his family should receive full advice and support. If he has to leave home for a foster home or hospital, temporarily or permanently, links with his own family should normally be maintained.

(vii) The range of services in every area should be such that the family can be sure that their handicapped member will be properly cared for when it becomes necessary for him to leave the family home.

(viii) When a handicapped person has to leave his family home, temporarily or permanently, the substitute home should be as homelike as possible, even if it is also a hospital. It should provide sympathetic and constant human relationships.

(ix) There should be proper co-ordination in the application of relevant professional skills for the benefit of the individual handicapped person and his family, and in the planning and administration of relevant services, whether or not these cross administrative frontiers.

(x) Local authority personal social services for the mentally handicapped should develop as an integral part of the services recently brought together under the Local Authority Services Act, 1970.

(xi) There should be close collaboration between these services and those provided by other local authority departments (e.g. child health services and education), and with general practitioners, hospitals and other services for the disabled.

(xii) Hospital services for the mentally handicapped should be easily accessible to the population they serve. They should be associated with other hospital services so that a full range of specialist skills is easily available when needed for assessment or treatment.

(xiii) Hospital and local authority services should be planned and operated in partnership; the Government's proposals for the re-organization of the National Health Service will encourage the closest co-operation.

(xiv) Voluntary service can make a contribution to the welfare of mentally handicapped people and their families at all stages of their lives and wherever they are living.

(xv) Understanding and help from friends and neighbours and from the community at large are needed to help the family to maintain a normal social life and to give the handicapped member as nearly normal a life as his handicap or handicaps permit (DHSS 1971).

Practices

Ordinary and special services

These general principles depend essentially on helping mentally handicapped people to take their place in society and to use the whole range of community services available to the general population. At the same time, it is recognized that these services have not always helped them adequately in the past and will not do so in the future unless provision is made for meeting additional special needs. It is a question of finding a balance between meeting needs through the ordinary resources of the community whilst at the same time ensuring that provision is also made for meeting those special needs which arise from the mentally handicapped person's disabilities. This calls for ordinary services staffed by people who have both the training and the attitudes to help mentally handicapped people to use community services, but who can call on more specialized back-up help from colleagues in the mental handicap services to meet additional needs which ordinary services cannot easily provide.

Finding the right balance between ordinary and special services is one of the tasks for the immediate future. In the past, services have tended to be specialized and segregated — hospitals, special schools and training centres and residential homes. But specialist staff were scarce and had to divide their time between working in their own agencies and working in the community. Because the specialists were often only able to provide a sporadic service, mentally handicapped people and their families were left unsupported and had to manage as best they could with occasional visits to specialists and as much support as they could get from community agencies such as general practitioners who lacked the knowledge to provide more detailed help.

Most people now agree that the dilemma must be resolved by bringing specialist services into the community and by providing better training for all staff who come into contact with disabled people, whether occasionally or regularly. A start has already been made, but there is a long way to go. For example, mental handicap specialists such as psychiatrists, psychologists and community nurses provide an advisory service both to families and to staff working in schools, hostels and Adult Training Centres. In contrast to rather artificial out-patient clinics in local hospitals, staff are tending to operate in more normal and natural settings, particularly in the home. The initial assessment of a handicapped child may be carried out in a hospital setting but the only true assessment of learning ability is in a setting where he needs to learn, just as the only true assessment of a child's ability to cope with the day-to-day demands of living and relating to people comes from observing him at home.

Going to the client rather than asking him to come to you is not only more natural but more instructive. A psychologist can devise an excellent training programme for a mother to teach her child either to dress himself or to become toilet-trained but the mother may be quite unable to carry out the programme in grossly over-crowded conditions or if the rest of her family is not in sympathy with what she is doing. Only an approach based on a knowledge of the family as a whole can hope to achieve results, no matter how good the training programme. This is why it is essential to include an experienced social worker as a full member of the team responsible for a particular mentally handicapped person.

Involving the family
One way of resolving the dilemma between ordinary and specialist services is through parental participation. By bringing elements of 'special' treatment into the home, we may well be able to achieve a balance that helps the child as well as the family.

The last ten years have seen a number of highly innovative schemes in which parents have been helped to become involved in depth and detail in working with their handicapped child and in helping him to reach the next stage of his development (Cunningham 1975). Parents have worked in close partnership with professionals in, for example, carrying out simple assessments which may consist of no more than a simple checklist of ordinary skills and behaviours. Parents' assessments of their own child generally agree closely with those carried out by 'trained' assessors but obviously have the advantage of being conducted in ordinary and natural surroundings, by those who know the child best. Assessments of this kind are very different from the classical intelligence test approach which depends on the tester eliciting behaviour from the child under fairly controlled and standardized conditions. It is particularly instructive to compare the results of assessments carried out in such artificial settings with those conducted in natural surroundings. Parents have also been helped to make more detailed observations of the child's behaviour — e.g. the frequency with which he does certain things, what precedes and succeeds these behaviours and what happens when certain changes are introduced into the environment. Above all, parents have been helped to work for specific goals, sometimes by relatively informal methods — e.g. the use of particular toys, games and activities — and sometimes by more systematic methods involving the use of specific behavioural techniques such as shaping, prompting, modelling and reward training. However, such parental participation is easier in the case of children than adults who may not welcome continued intense teaching by their parents.

Of course, not all parents are able or willing to be involved in working with their child in this way, but they are increasingly being given the opportunity to do so if they wish. There is little doubt that many parents have been deeply frustrated by the lack of such opportunities in the past; one result of this frustration is that some parents are willing to sacrifice a great deal of time and money to seek treatments abroad which allow them to provide specialized exercises or other forms of treatment for their child.

Planning joint services

Parents are also becoming more involved in the planning of services at local and national levels. This has been a slow development but there is now an increasing realization that parents have a special contribution to make as consumers. The former objection that parents are only interested in their own child or only in the age group of their own child has little validity; parents have shown that they are more than competent to distance themselves from their personal situation in considering the wider needs for local services and are often able to take a more dispassionate view than some officials who see the problem somewhat narrowly from the per-spective of specific departmental or professional loyalties, whether these are medical, educational or social.

One of the major obstacles to progress lies in the division of responsibility between various departments at local and national levels. This is the price to be paid for the principle that mentally handicapped people should use the existing range of community services. The alternative lies in a single co-ordinated specialized service specifically for the mentally handicapped. But whatever the benefits of a single service, it would probably be cut off to some degree from mainstream services for the rest of the population. This runs counter to the principle of helping mentally handicapped people to use community services so that they can eventually take their full place as local citizens.

A start has now been made in forging a framework within which collaboration can take place between the various service agencies and between all of these, the consumers and their representatives. But we are still far short of the kind of joint planning that is essential to an integrated and comprehensive local service for groups whose needs inconveniently cut across existing administra-tive boundaries (see NDG Pamphlet 1 (1976)).

Two of the more important bridges that have been built are the Joint Consultative Committees (JCCs) and the Joint Care Planning Teams (JCPTs). Both assume fairly close alignment between the geographical boundaries of the NHS and of Local Government — which was the aim of the 1974 reorganization. Although there are many places where the fit is far from perfect (especially in London), it should now be easier for health and local authorities to plan jointly for the needs of the people within given geographical and administrative boundaries. There are co-terminous boundaries within most of the counties between the Area Health Authorities (AHAs) and local authorities. This makes for more effective planning and collaboration between Social Services and Education Departments on the one hand and the AHA on the other. But much of the day-to-day decision making within the Social Services rests with Social Work Areas and Area Teams which cover population units of about 100,000 on average and which do not necessarily correspond to the post-1974 Health Districts. However, there is a need for co-ordination between the NHS districts and area social work teams. This is where the joint services are most needed.

The Joint Consultative Committee was established under NHS reorganization to advise AHAs and local authorities on matters of mutual interest; it is essentially an advisory body consisting of elected members, though officials also attend. The Joint Care Planning Teams (JCPTs) were only established in 1976, and consist largely of senior officers, reporting through the JCC to the main authorities who take the final responsibility for making decisions. The JCPTs replaced many of the existing Health Care Planning Teams which operated at the level of the health district and which were therefore frequently without adequate social services representation. The JCPT, being at area level, is better placed to develop an overall strategy for services, but is less close to local opinion than the HCPTs; these in turn were advised by Community Health Councils, again at district level.

The new arrangements for joint planning have been greatly helped by the provision of special funds known as joint financing. These are essentially NHS funds which can be made available to social services for projects which are 'in the interests of the NHS as well as the local authority, and can be expected to make a better contribution in terms of total care than if directly applied to health services' (Health Circular 77(17); Local Authority Circular 77 (10)).

Despite substantial administrative problems brought about by the restrictive conditions under which joint financing must be used, the scheme has brought about a considerable improvement in mental handicap services at a time when public spending was virtually at a standstill. 80 per cent of all the money made available was spent on mental handicap projects in the first year of operation (1976/7); the Government has now doubled the original amount of money in real terms to be made available for joint financing in the five-year period leading up to 1980, by which time the combined capital and revenue expenditure will total about £40 million at 1975 prices.

Joint financing can be used for any purpose which is in the

interests of the service as a whole, including any service which is likely to reduce the demand for long-term hospital admission. Services which have been funded out of joint funding include the building and staffing of hostels, group homes and short-term care arrangements; the appointment of social workers to mental handicap hospitals and other hospital services; building Adult Training Centres, particularly Special Care Units for the most severely handicapped, and the creation of co-ordinating posts to ensure that families obtain the services that are recommended by assessment and other teams. Joint funding can also be given to voluntary bodies such as the National Society for Mentally Handicapped Children and the Spastics Society; unfortunately joint funding cannot at this stage be provided for projects funded by education, housing or employment authorities.

Joint planning and the joint financing to pay for it is probably the most important single development for mental handicap services since the 1971 White Paper. Services are being made available for people living in the community, though much more slowly in some parts of the country than in others. There has been rather less improvement for people living in hospitals who no longer need hospital services. Although the number of hospital residents has been reduced, hospitals are still caring for many thousands of people who could be cared for outside if residential provision was available (Chapter 9).

Local authorities have understandably given priority to people already in the community rather than to those ready to leave hospital. Indeed, this priority was suggested in the White Paper. But perhaps the time has now come to try to include hospital residents in plans for community services. This might be done by joint assessment and review meetings between hospital and local authority staff in which an attempt might be made to identify the local authority that is in principle willing to take responsibility for each resident. Even if they do not have the facilities to discharge those responsibilities immediately, they will at least know the names and needs of those of their local citizens who are in hospital only because they need residential care and who are competent enough to be discharged to community facilities once these do become available.

Most people recognize that there are hospital residents who do not necessarily want to be discharged and for whom the hospital has become their home. But there are many others who can be helped to live and work in the community, who have responded well to hospital training and rehabilitation programmes but who have to remain in hospital because there is simply nowhere else for them to go. In some cases, they have lost all contact with the area from which they were originally admitted; in other cases, no local authority is willing to accept responsibility for them — these are the 'stateless people', whose needs cannot be met outside hospital for reasons that are almost entirely administrative. This problem is particularly severe in the Home Counties, where there are many mental handicap and mental illness hospitals which are geographically remote from their original catchment areas, filled by people who might be discharged to the area in which the hospital is situated if that area could be given additional resources to provide services for them. Counties such as Surrey and Hertfordshire are understandably reluctant to absorb many thousands of hospital residents who originated from outside their areas and for whom no additional funds are being provided. These are the lost citizens of this country who will undoubtedly spend the rest of their lives in hospital unless there is a political will to find an administrative solution to the problem of helping them to leave hospital.

The problem might be tackled, for example, by some form of ear-marked finance to reimburse local authorities for providing services to hospital residents (whether stateless or not); this might come out of joint financing, which would need to be supplemented for the purpose, or by ear-marking a part of the Rate Support Grant. Another possibility is for the Government to organize a central pool of resources which local authorities could use specifically for the purpose of providing services for discharged hospital residents. These suggestions are radical in so far as they violate the principle that nothing should ever be done for the first time, but a new approach to the problem is needed.

Targets for 1991

The 1971 White Paper suggested broad service targets to be achieved over a twenty-year period for the various components of the mental handicap services. These are summarized in *Table 1.1* in terms of targets per total population units of 100,000 people to be reached in stages by 1991. Figures indicating the approximate scale of provision in 1969, and in 1976/77 are also provided for comparison.

It is clear from this brief summary that the 1991 targets are much more likely to be achieved for some people than for others both nationally and locally. Thus, Adult Training Centre (ATC) places and hostel places for adults, remain reasonably on target; the number of children in long-term hospitals has gone down at a much faster rate than was foreseen in the White Paper, though very few

Table 1.1   *Plans and provisions of residential and day places 1969-91*

	1969 (provided)		1976/77 (provided)		White Paper target 1991	
	Total	per 100,000	total	per 100,000	total	per 100,000
Residential care (local authority, voluntary and private)						
Adult	4,200	9	11,276	24	28,900	60
Child	1,700	4	2,078	4	4,800	10
Total	5,900	13	13,354	28	33,700	70
Hospital						
Adult	52,100	113	44,696	96	26,500	55
Child	7,400	16	4,263	9	6,300	13
Total	59,500	129	48,959	105	32,800	68
Adult Training Centres	23,200	50	37,552	81	72,200	150

Source: Adapted from DHSS (1971, 1976a).

of these children were discharged to local authority residential accommodation. Residential accommodation for adults has increased from about 9 places per 100,000 in 1969 to about 24 places in 1977; if this rate is maintained it should be just fast enough to reach a target of 60 places by 1991.

But the number of hospital residents has been falling far too slowly to reach the target of 26,500 adult places. In fact, the slight fall in numbers is mainly due to deaths and to discharge of short-term admissions.

If these national figures present a mixed picture, those available for local provision show even more disturbing variation. For example, there were twenty-four local authorities in England that had no residential accommodation for mentally handicapped children in 1976 and a further twenty with less than 10 children's places in all. Eleven authorities had no adult residential provision and a further thirty-five had less than 10 places per 100,000. In contrast, provision for ATC places was rather less variable, all authorities providing one or more ATCs, some having got quite close to 1991 targets, though mainly as a result of local government boundary changes.

Both national and local figures could be much better known and more publicly debated. In particular, parent groups could arm themselves with the latest local figures and discuss the performance of their local area with officers of health and local authorities and with Community Health Councils.

The new Joint Care Planning Teams are an appropriate forum for reviewing local performance in relation to national targets; there may be genuine local reasons why national targets may not be relevant to a particular locality but they are a useful form of guidance, worked out with some care by the authors of the White Paper. They can at least be considered as basic minimum targets towards which local communities should be moving. They also represent one way in which local and health authorities can express accountability to the public and to their mentally handicapped citizens.

Central government has stated time and again that mentally handicapped people are a high priority group and have advocated not only the specific service targets set out in the White Paper but the relative degree of priority which might be given to different sectors of the service. The 1976 Consultative Document *Priorities for Health and Personal Social Services in England* (DHSS 1976a) suggested that the mentally handicapped were second in priority order, the first being the elderly; this priority was essentially confirmed in the authoritative five-year plan for Health and Personal Social Services (*The Way Forward* (DHSS, 1977)). This last document was difficult to interpret, since the figures for growth could not be related to the earlier document; furthermore, by referring to the difficulties of effecting a shift of resource from acute services to the 'new' priority groups, and by suggesting that health authorities would need to continue to provide services until local authorities were ready to make a bigger contribution, the Government provided ammunition to critics who argued that the White Paper policy was 'in shreds'.

Conclusions

Whatever the Government may say, decisions about the quantity and quality of mental handicap services are essentially made locally by Area Health Authorities and local authorities. Governments try to give guidance and leadership, and can provide independent advisory groups such as the National Development Group to develop policies and the Development Team to help authorities to improve their services. But in the last analysis the decisions made are by members and officials — that is by representatives of local communities. The decisions they make will be influenced by their attitudes to mentally handicapped people, and by their knowledge of what they can do, given skilled staff and the right facilities. This in turn depends upon them having access to the information which is already available on the achievements of mentally handicapped people and the staff who work with them.

This book aims to provide some of that information by discussing advances in our knowledge of what can be done by mentally handicapped people if they are given the chance to learn and to develop their skills and abilities. The Minister for the Disabled has expressed the hope that this country will have no second class citizens. If this hope is to be realized, and if we are to move from negative to positive discrimination, much more will need to be done to establish the rights of mentally handicapped people as citizens. And that includes their rights to resources.

2
DEFINING MENTAL HANDICAP

Every society intuitively arrives at a consensus of attitudes to handicapped people. Unfortunately, the heritage of one generation's attitudes have a survival value far beyond their useful life, as a visit to one of our older hospitals quickly demonstrates. The late Victorians were so haunted by the spectre of a declining national intelligence that they pursued a ruthless segregationist policy which led to many thousands of people being identified as mentally handicapped and incarcerated in asylums and colonies. The fact that their names were later changed to hospitals does not alter the fact that they were sited and designed to meet the needs of the time to segregate the handicapped from the rest of society and to do everything possible to prevent them from multiplying.

Not surprisingly, the criteria by which people were described as mentally handicapped were not only subjective but grossly unfair. As a result, many people were permanently institutionalized on the grounds of social incompetence or because of a mild transgression of the law, and were labelled as 'mentally deficient' on evidence of the most impressionistic kind. In certifying people as mentally handicapped, the emphasis until 1959 was placed on what they could not do, rather than on what they could do.*

To define mental handicap is at once easy and impossible. It is easy because some people are obviously so severely handicapped that it is immediately possible to recognize them. It is impossible because mental handicap merges imperceptibly into 'normality'.

It is obvious that societies will vary greatly both in their definitions of the milder grades of handicap, and in the provisions which they make. Once services are available, it becomes necessary to identify the people for whom they are intended. The more severely handicapped will come to notice more quickly, since they will have

---

*A study of the former 'Special Reports and Certificates' would reveal some curious examples to the historian of social attitudes. My personal favourite is: 'He cannot tell the difference between a bloater, a kipper and a herring'.

obvious pressing needs; in the case of more mildly affected individuals, nothing may be noticed until the child has been at school for some time, and is obviously not learning at the pace of his peers. Even then, it is not easy to decide whether special measures are needed, and what form they should take, or whether he will 'catch up' with other children given time and a little extra attention and encouragement.

These problems will be discussed in greater detail elsewhere (Chapter 5). At this point it is necessary to review attempts at definition which have been made both internationally and nationally. Emphasis will be placed on the present position; information on earlier practices will be given whenever a historical context is required to understand existing policies. Fuller accounts of earlier legislation are freely available in Hargrove (1965).

Criteria based on social competence

Underlying all attempts to define mental handicap is the problem of defining adaptation to the demands of the society in which the handicapped person is living. Mental handicap is not a single condition, nor is it a disease or illness in the generally accepted sense, though it may be caused by illness or disease. The criteria which any given society uses to decide whether someone is mentally handicapped will vary greatly from one time to another, and will also depend on what help it is able to offer to those it categorizes as handicapped. But it is probably true to say that most countries have used criteria based on social competence and ability to adapt to the demands of the society.

But how does one decide whether someone can or cannot adapt to the demands of society? This is obviously less difficult in respect of the most severely handicapped groups, though even here serious mistakes have been made in assuming that an apparently unresponsive and 'incompetent' person was mentally handicapped, when other factors, such as deafness or blindness may have been overlooked. Similarly, severe physical handicap such as certain forms of cerebral palsy may be mistaken for mental handicap because the affected person has such limited means of self-expression that it is easy to assume that he is 'unresponsive to his environment', incapable of speech, etc. It is not uncommon even today to encounter individuals who have been misdiagnosed in this way and been deprived of educational and other opportunities, but who respond dramatically to a planned programme of individual help suited to their needs.

The problem of misdiagnosis raises a second issue — that of the self-fulfilling prophecy. If an individual is regarded as severely mentally handicapped, placed in a hospital and treated in every way as mentally handicapped, then, unless he is very resilient and resourceful, he will for all practical purposes function at that level. The concept of the self-fulfilling prophecy thus applies not only to the probably small numbers who are misdiagnosed, but in a sense to all handicapped people on whom society makes only limited demands.

Research from many sources has suggested that people respond to the demands made on them; if we expect little or nothing from the handicapped, then that is all that we shall get. If we fail to provide schools that are properly equipped and staffed by trained specialist teachers, we must not be surprised if handicapped children fail to learn. If we design Adult Training Centres on the assumption that the handicapped need to be protected from the competitive pressures of the world of work, we should not be surprised if they fail to adapt to the demands of a system for which they have been inadequately prepared. If we provide segregated housing and leisure, and restrict opportunities for the fulfillment of social and sexual needs, we must not expect handicapped people always to behave according to the accepted conventions.

We may refer here to an educational parallel from the normal educational system. Longitudinal studies of some 5,000 children have suggested that children placed in lower streams of junior schools obtain poorer educational results than those placed in higher streams, even when the groups are equated for ability. Furthermore, the brightest children in the lower streams stood to lose most, and the dullest children in the higher streams gained most over a four-year period, suggesting that there is a differential effect of being placed in one or the other stream (Douglas 1964).

It would be an oversimplification to suggest that the principle here is 'you get out what you put in'. This would underestimate the contribution of the individual person who is more than just the product of environmental demands. On the other hand, the person with fewer resources is probably more vulnerable to the adverse effects of being placed in an inappropriately undemanding environment than a more able individual.

We can see, therefore, that decisions about social competence depend partly on the kind of demands made on the individual, and on whether he has in fact been given opportunities to develop such abilities as he has. If a mother never allows her child to play with other children on the grounds that they might not understand his special needs, he is likely to be socially handicapped as a direct result of being deprived of such experiences, with the result that he might be labelled as excessively shy or withdrawn when he finally does have to mix on terms of equality with other children at school. Similarly, a handicapped adult who is not allowed to use public transport or go shopping by his parents because he might 'get into difficulties' or be 'unable to talk to strangers' is more likely to be regarded as 'unable to adapt to the demands of society' than an equally handicapped person who has been encouraged by his family to be as independent as possible, even at some risk to himself, not to mention anxiety to his family.

Faced with a young person alleged to be mentally handicapped, one has not only to judge his existing social skills, but also whether his previous history and circumstances might have unduly deprived him of appropriate opportunities of acquiring them. Furthermore, a decision is also needed on whether he could make up for his lack of social competence by a special regime of training. If he can do this, then it is obviously unfair and unwise to label him as mentally handicapped on the basis of a social incompetence which might be alleviated without undue difficulty by a training programme.

Adults admitted to hospitals for the mentally handicapped are often more socially than intellectually handicapped, and much has been done to rehabilitate them by programmes of social education designed to help them acquire specific skills as well as confidence — for example, in shopping and handling money, simple sign reading, use of telephones, post office procedures, public transport and so on.

Problems of judging social competence are even more insoluble in the case of children who develop at different rates, not only because of differences in intelligence as such, but for a variety of reasons which are poorly understood. However, children tend to be assessed in relation to their educational attainments relative to other children; judgements of social competence are comparatively rarely invoked as a single determinant of mental handicap in children.

Criteria based on intellectual abilities

Intelligence constitutes an obvious criterion for judging the presence of mental handicap, but it is by no means an adequate or reliable criterion by itself, and the use of intelligence tests is beset by many problems. No one therefore advocates the use of intelligence tests as the *sole* measure of mental handicap; the present situation as far as Britain is concerned is that for a person to be described as mentally handicapped, 'subnormality of intelligence' must be shown to be present. In other words, even if a person is obviously socially incompetent (by whatever criteria are being adopted) it must be shown that he is *also* intellectually subnormal for a classification of subnormality to be legally valid. However, although this is the position as defined in the Mental Health Act of 1959, it is often disregarded in practice.

Moreover, the Mental Health Act itself is in process of revision, and there is argument about whether the mentally handicapped should not be excluded from a revised Act.

At first sight, intellectual assessment seems to offer a procedure that is both more fair and more objective than decisions based on social competence alone. Intelligence testing has a long history, its procedures have been scientifically investigated since the turn of the century, and an enormous amount of information is available on the performance of children and adults of all ages on a variety of different tests and procedures. Tests have been standardized on many thousands of subjects, and elaborate precautions taken to ensure that the people tested constituted a representative sample of the general population. Because it is possible to compare the score obtained by any single individual with that recorded by a large number of comparable people of similar age, any given score can be expressed in such a way as to indicate its probable frequency in relation to the general population.*

Despite the massive research on the use of intelligence tests with both normal and handicapped people, most psychologists are now well aware of the limitations of placing too much emphasis on an IQ score in judging the presence or extent of mental handicap.

It is important to stress that the IQ is in no sense a 'magic number'. Unfortunately, it has been credited with a degree of psychological significance out of all proportion either to its scientific status or to its relevance to the practical problems of normal or handicapped individuals. Over the years it has acquired an extraordinary mystique by a process which is understandable, though regrettable. Due to its previous importance in the selection of children for secondary education, the general public at first became morbidly interested in the IQ scores of their children; some parents began to buy 'IQ crammers' in order to prepare and coach their

---

*Thus, one child's score may be so low that only one child in every hundred would be expected to score at that level, or below. We then say that his percentile score is 1. At the other end of the scale, a score may be so high that it is likely to be equalled or exceeded by only one child in a hundred; his percentile score is 99. If the percentile score is 50, this means that half the population would score higher and the other half lower than a person scoring at this level. Similarly, a percentile score of 10 means that 90 people out of every 100 would score at or above this level. (See Clark (1974) and Mittler (1973) for more detailed treatment of measurement problems.)

children for the tests that were held to determine their educational future. But it soon became clear from research studies that while practice on tests might help to make the items more familiar and help the child to be less anxious, his IQ score was only marginally affected by such practice. Even systematic coaching in the strategy of tackling the questions only resulted in temporary rises in scores. Eventually, the public's hostility to the whole selection machinery for 11-year-olds was focused on the use of intelligence tests, which became discredited, despite a change of name to 'verbal reasoning tests'. We might add that whatever the imperfections of the selection system on social and educational grounds, the tests were reasonably effective in selecting children for grammar school education — that is, in doing the job which was set them under the prevailing system of selection (Vernon 1957).

The use of tests in special education has taken a number of forms. In the first place, tests were used for many years in deciding whether a child was 'educable' at all. An IQ between 50 and 55 was widely used as the cut-off point below which children were declared 'ineducable' (before 1959) or as 'unsuitable for education in school' (between 1959 and 1971). Not surprisingly, following the eleven plus precedent the opprobrium that fell on the whole machinery of deciding whether children were 'ineducable' or not was concentrated largely on the intelligence test. Once again, intelligence tests were being used to segregate children into different streams — with the difference that the tests were on this occasion being used to exclude the child from the mainstream of education altogether. To add insult to injury, the tests were often administered in hospitals or clinic settings unfamiliar to the child by a tester previously unknown to the child, who in many cases was not a qualified psychologist but a medical officer with only two or three weeks formal training in testing.

These procedures illustrate the use of tests for administrative purposes — in this instance to decide whether the child should be educated in one type of 'school' or another. In no sense could they be used to help the teacher to carry out a detailed study of the child's various cognitive strengths and weaknesses with a view to planning a programme of education suited to his particular needs. Indeed, it is the irrelevance of most intelligence tests to teaching rather than their unreliability as selection instruments which has made them increasingly unpopular with psychologists themselves.

Intelligence tests are used somewhat differently in selecting children for special schools for mildly educationally subnormal children (ESNM). If a child in a normal primary school is failing to learn adequately, decisions about special educational treatment, either in an ESNM school or class attached to an ordinary school, tend to be made principally by reference to the extent of his *learning* difficulties compared to those of his peers. Thus, if his educational attainments (measured in terms of reading age, arithmetic age, etc.) are less than those of children who are 20 per cent younger, tests are carried out by a psychologist. In many cases it is then found that the child also scores relatively badly on an intelligence test. The IQ, however, is not necessarily the main instrument of selection for an ESNM school, although practices undoubtedly vary in different parts of the country. In the past, children in ESN schools tended to have IQs below 70, but for the last ten to fifteen years the *average* IQ of children in ESN schools has been in the low 70s, and a large proportion have IQs above 70 (Williams and Gruber 1967). It is quite feasible and within the spirit of the legislation to suggest special educational treatment for, say, a child of 10 with a reading age of under six, even if his IQ is within the average range. This rarely happens in practice, but it is important to realize that the IQ should not be the main determinant of placement in an ESNM school.

Intelligence tests can be legitimately criticized on the grounds that they are in many ways unsuitable for children from different cultural and linguistic backgrounds, but it is the child's failure to *learn* in the ordinary school (for whatever reason) that raises the need for special measures in the first place.

The use of intelligence tests in general, and in the field of mental handicap in particular, has both strengths and weaknesses. Its strengths derive from the objectivity of the procedures, and from the fact that they enable fairly accurate comparisons to be made between the person being assessed and a representative sample of the population, comparable to him in age and general background. The IQ, though no magic number, does provide a measure of the rate or speed of intellectual development in comparison with others, up to the time of the test. Moreover, the tests are of known reliability and validity; they are reliable in so far as they provide a reasonably consistent set of scores, and valid in so far as there is good evidence that, within certain limitations, they measure what they purport to measure. Properly chosen and interpreted tests are also valuable in so far as they can help to pinpoint specific areas of strength and weakness and suggest special programmes of remedial treatment.

The main weaknesses of intelligence tests lie partly in the procedures themselves and partly in the way in which they have been used. Taking the external weaknesses first, the main problem has been due to the use of tests for predictive purposes. It has been assumed, not without some supporting evidence, that because the IQ does not vary greatly over the years, an IQ score obtained at a particular point in time can be used to predict the individual's future development, and therefore provide some 'scientific' justification for treating him as mentally handicapped. People have therefore been placed in special schools or hospitals, or in many cases deprived of appropriate education at all, at least partly on the basis of IQ scores. Others have lost opportunities for employment and other civil rights.

This is more likely to happen if the individual is thought to be severely subnormal, within the meaning of the 1959 Mental Health Act. Injustices may arise in the many borderline cases where the person concerned might be regarded as either severely subnormal or as mildly subnormal (IQ around 50 to 60). These decisions are not easy to make, and an IQ result might therefore be crucial in determining what a person can or cannot do in society and in law. The use of the IQ as a predictor of future development is a technical question of some complexity. A comprehensive review of the evidence and issues will be found in Clarke and Clarke (1976); see also Clarke (1978). At this point we should draw attention to the important distinction between the results of research findings on large numbers of people and the strong possibility that any individual handicapped person will provide an exception to a rule that holds for many but by no means all. From a statistical point of view, it is unlikely that a person with an IQ of 25 will later turn out to have an IQ of 65, or that an IQ of 65 will later rise to an IQ of 100.

Nevertheless, it cannot be too strongly emphasized that such exceptions do occur, perhaps more frequently than we think. There is a growing body of evidence both on individuals and on groups showing substantial IQ increments over a period of years. Many of the studies showing such increments claim that they are related to particular types of treatment, such as removal from adverse to more benign environments, the introduction of better child care or management practices, including higher staff ratio, the introduction of special educational provision and so on.

Two points should be made at this stage. In the first place, such studies do not yet provide enough evidence to discredit the IQ, though they do justify great caution in using IQ as a predictor for any given individual. Second, it should be emphasized that what really matters is not the prediction from one IQ to another IQ at a later point in time, but whether the IQ tells us anything important about *behaviour*. This raises the whole issue of the relevance of the IQ as a predictor of what a handicapped person can do, and what he can learn.

As an example of the insensitivity of the IQ, we can consider Jim and Bill, both with IQs of 70. Let us suppose that Jim has never been to a special school, although he was regarded as a slow learner, and needed extra help from the teachers. Nevertheless, he attracted no special attention at school and was not thought to require any special help from the statutory or voluntary services. After leaving school, he had little difficulty in obtaining and keeping a job. His subsequent life was unremarkable, and not noticeably different from that of his contemporaries, except perhaps that at first he found it a little difficult to learn a new skill.

Bill, also with an IQ of 70, came to notice in his first two years at school on account of his failure to learn, his difficult, aggressive behaviour and inability to adapt to the work or social life of the class or the school as a whole. He was soon sent to a special ESN school at the age of 7, but even there, despite the smaller classes, the less-demanding curriculum and a great deal of individual help, he learned little and left school at 16 barely able to read at a six-year level, and virtually innumerate. Not surprisingly, his behaviour difficulties, now exacerbated by a stormy adolescence in which he was continually at odds with his family, made him unpopular both with his fellow pupils and the staff of the school. Every effort was nevertheless made to help him both through individual attention from the staff, and also by enlisting the help of social workers and psychologists. On leaving school, he was sacked from five jobs in as many months, and became involved with three other boys in an attempt to break into a post office at night, though he was the only one to be caught by the police. He was remanded for medical reports which described him as 'borderline subnormal with psychopathic tendencies', recommending that he be placed on probation so that he could form a 'stable relationship with an older man'. However, he failed to keep appointments, and was later charged by the police for trying to steal a car, and resisting arrest. He was then seen by a consultant psychiatrist who reluctantly agreed to admit him to a subnormality hospital 'for observation and training'. He objected strongly to the routine of the hospital, and could only with difficulty be persuaded to attend the hospital's sheltered workshop where he was given intensive work and social training. He absconded repeatedly from the hospital, and since he was a voluntary patient, it was his parents who brought him back, insisting that the hospital should deal with his tempers and his attitudes to work. Despite intensive efforts to train and rehabilitate him back into the community, Bill remained in hospital until his mid-twenties, when he was eventually discharged by small degrees to work in a small family business. He remained virtually illiterate, though his behaviour became calmer and he kept out of the hands of the police.

The contrasts between Jim and Bill could be repeated in many case histories of people with the same IQ but with totally different histories. Even when the problems are not further complicated by totally different personalities or behaviour difficulties, two children of the same age and IQ, coming from similar backgrounds (perhaps even from the same family) may respond quite differently to the same learning situation. Experts can rarely explain why this should be, and tend to refer vaguely to 'individual differences'.

We took an IQ of 70 as a convenient illustration for the two case histories because this is conventionally regarded as the borderline between subnormality and 'normality'. But it is obvious that many people with IQs lower than 70 manage reasonably well and do not require special help, whereas many others with IQs considerably higher than this experience serious difficulties in learning and living.*

The discussion on the relevance of intelligence testing has so far concentrated on the expectations which are placed on the tests by others, and not always by the users themselves. For reasons which we can only guess at, people have come to expect more of IQ tests than is now seen to be scientifically acceptable or valid. Current thinking about the use of such tests in handicap is much more guarded than it would have been twenty years ago, mainly because of the uncertain nature of the relationship between test results and the individual's actual behaviour, particularly at the borderline between mental handicap and normality, where the IQ may be a relatively unimportant and trivial piece of information, compared to other variables which will contribute more powerfully to the possibility of living in and adjusting to the demands of the community.

A second reason for a certain loss of confidence in tests is that we now have more evidence that a person's performance both on intelligence tests and in social situations generally is greatly affected by his opportunities for gaining experiences. If he has been deprived of opportunities for learning and development, and if he lacks the experiences that are essential to intellectual and social

*The insensitivity of the IQ is also illustrated at high levels of intelligence. The rare person with an IQ of 160 is not necessarily any better off than someone with an IQ of 140, but perhaps both are likely to be more successful in life than a third person with an IQ of 120, though one has to add a cautionary 'other things being equal'. This is because at all levels of intelligence, but perhaps especially at the extremes, other factors are of equal or greater importance, and interact with intelligence in ways that we have hardly begun to study or understand. The obvious 'other factors' include personality, motivation and drive and, of course, opportunity and sheer luck.

development in the widest sense, it is impossible to judge how he will respond to an appropriate regime of treatment which provides him with learning experiences designed to suit his particular needs.

In addition to the unrealistic expectations which have been placed on tests, it is also important to be aware of their technical limitations in general and for subnormality in particular. These will not be discussed in detail here; fuller discussions are available, particularly in Clark (1974). But it is important to be aware of the kind of questions that need to be asked when test information is being used in determining whether a person is going to be regarded as mentally handicapped, and what kind of help is to be provided for him.

In the first place, it is important to establish which of the many tests is being quoted. A disembodied IQ without reference to the name of the test is valueless, and should never be allowed to appear on any official documents. This is because different tests are constructed in different ways, and an IQ of 60 in one test may not mean the same thing as an IQ of 60 on a different test.

The two main individually used tests are first, the Revised Stanford Binet, sometimes known as the Terman Merrill (hopefully in the 1960 revision), which should not be used on adults, unless they are very severely handicapped, and second, one of the Wechsler scales — either one of the children's scales, the Wechsler Intelligence Scale for Children (WISC) or the Wechsler Preschool and Primary Scales (WPPSI), or the main adult scale which must be used at sixteen plus, the Wechsler Adult Intelligence Scale (WAIS). The Wechsler scales yield separate IQs for verbal and performance items, as well as a composite of the two scales known as the Full Scale IQ. This is designed to overcome the verbal bias of the Stanford Binet, and to allow separate estimates of verbal and non-verbal abilities to be made. Many other tests are also used, so that it is important to know the characteristics and limitations of the test before quoting any results derived from it.

A second consideration is one of reliability. The reliability of a psychological test is measured in a number of different ways, some concerned with the extent to which individual items contribute to the overall score, and others concerned with test-retest reliability of the test as a whole. This is obviously crucial, since a test must give similar results when administered twice over a short period to the same subjects. Similarly, two groups of subjects of the same age and from similar backgrounds should not differ markedly from each other. All published tests contain details of reliability which must be consulted before any test interpretations can be made. It is not always appreciated that even with a very high level of reliability (expressed in a correlation coefficient of 0.90), the statistical effect of errors of measurement is such that one third of a group of children all scoring an IQ of 100 on a standard test would be likely to score at a level of 107 or more on a retest, and another third would score at a level of 93 or below. The dangers of excessively narrow adherence to IQ measurement is illustrated by the estimate that a variation of as little as 5 IQ points from 70 to 75 would increase the overall prevalence of mental handicap approximately twofold (Begab 1977).

A third point of crucial importance is the date of the test — a vital piece of information which is often omitted from documents. Its importance derives not only from the fact that decisions taken at one point in time should not be based on test performance obtained at an earlier time, but also because intellectual development is a continuing process; substantial changes may have taken place in the individual as a result of special educational treatment or training, of being removed from an adverse environment which masked his true ability or at least had prevented proper development at the time of the earlier test, and also because of sheer maturation. Inspection of records in hospitals often shows that no tests have been given to the individual for a very long time (sometimes no tests are recorded at all). In any event, it is scientifically invalid and probably ethically unjustified to continue to use or quote test results that are many years out of date. Finally, it is usually worth establishing whether the test was carried out by an appropriately qualified psychologist, and where it took place. It is easier to have faith in a test result if one knows that the tester was already known to the subject, and that it took place in a reasonably familiar environment.

Classification systems

Having discussed both social and intellectual criteria for defining mental handicap in general terms, we must now examine some of the main classification systems in current use. But before we can begin to consider the various attempts which have been made to grade the condition, we shall have to deal with the problem of terminology.

Although we have mainly used the term mental handicap up to this point, it is obvious that a number of other general terms are in widespread use both in Britain and elsewhere. Among the most common terms are 'mental retardation' (mainly in the USA), 'mental deficiency' (now obsolete in England) and 'mental subnormality' (which includes subnormality and severe subnormality, as defined by the Mental Health Act of 1959). 'Developmental disability' is increasingly used in North America. The Department of Health and Social Security now favours mental handicap and severe mental handicap to denote mild and severe subnormality, but mental handicap is frequently used as a generic term for both groups combined. Some guidance on terminology is overdue for professionals and public alike. Despite many campaigns of public education and many appeals, the distinction between mental handicap and mental illness is far from clear to many.

Two general definitions and classification systems will be discussed here — from the Mental Health Act, and from the American Association for Mental Deficiency.

The Mental Health Act (1959)

The Mental Health Act, based largely though not entirely on the *Report of the Royal Commission on the Law Relating to Mental Illness and Mental Deficiency* (1959) defined mental subnormality in general terms as a state of 'arrested or incomplete development of mind'. Two sub-categories were identified, as follows:

(a) *severe subnormality*: 'a state of arrested or incomplete development of mind which includes subnormality of intelligence and is of such a nature or degree that the patient is incapable of living an independent life or of guarding himself against serious exploitation, or will be so incapable when of an age to do so'.
(b) *subnormality*: 'a state of arrested or incomplete development of mind (not amounting to severe subnormality) which includes subnormality of intelligence and is of a nature of degree which requires or is susceptible to medical treatment or other special care or training of the patient'.

Although the Mental Health Act is soon to be revised, these definitions still constitute current legal practice in England and Wales (Scottish practice and terminology are different).

One notable advance of the 1959 legislation lies in the phrase *'including subnormality of intelligence'*. This was adopted because it was realized that 'mind' could not be properly defined, and that under the previous Mental Deficiency Acts of 1913 and 1927 it was quite legal to interpret mental development without any reference to intellectual development or to intelligence test scores. Indeed, most of the witnesses to the Royal Commission argued that the previous criterion based on social competence should be retained. For example, the Royal Medico-Psychological Association (now reconstituted as the Royal College of Psychiatrists) stated in its evidence that 'the undeveloped mind may be manifested chiefly by failure to attain normal control of the emotions or to achieve the qualities needed for normal social behaviour'. Similarly, the Board of Control whose job it was to supervise the workings of the previous Mental Deficiency Acts in the interests of patients, reported as follows: 'We regard the present definitions as enabling medical practitioners to certify mentally defective patients on the grounds that they have .characteristics from early youth which make them anti-social, although their intelligence might be quite normal' (quoted by A.M. Clarke 1974).

The results of this situation may be imagined, and will be remembered by all who worked within the previous legislation. Indeed, the results are still all too apparent in the many people still living in hospitals who were detained under the old legislation not because they were of low intelligence but because of social or emotional difficulties which were attributed to 'incomplete development of mind'. (The difficulties involved in the rehabilitation of these people will be discussed in Chapter 9; at this point we should note that their presence in hospitals is directly related to the practice of adopting a comprehensive definition of 'mind'.) It is against this background that the British Psychological Society argued strongly for the adoption of a criterion related to intelligence, on the grounds that subnormality of intelligence should be shown to be present if a person was to be classified as mentally subnormal, and perhaps deprived of his liberty and civil rights.

This, however, raised the problem of what is meant by subnormality of intelligence. A BPS working party addressed itself to this problem (British Psychological Society 1963, 1966; Castell and Mittler 1965). After surveying admissions to a sample of hospitals in 1961 and 1962, and finding that many people were still being labelled as subnormal or severely subnormal without reference to their tested intelligence, it recommended the adoption of IQ classifications which would conform more closely to international practice. In defining subnormality of intelligence, it was suggested that the *upper* limit of subnormality should be IQ 70, and that for severe subnormality IQ 55. (These figures presuppose the use of a test where the mean is 100, and the standard deviation is 15, e.g. the Wechsler scales.). Another way of expressing the same recommendation would be in terms of standard deviation (SD) units. An IQ of 70 corresponds to a distance of two SDs from the mean, one of 55 represents three SDs from the mean. If these recommendations were strictly followed, the severely subnormal (SSN) would be those with IQs below 55, and the subnormal (SN) those with IQs between 55 and 70. No one with an IQ of over 70 should really be called subnormal, though the need for a 'borderline subnormal' classification was recognized (somewhere in the range IQ 70-80).

One of the difficulties of implementing such recommendations is that many people are still not properly tested, with the result that decisions about grades of handicap (which are important in affecting the person's civil rights) are still necessarily made on the grounds of social competence alone.

The definitions of mental subnormality provided in the Act have a somewhat old-fashioned ring about them because of the emphasis they place on prediction. The fact that someone is judged to be 'incapable of living an independent life' should not mean that he can never do so even after suitable training. Even more dogmatic is the insistence on predicting in the case of a child that he will be incapable of independence for the rest of his life. This definition does not appear to allow for what can be achieved in some cases by an effective educational programme. This is not to argue that mental handicap is 'curable' — only that prediction from current levels of performance is invalid and unjustifiable, given modern methods of rehabilitation.

In fact, the definitions reflect the predominantly medical approach to mental handicap which was prevalent in the 1950s, and which is now being replaced by a growing emphasis on education and social training. It is perhaps symptomatic of the then prevailing climate of opinion that the Ministry of Education was not even asked to give evidence to the Royal Commission.

Finally, we should briefly note some of the practical implications for the handicapped person himself of being labelled subnormal or severely subnormal. In the first place, it is much easier to enforce compulsory detention for the SSN if they are over 25, whereas only short periods of detention are possible for the SN. However, the majority of residents in hospital are now voluntary, and there is little evidence of abuse. Hospitals are only too anxious to discharge people wherever possible. Difficulties occur after discharge in obtaining permission to vote, in applying for a driving licence or in marrying, though the precise legal situation is not clearly laid down.

The AAMD classification

The American Association on Mental Deficiency adopted a classification system which is considerably more complex and comprehensive than the British system. In its most recent revision (1973), the overall definition of mental retardation is given as follows: 'Mental Retardation refers to significantly sub-average general intellectual functioning existing concurrently with deficits in adaptive behaviour, and manifested during the developmental period.'

The AAMD classifications are incorporated in a detailed manual (Grossman 1973) which offers a number of principles to assist interpretation. Intellectual functioning is to be measured by an acceptable objective test, while sub-average refers to performance which is more than two standard deviations below the population mean. A score which is only one SD below the mean used to be regarded as 'borderline intelligence' (not borderline retardation) but has now been abandoned. The developmental period is approximately placed within the first eighteen months.

The emphasis on intellectual assessment, while welcome in some respects, has always been under criticism, and in recent years the AAMD has made a great deal of progress in defining and measuring important aspects of adaptive behaviour. Adaptive behaviour is defined as 'the effectiveness with which the individual meets the standards of personal independence and social responsibility expected of his age and cultural group'. These are assessed in terms of (i) maturation, (ii) learning and (iii) social adjustment, each of which assumes differing degrees of importance at different ages and stages of development. The AAMD has also produced a wide ranging set of Adaptive Behaviour Scales which aim to assess adaptive behaviour as objectively as possible. These are available for both children and adults. The children's scales cover areas such as degree of self-sufficiency, sensory-motor development, language development and socialization; the scales for older people include additional items concerned with domestic skill, vocational potential and responsibility. A great deal of research went into the development of the scales, and they certainly represent important attempts to objectify the rather vague and subjective way in which social competence has been defined. However, their value obviously depends entirely on the way in which they are filled in and interpreted. The rater must know the subject well, and must try and carry out the ratings on the basis of the individual's behaviour, and not on his own opinion of what the person might or might not be able to do. The main value of the scales probably derives from their use in hospitals and residential settings. It is not yet clear whether they can be used in the setting of an initial or diagnostic interview.

A second important feature of the AAMD system lies in its attempt to define grades of retardation. It does so by defining two parallel systems consisting of four grades, one based on measured intelligence (see *Table 2.1*) and the other concerned with adaptive behaviour.

Table 2.1

Measured intelligence	Level of deviation	IQ range
Mild	-2	55-69
Moderate	-3	40-54
Severe	-4	25-39
Profound	-5	24 and below

We can also consider an example of a series of adaptive behaviours listed in the AAMD manual. The particular examples refer to levels of adaptive behaviour. Not to have achieved these levels would be considered mild at 3 years, moderate at 6, severe at 9 and profound at 12 years or older.

Illustrations of highest level of adaptive behaviour functioning

Age and level indicated:
3 years: mild
6 years: moderate
9 years: severe
12 years
    and above:
    profound

Independent functioning: Feeds self with spoon (cereals, soft foods) with considerable spilling or messiness; drinks unassisted; can pull off clothing and put on some (socks, underclothes, boxer pants, dress); tries to help with bath or hand washing but still needs considerable help; indicates toilet accident and may indicate toilet need. *Physical:* May climb up and down stairs but not alternating feet; may run and jump; may balance briefly on one foot; can pass ball to others; transfer objects; may do simple form-board puzzles without aid. *Communications*: May speak in two or three word sentences ('Daddy go work'); name simple common objects ('boy', 'car', 'ice cream', 'hat'); understands simple directions ('put the shoe on your foot', 'sit here', 'get your coat'); knows people by name. (If non-verbal, may use many gestures to convey needs or other information).

> *Social*: May interact with others in simple play activities, usually with only one or two others unless guided into group activity; has preference for some persons over others.

Source: Adapted from Grossman (1973).

This division into grades of handicap has certain advantages over the British two category system. The severely subnormal population is a very varied one, containing at one extreme an utterly helpless, non-ambulant and unresponsive person needing maximum care, and at the other end a reasonably competent individual with well-developed cognitive and language skills, who can respond to training and be helped to live in the community, while contributing at least partially to his support. The problem about the American system is that it is unlikely that a classification once made will be changed. For example, if someone is regarded as profoundly or severely handicapped, he may be deprived of appropriate treatment on the grounds that he is 'unlikely to benefit'. We have already discussed the dangers of self-fulfilling prophecies of this type. But perhaps the British system is going too fast and too far towards increasingly comprehensive categories, and tending to blur the distinctions within each group. The creation of comprehensive categories is understandable in terms of the need to dispense with excessive labelling, but is more debatable on educational grounds, since it can be argued that the two groups (ESNM and ESNS) are in some respects different in relation to the kind of teaching which they need (see Chapter 5 for a fuller discussion).

The AAMD classification also includes a 'biomedical' approach, which distinguishes between different causes or presumed causes of retardation. Diagnostic advances are now being made on a considerable scale, and an increasing number of specific disease entities are being identified with advances in the technology of diagnosis. The system proposed is designed to run in parallel with the International Classification of Diseases (8th revision, World Health Organisation 1968). The following broad categories are used, each of them containing sub-groups:

> following infection and intoxication (e.g. maternal German measles);
> following trauma or physical agent (e.g. prenatal or perinatal injury);
> with disorders of metabolism or nutrition (e.g. phenylketonuria);

associated with postnatal gross brain disease (e.g. tuberous sclerosis, tumours);

associated with diseases and conditions due to unknown prenatal influence (e.g. hydrocephalus);

with chromosomal abnormality (Down's Syndrome);

gestational disorders (prematurity);

following psychiatric disorders (e.g. childhood psychosis);

environmental influences;

other conditions.

Additional categories are concerned with genetic components, impairment of special senses, disorders of perception and expression, convulsive disorders, motor dysfunction and psychiatric impairment.

Comprehensive classification can only begin to work if it is based on a recognition that mental handicap represents a complex interaction between different factors. For example, a child may be a clear case of Down's Syndrome, and functioning within a particular intellectual category, but the level of his adaptive skills may depend on the kind of home environment in which he has been living, and the kind of education and, training that he has been receiving. One or all of his adaptive skills, as assessed by the Adaptive Behaviour Scales, may be at a low level not because of his medical condition or his intellectual classification alone, but simply because he has not been taught or encouraged to learn the relevant skills and behaviours.

All classification systems are in danger of degenerating into sterile academic exercises which look impressive on paper but which do not lead to action to help the handicapped person. The recent AAMD system is a considerable improvement on earlier versions, not merely because it is more comprehensive but because its emphasis on objective assessment of adaptive skills can and should highlight areas of strengths and weaknesses in the individual person, and also in groups. But it remains a classification system, and should not replace assessments leading directly to programmes of treatment and remediation.

A radical alternative

In view of the limitations of classification systems, we will conclude by referring to one radical alternative to traditional classification systems which has been proposed by a number of behaviourists, of whom Bijou is the clearest spokesman (Bijou 1966).

Bijou's starting position is that we should stop using terms such as intelligence, mental retardation and even adaptation because these are nothing more than hypothetical constructs, and cannot be directly observed. We merely infer the presence of low intelligence from our observation of behaviour, but fail to study the behaviour itself. Certainly, we rarely try to establish what relationships might exist between a specific behaviour and what precedes or follows it.

Bijou sees the retarded person as someone who has a limited repertoire of behaviour, due to limited and unrewarded contacts with the environment. These he describes in terms of inadequate reinforcement, frequent punishment and other terms derived from learning theory and operant psychology. He is not, of course, saying that there is no such thing as mental retardation, or that it can be completely explained in terms of learning theory. But he does warn against assuming that 'intelligence', 'mind' or 'retardation' are real *things*. Instead he asks us to look at the underlying behaviour, and to consider the possibility that part of what we call retardation is the result of the kind of history and the nature of the learning environment experienced by the retarded individual.

Bijou's emphasis on the need to study what can be observed and to avoid what can only be inferred should be seen as one of the foundation stones of the behaviourist approach to mental handicap. This will be described in detail in Chapter 5, but we can note at this point that the essence of the approach lies in its stress on ways in which specific events in the environment affect specific behaviours in the here and now, and also on what can be done to increase the limited behavioural repertoire of the retarded person. This approach is obviously more interventionist in nature than one that is preoccupied with allocating people to categories or grades of retardation.

Conclusions

The ways in which a society goes about identifying its handicapped members tells us more about the society than about the handicapped. The values that a society sets on the importance of helping its handicapped members, the kind of services it provides and the resources that it is prepared to allocate reflects its standards and priorities.

Whether our own society will be found wanting by these criteria is still an open question. On the positive side, a great deal of progress has been made in the last twenty years, and it seems likely that the rate of progress will not merely continue but also gain momentum. On the negative side, we are hampered on the one hand by a lack of clarity in defining our objectives and on the other by a poorly integrated administrative framework within which they might be attained.

Despite the subjective nature of the decisions, it has always been felt that social competence, or the ability to adapt and conform to the demands of society, is a central feature of mental handicap. We have discussed the difficulties of a social competence criterion, and reviewed some of the attempts which have been made to devise more scientific and objective measures of social competence. Although the Royal Commission on Mental Illness and Mental Deficiency accepted the views of the majority of expert witnesses who argued for the retention of social competence as a sole criterion, the Mental Health Act incorporated the views of the British Psychological Society by defining mental subnormality in terms which included subnormality of intelligence. Under existing law, therefore, no one can be regarded as mentally subnormal unless he can also be shown to be of subnormal intelligence. The fact that this part of the law has been impossible to implement in practice is once again a reflection of lack of resources which continues to make it necessary for the mental handicap services to provide for many people who cannot be described as being of subnormal intelligence but who are unquestionably in need of professional help and public sympathy.

Unfortunately, recourse to objective tests of intelligence is also beset by problems. We have discussed these at some length, because it is important to arrive at a realistic appraisal of what tests can and cannot do, and to realize in particular that an IQ is not a magic number, but simply reflects the number of items scored on a particular test. Its ability to predict future development, or even to correlate with a current learning situation is much more limited than is generally supposed. Nevertheless, despite its limitations, it does provide a more objective basis not only for classification and diagnosis but also for a more detailed investigation of a person's intellectual strengths and weaknesses.

In the last analysis, we must conclude that a classification system is only as good as the use to which it is put. We may use it merely to describe people and to pigeon-hole them into precise categories. In fact, the less we are able to do for people, the more preoccupied we tend to be with classification systems. On the other hand, now that we are able to offer much more by way of rehabilitation, we are in a better position to see the problem of definition in its proper context — as the first step in a rational and systematic programme of treatment.

One of the main tasks that confronts anyone working with

mentally handicapped people, whether as individuals, in small or large groups, or as a planner of services for many thousands, is that of differentiating between the multiple and complex disabilities involved. In the first place, there are the 'real' or 'actual' disabilities that prevent the individual from learning and responding to those around him in the same way as others. These disabilities are biological in the broadest sense of the term; they cannot be cured and of course they must set limits on how much can be done to help the individual, no matter how skilled the teaching or how good the facilities.

Although it is important not to lose sight of the severe disabilities of mentally handicapped people in one's enthusiasm to stress their more positive achievements, neither should we be over-whelmed by the biological obstacles that mentally handicapped people experience in learning. There is little that we can do to minimize the biological impairments in themselves, but the emphasis nowadays lies in modifying the environment in such a way that maximum opportunities for learning are provided from the start. We know that in general people respond if demands are made on them and that they do not learn if they are not taught. We also know that human behaviour cannot be explained by invoking just one set of causes, whether these are biological, social or educational. A profoundly handicapped person, functioning for most purposes at a developmental level of only three or four months, can nevertheless be helped to take a small and significant step forward in his development, provided that the goal meets his needs and the teaching is carefully defined. On the other hand, an individual whose intellectual impairment may only be minimal might nevertheless fail to develop adequately if he is placed in an unstimulating environment, if no demands are made of him and if he lacks the motivation to learn.

Mental handicap presents an exciting challenge precisely because it involves a dynamic and complex set of interacting forces, some biological, some social, some educational. This book largely stresses what can be done by those environmental means which are within our control. Of course, there are limitations to what a handi-capped person can do, but we are less confident than we used to be that we know what those limitations are. Our task is to beat prediction if we can.

3

NUMBERS

Anyone concerned with planning needs to know the sheer number of people who will require services. This is more than ever necessary now that local government boundaries have been drastically revised; smaller authorities have been absorbed into larger units, and many local government boundaries have become coterminous with National Health Service administrative units. This reorganization provides for the first time a structure within which we might, if we so chose, embark on a more integrated and comprehensive service for the mentally handicapped.

Severe mental handicap

The most recent estimates currently available suggest that there are about 160,000 severely mentally handicapped people in Great Britain (Office of Health Economics 1978). This corresponds to a figure of between 4 and 5 out of every 1,000 children, and two out of every 1,000 adults, or a total of around 240 people out of every 100,000 of the total population.

The severely mentally handicapped are people with IQs around or below 50, whose abilities are obviously seriously impaired, and most of whom show evidence of anomalies to the brain or central nervous system; many have additional handicaps. By far the largest single group are those suffering from Down's Syndrome (mongolism), who make up about a third of all ESNS school children and about a quarter of adults in ATCs. In many cases, however, the precise cause of the handicap still remains unknown, even though it is usually clear that the child is in a general or specific sense biologically impaired.

Although the figure of 4 per 1,000 population is widely quoted, it represents no more than a rough approximation based on combining data from epidemiological surveys carried out in three different parts of the country — the Wessex Regional Health Authority (covering a population of some two million), the

Newcastle area and the London borough of Camberwell. Although there are common points of agreements between the three surveys, it is open to question whether the results of surveys from three such different areas should have been combined into a single national prevalence figure in the 1971 White Paper. Quite apart from variations which occur from area to area, prevalence figures vary markedly with the age of the people being studied. Some years ago it was common to estimate prevalence by studying the age group 15 to 19, on the grounds that most people requiring services would have been discovered by that age. But since the advent of compulsory education for ESNS children in 1971 and the growth of educational provision for virtually all children of school age, it seems reasonable to assume that all severely mentally handicapped children would have been identified by the age of 10. Indeed, there is a risk that considerable numbers of the 16-20 age group might not be identified after they leave school, especially if they are not attending ATCs or receiving other services.

Recent surveys in this country and Europe suggest that the figure of 4 per 1,000 may be an underestimate as far as children are concerned. More recent estimates from both Camberwell and Salford (the first with a declining and highly mobile population, the second with a more constant population) suggest a marked increase in the survival of the most severely handicapped, (including profoundly and multiply handicapped children) and a larger number of surviving children in the 15 to 19 age-group than had originally been estimated (Fryers 1978). Some careful surveys in Holland suggest that the prevalence of severe mental handicap in the 10 to 14 age group was around 5.65 per 1,000; they attribute these higher rates to their relatively lower rates of infant and child mortality compared to Anglo-Saxon countries (Verbraak 1975). Figures given in the Court report certainly suggest that Britain has now fallen seriously behind most other European countries in respect of infant mortality rates (DHSS 1976).

In view of the variations in prevalence, it is doubtful whether we should go on talking about a single prevalence rate at all. However much different studies agree about overall prevalence, there is no doubt that the figures vary greatly with the age group being studied. Local planning groups who are developing services for their area will therefore need to base themselves on the age structure of their own population. Thus, a population with a higher than average number of elderly people will have relatively fewer mentally handicapped people in its midst or being born; conversely a higher prevalence is likely in areas of high urban density, with poor uptake of antenatal services and poor resources in screening, identification and detection of handicapping conditions. Despite the fairly even distribution of severe mental handicap across all social classes, there is still a higher element of risk among older mothers — not just for Down's Syndrome but for other reproductive complications — and among poorer and socially disadvantaged families. Similarly, poorer families are more at risk when it comes to low birth weight and 'small-for-dates babies', as well as postnatal infections such as meningitis and encephalitis. More recently, anxieties have been expressed about children whose mental handicap may be due to child abuse and non-accidental injury. Children also become mentally handicapped as a result of severe head injury resulting from road accidents. Finally, a number of studies are beginning to suggest that there is after all some over-representation of Social Classes IV and V (e.g. Bayley 1973) though this is nothing like as marked as the Social Class V skew in ESNM children.

It has been estimated that the average population unit of 100,000 people can expect to have between five and six children born every year who will turn out to be severely mentally handicapped. Here again, these numbers will be significantly higher in some areas than others. One can also think in terms of 5 to 6 per 100,000 as the number of children in each year group in ESNS schools. This is about the number of children per year who are reaching the school leaving age of 16 in ESNS schools for each population unit of 100,000 and for whom provision will need to be made (see Chapter 6 for more detailed discussion). The numbers remain constant at 5 to 6 per year group partly because those who die early (a relatively small number) are balanced out by those whose mental handicap is not recognized for the first few years, as well as those whose handicap is acquired rather than present at birth. Nationally, therefore, we are talking about some 48,000 children between birth and 16, out of a total of about twelve and a quarter million — i.e. just under four mentally handicapped children in every thousand children.

4/1000

Mild mental handicap

Although this book is mainly concerned with the needs of severely mentally handicapped people, it is important to bear in mind that a proportion of people with relatively mild degrees of handicap are also being catered for within our existing mental handicap services. For example, at least a third of the people living in mental handicap hospitals are graded as only mildly handicapped by the staff of the hospital (DHSS 1972). Similarly at least 10 per cent of students attending ATCs were admitted from ESNM schools

(Whelan and Speake 1977); the numbers attending from this source are likely to increase as a result of the severe unemployment among handicapped school leavers. If we take an IQ of 70 as the *upper* limit of all grades of mental handicap (as recommended by the World Health Organisation 1968), 75 per cent are mildly handicapped (IQ 50 to 70), 20 per cent have IQs between 20 and 50, and 5 per cent have IQs below 20. Thus, mild mental handicap is by far the most common form, though it is impossible to measure prevalence at all accurately, since many never come to notice or require services. Total prevalence is roughly estimated between one and one and a quarter million — i.e. some 2 per cent of the total population in all.

Difficult as it is to draw a distinction between the severely and mildly mentally handicapped in terms of IQ or any other single criterion, it is virtually impossible to define the upper limits of mild mental handicap. The previous chapter reviewed a number of approaches to definition, including the suggestion that no one with an IQ above 70 should be regarded as mentally handicapped, and that the previous borderline category between IQ 70 to 80 should be abolished. But human intelligence, whether measured by tests or by adaptive behaviour, is a finely graded characteristic and moves by almost imperceptible steps from levels that are obviously a reflection of gross biological damage into the 'normal', however defined. There is no sharp dividing line whether set by IQ or by any other measure between the mildly handicapped and the normal. Once we reach levels of IQ 80 we are in any case talking about some 10 per cent of the population.

The vast majority of people with IQs at or above 70 manage to adapt quite competently to the demands of society and require little specialized help, even though some will experience more than their fair share of difficulties and may make correspondingly greater use of social and employment services, social security etc. But others will at some time come into the framework of services designed for more severely mentally handicapped people. The same applies to the smaller number of people within the IQ range 50 to 70; many of them who have attended special schools or classes for the ESNM will be able to get jobs, 'adjust to the demands of society', and make no further demands for specialized services, but a minority will experience more serious difficulties for shorter or longer periods and may well receive help from the mental handicap services. This is particularly the case if they have been convicted by the courts, even for relatively minor offences.

Fortunately, the majority of ESN children are able when they leave school to find a job and require little further help — although this is less the case today, than under reasonably favourable economic circumstances. Of those that experience continuing difficulties in finding and remaining in employment (about 30 per cent of all ESNM leavers), about half come from families marked by particularly severe stress or exceptionally poor relationships (Stein and Susser 1963).

Social disadvantage

The mildly handicapped have to contend not only with low intelligence but a variety of social and environmental handicaps which may restrict intellectual development and learning even further. These include severe poverty, poor housing, large families, parental ill health and continued unemployment.

. The National Child Development Study (Davie, Butler and Goldstein, 1972) has documented the educational and social handicaps of children brought up in poor circumstances. The definition of 'disadvantaged' adopted for the purpose of their study was concerned with all three of the following criteria:

  (i) Family composition: a child living in a one-parent family (6 per cent of all children in Britain)* or a child living in a family with five or more children (18 per cent);
 (ii) Low income: this was defined in terms of children receiving free school meals or whose families were receiving supplementary benefit (14 per cent);
(iii) Poor housing: families where the room density exceeded 1½ persons per room or where there was no hot water supply exclusively for the use of the family (18 per cent).

The number of children who fell into all three of these groups amounts to 1 child in 16 — on average 2 children in every British classroom. Although the prevalence was 1 in 16 for Britain as a whole, there were substantial regional variations: 1 in 47 in Southern England, 1 in 12 in Northern England and Wales, and 1 in 10 in Scotland.

It is not surprising that children brought up under such adverse conditions should experience serious learning difficulties. This would be expected even if they were within the average range of intelligence (as most of them are) but when low intelligence is added to many other disadvantages, the chances of satisfactory educational progress become slim indeed. Thus, 1 in 20 of the disadvantaged group as defined by the three criteria adopted by the study (i.e. excluding low intelligence) were said to be educationally sub-

*This figure would be nearer 10 per cent today.

normal (ESNM), compared with 1 in 150 among other children.

The need for special educational treatment arises from many causes, of which low intelligence is only one. In the case of ESNM children, however, there is general agreement that many of the learning difficulties which they experience are related to environmental factors, including poverty, poor housing and deprivation of experience.

> With more freedom from parental stress, perhaps there would have been fewer of those children whose educational subnormality might be ascribed to lack of home stimulation. The need for special educational treatment that arises because of overcrowding, poor amenities, low incomes etc. is surely avoidable (Wedge and Prosser 1973:43).

We noted earlier that not all children classified as educationally subnormal are of low intelligence and that the *average* IQ of children in ESN schools is around 70, so that these special schools contain many children with IQs between 70 and 100. Low intelligence is not the main factor that determines selection for ESN education. The decision is usually made in the light of the child's attainments — e.g. in reading and number work. Conversely, a substantial number of children with either a low IQ or poor attainments (or both) are not in special schools at all, and are not thought by their teachers to need them.

The National Child Development Study has richly documented the strong associations between educational achievement and social class. The study shows that the child of an unskilled manual labourer in Social Class V is fifteen times more likely to be a poor reader than the child of a professional man in Social Class I. These differences are maintained and in some cases increased after the age of 11 and are still strongly present in the same children at 16 (Fogelman 1976). They can by no means be accounted for in terms of intelligence alone but are multiply determined by a combination of complex interacting factors.

It is now accepted that early educational intervention in the form of universal nursery education or variations of Headstart programmes cannot by themselves disturb these fundamental differences in later school achievement; as Bernstein put it, 'Education cannot compensate for society'. Nevertheless, it is all the more important that such educational measures as are taken either before the child enters infant school or later are clearly focused on definite educational objectives. This becomes even more crucial since social class differences are already clearly apparent at the preschool stage. For example, marked social class differences in language skills were noted in a group of 100 normal children aged 48 months who were all already attending nursery schools (Mittler and Ward 1970). Teachers are now beginning to develop structured approaches to helping children to make better use of existing language abilities (Tizard 1975).

The recommendations of the Warnock report (DES 1978) are disappointing in this connection. Although the report as a whole widens the definition of special education to include between 16 and 20 per cent of the school age population, and thus goes far beyond the 2 per cent of handicapped children now in special schools, it makes few proposals which are designed to identify such large numbers at the preschool stage. Now that services for preschool children who are obviously handicapped are beginning to develop, we need new initiatives to identify and cater for the needs of young children who are likely to be regarded as having special needs when they reach school. Merely expanding nursery provisions — even if the resources could be found — is not going to be enough. Some innovative studies in the USA and Britain have suggested that the development of children can be significantly helped by a comprehensive programme of educational and social help for both the child and the family. The success of such measures depends on full parental involvement and also on continued follow-up into the infant school if the effects are not to 'wash out' (Bronfenbrenner 1974; Stedman 1977; see also Mittler (1978) for a critical review of the Warnock proposals for under fives).

Social class and severe mental handicap

Severely mentally handicapped children are fairly evenly distributed across all social classes. Furthermore, siblings of ESNS children are normally distributed within the entire range of intelligence (Roberts 1952). This contrasts strongly with the siblings of children in ESNM schools, who are themselves more likely to attend special schools, and whose parents are found largely in Social Classes IV and V (Birch *et al.* 1970).

Interestingly enough, there is no suggestion in the literature that the influence of social class on educational attainment is anything like as powerful in the mentally handicapped as it is in normal children in whom, as we saw, the effects are already quite apparent before the age of 5. One of the first studies to consider social class effects was carried out by Carr (1970) in the London area. She found no evidence of social class differences on the Bayley mental and motor scales in a sample of young Down's Syndrome children. The Schools Council survey of the language abilities of some 1,400 children attending nineteen schools for ESNS children in the North West likewise failed to detect any association between parental social class and language skills, as rated by teachers using a standard questionnaire (Swann and Mittler 1976; Leeming *et al.* 1979). The surveys nevertheless reflected gross differences in environmental settings — for example children in hospital scored significantly lower than those living at home, though these in turn did not differ from children living in residential hostels.

Several kinds of explanation have been offered to account for the lack of any clear relationship between social class and intellectual or educational achievement. It has been suggested, for example, that the children are too severely handicapped to be affected by the marked differences in child-rearing practices that occur across social classes in ordinary families and that have been well documented by many writers (e.g. Newson, Newson and Barnes 1973). An alternative explanation suggests that middle-class mothers do not treat their handicapped children in the same way that they would treat their normal children, in particular in respect of the kind of language codes they use. For example, a number of studies have compared the language of parents in both structured and ordinary unstructured situations and suggested that parents of mentally handicapped children use a larger number of commands and tend to fire questions demanding only single word responses. More recently, however, Rondal (1977) has shown that such differences disappear when groups of normal and handicapped children are carefully matched in terms of the language maturity of the child. In other words, mothers adjust the language they use to the maturity of the child, irrespective of whether he is handicapped or not.

In any case, social class provides only a crude measure of the kind of influences brought to bear on a child by his family. Even though it may be insensitive as a measure of environmental influence, other studies demonstrate that mentally handicapped children certainly do respond to much more specific and structured types of teaching and intervention. We shall begin to consider these in the following chapter.

Specific abilities and disabilities of the severely handicapped

The White Paper *Better Services for the Mentally Handicapped* (1971) provides a detailed breakdown of the kind of handicaps and disabilities which are found in the population who come into the category of severe mental handicap. *Table 3.1*, adapted from the

Table 3.1 Incapacities associated with mental handicap. (Rate per 100,000 population)

Place of residence	Degree of mental handicap	Non-ambulant		Behaviour difficulties requiring constant supervision		Severely incontinent		Needing assistance to feed, wash or dress		No physical handicap or severe behaviour difficulties		Incapacity not assessed		Total	
		0–14 years	15+ years	0–14 years	15+ years	0–14 years	15+ years	0–14 years	15+ years	0–14 years	15+ years	0–14 years	15+ years	0–14 years	15+ years
Home	Severe	10·49	3·18	4·83	3·17	5·00	1·69	15·90	9·29	12·79	53·90	0·73	0·94	49·24	71·65
Hospital or other residential care	Severe	6·10	7·23	4·86	15·58	3·65	6·97	3·63	16·58	1·69	49·36	0·10	0·94	19·96	96·19
	Mild	0·34	1·51	0·88	5·29	0·15	0·64	0·23	1·96	3·85	42·20	0·21	0·15	5·55	53·17
Total		16·81	11·92	10·27	24·01	8·75	9·30	19·68	27·82	17·04	145·46	1·04	2·03	72·90	221·01

Source: Adapted from DHSS (1971).

White Paper and based on the surveys in Wessex, Newcastle and Camberwell, shows the number of people with specific difficulties which are likely to be found in a unit of population consisting of 100,000 people. Anyone wishing to make a provisional estimate of the relevant figures for his own district or area needs only to make a simple extrapolation. National figures can be roughly estimated by multiplying by 550.

These figures are a useful starting point in considering the range of disabilities found among a group of mentally handicapped people living either at home or in residential care but they can only be taken as a rough guide and need to be interpreted with caution. Problems arise because criteria for defining the disability levels were not standardized between the three areas studied. Similarly, people were originally classified as CANs if they were Continent, Ambulant and Not behaviour disordered; at a later stage, their numbers were raised by including those who needed help to wash, feed or dress themselves. Taking the former criterion, therefore, 75 per cent of adults living at home were graded as CANs, as against 51 per cent of those living in hospital; corresponding figures for children are 25 per cent for those at home and only 8 per cent for those in hospital.

The DHSS conducted a large-scale census of one in three of all those who were residents of mental handicap hospitals on 30 December 1970 — just under 20,000 people. The results of this survey were published in 1972 and were not therefore included in the calculations which went into Table 1 of the White Paper reproduced (with slight modifications) above.

Although people living in hospital are likely to be more severely handicapped, it is worth noting that 81 per cent of adults were fully ambulant, 74 per cent were fully continent, 63 per cent required little or no help with feeding, washing or dressing, and 69 per cent were free of behaviour disorders. More recent estimates have been made by the Development Team for the Mentally Handicapped (1978), on the basis of information provided by staff in respect of some 7,000 adults and also by the Office of Population Censuses and Surveys (OPCS) on behalf of the Jay Committee (OPCS 1979). These are in broad agreement with the results of the 1970 census, though there are a number of areas where the figures are inconsistent — e.g. the Development Team estimates for severe incontinence among adults is only 8 per cent compared with 16 per cent estimated by the 1970 Census.

It is worth emphasizing the positive aspects of these figures because it is often assumed that the majority of hospital residents are too severely handicapped to be rehabilitated to community provision, at least in the form in which it is available today. There is a sense in which this is true, since an examination of the disability levels of those living in local authority hostels certainly indicates that these are minimal. The parallel census of mentally handicapped people living in local authority and voluntary homes on 30 April 1970 undertaken by Morgan for the DHSS (1975) showed that none of the adults required any help in feeding and that well over 90 per cent required no help in washing or dressing and were fully continent. Only 7 per cent were graded by staff as being appreciably or heavily dependent. Although the number of adults living in hostels has risen from 3,200 in 1970 to just under 12,000 in 1977, it seems from recent surveys that the ability levels of residents have not changed appreciably in the last eight years. The OPCS survey of a sample of 1,760 hostel residents conducted for the Jay Committee in 1976 certainly provides no evidence that hostels are now admitting people with greater degrees of dependency. Following a survey of NHS and local authority residential provision in the NE Thames Regional Health Authority, Tyne (1977) concluded that 'local authority hostels have been prepared to accept only the least handicapped of all' (p.44). However, he notes two hostels (in Camden and Southend) which specifically set out to cater for a proportion of the more severely handicapped; this is particularly necessary not only for children for whom a definite policy of preventing inappropriate hospital admission has now been suggested by the Government but also for those adults who are now beginning to be provided for in Special Care Units of Adult Training (Social Education) Centres. In a later publication Tyne (1978) argues that whereas staff at living-unit level need greater control over the resources of daily living, they should have far less control over who is admitted to their units. This would bring them into line with hospital staff who now complain (rightly) that they care for those whom others reject.

Implications for services

What are the implications of the available figures for services?

Although the information to hand is incomplete and not fully reliable, it does provide a rough and ready guide to help local planners to arrive at approximate estimates of the number of people who are going to require various kinds of services. The existing figures have been largely incorporated into Table 5 of the White Paper (summarized in Chapter 1) in which service needs are expressed in terms of population units of 100,000. More recently, it has become convenient to think in terms of larger units of 200,000 people, since these correspond to the size of the average NHS Health District; unfortunately these in turn do not have precise local government counterparts.

From the point of view of long-term planning, it makes sense to assume that services for mentally handicapped people will be co-operatively planned between the NHS and local authorities; in practice, this means that each local authority will need to provide not only for people now living in the community but will also need to know about and make plans to provide services for those of its local citizens who are living in long-stay hospitals. The hospitals themselves are beginning to group their residents according to their area of origin and to relate teams of staff to given geographical districts (see Chapter 9; also NDG's report on hospital services 1978).

The revision of the 1971 White Paper which has now begun will need to make comprehensive plans for the provision of both hospital and local authority services for given population units. Hospitals of the future are likely to cater for much smaller numbers of people or to be organized into sectors or divisions for this purpose, while each local community, whether functioning as an NHS Health District or a local government unit, will in future be expected to meet all but the most specialized needs of all of its mentally handicapped citizens.

Are numbers increasing or decreasing?

Whether there is an increase or decrease in the number of mentally handicapped people being born and needing services is a question often asked by people planning services. In general, it is probably true to say that there is a decrease in the number of mentally handicapped children being *born* but an increase in the number of children surviving into adulthood, at least for certain conditions, particularly Down's Syndrome. Thus, there are four times as many adults per 1,000 population with Down's Syndrome as there were in 1930, mainly due to the fact that antibiotics and other forms of chemotherapy have reduced the very large numbers who previously died as a result of untreatable chest and respiratory infections. The life expectancy of a five-year-old child with Down's Syndrome is now not far below normal, whereas in the 1920s only one Down's baby in ten survived to the age of 5 and very few lived beyond their twenties. However, as babies they are still highly vulnerable to chest infections; recent evidence suggests that as many as one fifth of Down's babies die before the end of the first year of life (Cowie 1970) and even more die before birth.

Evidence for a slight fall in the incidence of severe mental handicap comes mainly from a comparison of present-day data with information collected in earlier surveys. Tizard (1964) compared his own findings in Middlesex with those obtained by Lewis (1929) fifty years ago on children between the ages of 7 and 14. Lewis's figures were 3.71 per 1,000 for urban areas and 3.88 for rural areas, whereas the corresponding rate in 1960 for Middlesex was 3.45. These differences do not seem large at first sight, but when allowance is made for the known increase in the number of Down's children in the intervening period, the decline in incidence may be as high as 30 per cent for the remaining non-mongols. Thus, prevalence figures excluding Down's Syndrome were 3.37 in the 1920s and 2.31 today.

Tizard lists a number of factors which may be responsible for the lower figures today, though it must be added that we cannot be certain how much (if anything) any of these factors contributes to the reported changes, nor can one be completely certain that the differences are not spurious. For example, Lewis noted that 40 per cent of the children aged 7 to 14 were not receiving any form of training or education; his IQ estimates may therefore have underestimated children who were not being stimulated. Similarly, Lewis's numbers may have been raised by failure to distinguish physical from mental handicap, with the result that children suffering from, say cerebral palsy were assumed to be mentally handicapped without the more detailed investigations which would be made today. Despite these possibilities of artefact, Tizard and others believe that there has been a true fall in prevalence, and that this may be due to a combination of factors.

Environmental aspects

The most important constellation of factors can be related to the vast improvement in social conditions, public health and medical services.

(1) The increase in maternal and child health is best reflected in changes in the incidence of infantile mortality from about 154 per 1,000 live births in 1900 to around 17 in 1973. Deaths in the first year fell from 87 to 6 per 1,000 live births in the same period. On the other hand, damaged babies who might have died now survive. This is particularly true of children of very low birth weight, who are at risk both for cerebral palsy and mental handicap.

(2) The increased risk of giving birth to a handicapped child that is associated with greater maternal age is offset by the lower age at

which families are being completed.* More effective and more universal family planning is reducing the number of children born to older mothers. This reduces the number of Down's Syndrome children as well as those who suffer from the results of reproductive complications. Thus, the number of Down's Syndrome babies born in 1970 was some 200 fewer than in 1964, mainly due to the lower age at which families are being completed (Wynne Griffiths 1973).

(3) The better use of antenatal services, including genetic counselling and risk registers, is also an important element. Vitamin and iron deficiencies, and other forms of mild malnutrition can be spotted early, and preventive action taken. It is clear from recent evidence in Jamaica and also in Europe that maternal malnutrition represents a definite risk to the foetus, as does heavy smoking (Mittler 1977). Much greater caution is now expressed about the administration of any drug in pregnancy, in contrast to the blithe optimism of a previous era in which it was believed that the foetus was immune behind its placental barrier.

(4) Certain specific antenatal causes of handicap are not only known but preventable. The effect of German measles (rubella), and of rhesus incompatibility can be counteracted in an increasing number of cases, and will in future constitute a much smaller proportion of causes of handicap, much as maternal syphilis is no longer a significant aetiological factor.

(5) There is also evidence of a reduction in the number of children whose handicap is acquired some time after birth. Cases of acquired mental handicap are often due to infections or severe illnesses involving the central nervous system, particularly encephalitis or meningitis. These illnesses do not always affect the development of intelligence, and can now in many cases be successfully treated in the earliest stages. Before the advent of modern treatment methods, however, meningitis was frequently assumed to be the cause of the mental handicap, though the diagnosis of meningitis cannot be reliably made retrospectively, and precise figures are hard to obtain. Nevertheless, parents sometimes report that a child appeared to all intents and purposes to be developing quite normally until the advent of a severe febrile illness somewhere between 12 and 24 months, and that his development was subsequently distorted or delayed. Unless very thorough investigations were carried out at the time of the illness, it is difficult to be sure

*Less than 6 per cent of all births occur to women of 35 or more today, compared with about 11 per cent ten years ago (Office of Population Census and Surveys 1976).

whether the mental handicap is related to an infection or inflamma-
tion of the brain, or to some other unknown cause.

In general terms, significant improvements in maternal health
which have been taking placé in the last twenty-five years or so are
likely to reduce the risk of many, if not all, reproductive complications. However, these improvements are by no means equally
distributed throughout the community. It is apparent from
national surveys and from the Court Report (DHSS 1976) that the
incidence of reproductive complications, including infant mortality, is much higher in some parts of the country than in others, and
that some women are still at high risk. A small, multiparous,
heavy-smoking wife of an unemployed, unskilled labourer in the
industrial North is much more likely to have severe reproductive
difficulties than an affluent director's wife from the Home
Counties. These inequalities are more complex than they seem, and
we have yet to learn which factors are more critical than others. It is
not merely a matter of variations in the quality of medical services
in different parts of the country but another instance of the
complex interaction between biological and social influences which
we encounter time and again in studying handicapped individuals.
The fact of biological damage does not rule out the possibility
of environmental factors, and we need to find out much more
about the ways in which biological and environmental factors interact in a given individual. For example, prematurity (i.e. children
with a birth weight under 5½ lb.) and toxaemia are found more
frequently in working-class than in middle-class families (Davie,
Butler and Goldstein 1972).

Conclusions

Although there is a great deal we do not know about the mentally
handicapped, and how we can best meet their needs, we do now
have in our possession a substantial body of information which can
be used as the basis of a rational community-based service. It is
clear from numerous surveys in this country and elsewhere that the
frequency of severe mental handicap (IQ under 50) can be reckoned
at about 4 per 1,000 of the child population, or about 240 affected
individuals of all ages of a total population of 100,000. We also
have detailed analyses of the competence of various groups of SSN
individuals in respect of certain skills; for example, we know that
of the SSN adults now in hospital, over half are continent,
ambulant and free of serious behaviour disorders, and that most of
these can also feed, wash and dress themselves without help. The

problem of providing community services for this group is not therefore an insuperable one, because the individuals concerned are reasonably competent and certainly not heavily dependent, though many are undoubtedly severely 'institutionalized' and in need of active rehabilitation training to help them to live in the community.

Nevertheless these figures mask a considerable amount of local variation and have to be interpreted with great care. Prevalence figures vary slightly from one area to another, depending for example on the age structure and social composition of the population, the availability of good antenatal and perinatal facilities and the extent to which these are in fact used by those most at risk. It is one thing to provide the services, another to ensure that those for whom they are intended have access to them and are encouraged to use them. In planning new services, local planning groups could therefore usefully consider the kind of problem experienced by people in using those services that are already available.

Despite these local variations, considerable confidence can be placed in the information which is already available. We know roughly how many severely mentally handicapped people we may expect to find in any given area, how many are likely to be born each year, how many will be coming up to school leaving age and therefore require adult services. We also know a good deal about the characteristics and abilities of people living in hospital.

We need to use the information already available in order to plan and provide a comprehensive service for mentally handicapped people and their families. Proposals for joint planning, helped by joint financing monies, provide a framework within which local groups can use what national information is available and relate it to local needs and local conditions.

4
EARLY HELP

Introduction

Imagine that you have just become the parent of a severely handicapped child: what kind of help could you expect to receive from local and national services?

The answer to this question depends very much on where you live and on the degree of priority given at local level to early help for handicapped infants and their families. Until comparatively recently, very little practical help was available anywhere until the child was old enough to go to school or possibly to attend some form of preschool facility. Parents were left to cope as best they could, sometimes with little or no help or advice from anyone, sometimes with occasional visits to an out-patient clinic of the local hospital or a visit from a health visitor, family doctor or social worker, few of whom could claim any particular experience or specialized knowledge of severe handicap. The average general practitioner, for example, with a list of some 2,000 people, may expect only one newly-born mentally handicapped child in his practice every two or three years; the average health visitor or social worker with general case loads cannot be expected to build up a detailed working knowledge of the needs of handicapped infants or of ways in which parents can best be helped to cope with the day-to-day problems that may arise. They can offer support, warmth and sometimes access to people with more specialized knowledge, but many of them are only too aware of their lack of training and knowledge of this field. Some will tend to stay away, feeling that there is little that they can do, others will do what they can to help.

There is now general acceptance of the principle that one cannot begin early enough to work with a handicapped child and his family. Services have to be provided right from the start; it is certainly no use waiting for the child to go to school before providing skilled professional help. But this does not mean that the child has to be marked out as 'different' or to spend hours of his time attending specialized clinics and facilities. Although these need to be available in every district as a back-up service, the emphasis now is on bringing special services into the home, and on helping the family to mobilize its own skills and resources and to be active in working systematically but naturally for the development of the baby.

This chapter will therefore review the kinds of help which parents may expect to receive in the first few years, beginning with the primary prevention of handicap.

Primary prevention

Dramatic progress has been made in the last twenty years or so in prevention of handicap; even more progress could be made if we made better use of knowledge that is already available. This is a matter of educating not only the general public but also professional workers. We are beginning to provide the services but those who need the services most do not always receive them.

Some forms of screening and early detection of potentially handicapping conditions have been running well for many years; for example virtually every newborn baby is now screened by a simple blood test for the presence of phenylektonuria (PKU), an inborn error of metabolism which can lead to severe mental handicap unless treated by a special diet from the first few weeks of life. Although the condition is quite rare — less than fifty births a year — it is nevertheless considered worth while to screen 10,000 normal babies in order to find one baby who can be successfully treated.

Progress in recent years has taken the form of screening before birth, particularly by means of amniocentesis. This involves withdrawing a small amount of amniotic fluid, and examining cells from the foetus for the presence of the additional chromosome associated with Down's Syndrome (mongolism); some other abnormalities can also be detected prenatally including spina bifida.

Since the risk of having an affected child rises sharply as the mother gets older, women over 40 (and in some parts of the country those over 35) can be screened for the presence of a foetus with Down's Syndrome. It has now been shown that this procedure is almost free from risk, and is certainly cost-effective. The cost of a single amniocentesis examination was about £80 in 1976; if all women over 40 were to be screened, the cost of detecting a single case of Down's Syndrome would be about £8,000. However, this is still much less than the cost of providing the services needed for a handicapped person throughout his life. But even if all women over 35 who were found to be carrying an affected foetus were to choose to have the pregnancy terminated, we should only be able with present knowledge to prevent the birth of about one third of babies with Down's Syndrome. This is because most babies are still born to younger mothers; it would be impossible with present resources to offer amniocentesis to all (DHSS 1976b). Fortunately, there are strong signs of a national fall in the number of Down's children being born — mainly because women are choosing to complete their families at an earlier age — but the numbers could be further reduced by an energetic programme of public education, and by ensuring that all women at risk were routinely offered screening to detect the presence of an affected foetus. A recent study has shown that 58 per cent of women over 40 and 44 per cent of women over 35 do not report their pregnancies until after twenty weeks, by which time it is too late to perform an amniocentesis (Duncan 1978). It has been estimated that less than 10 per cent of women over 35 receive amniocentesis.

Other medical advances are also contributing to a reduction in handicap. For example, handicap due to rhesus incompatibility is now comparatively rare; better antenatal and perinatal care, including prenatal sonic foetal scanning, careful monitoring of foetal size and condition during labour, rubella (German measles) vaccination, and screening of newborns for biochemical abnormalities which respond to early treatment are all likely to contribute to a significant reduction in the number of children born with severe handicaps. Expert genetic counselling is also likely to make a considerable impact.

But advances in medical knowledge are not in themselves enough. Positive steps have to be taken to ensure that those 'at risk' get access to the services.

There is the usual differential uptake of mental handicap services between social classes which has been documented in social medicine for many years. This is why ensuring access to services is a matter of public and professional education and of direct concern to those responsible for administering our services. The Court Report on Child Health Services (DHSS 1976) has shown that Britain has fallen badly behind in the quality of its health provision around the time of birth, as measured by indices of morbidity and mortality in early childhood. In France and Austria, for example, a series of regular health checks during pregnancy and for the first year after the birth of the child are directly linked to generous financial incentives. Programmes of this kind have already made a dramatic impact on the figures of infant mortality and severe handicap.

Early identification

Despite considerable progress in prevention, it has been estimated that in the average health district of some 200,000 people, there will probably be about fifty children born each year with congenital malformations recognizable at birth, and a further thirty with handicaps that will be detected in the first seven years of life (Spain and Wigley 1975). By no means all these children will necessarily be severely mentally handicapped, perhaps ten to twelve per year (Kushlick and Blunden 1974); but the principles of providing services at an early stage apply to all children with severe delays or disorders of development.

There has been considerable discussion recently about the problems of communicating with a family who have just given birth to a handicapped baby. Clearly, there are no universal prescriptions which can be recommended, though there can be no doubt that such communications are often insensitive and brusque. The book edited by Spain and Wigley (1975) reports a number of examples of attempts to develop good practice both in the initial communication and in providing immediate support and practical help for the family.

Where the defect is obvious at birth, as in most cases of Down's Syndrome or spina bifida, the staff will have to decide how and when to 'break the news'. Many mothers report that although told with sympathy and understanding, they were unable to take in any information that was given at the time. Parents may remember statements about chromosomes, but may not appreciate the significance of what they have been told for some time. Many imagine that the babies will be abnormal in every respect, and are often surprised about the many ways the baby is like other children and presents fewer problems than anticipated (Carr 1975). It is important, therefore, to provide ample opportunities for discussion after the initial communication has taken place. The paediatrician may, for example; offer to come back in a few hours or the next day, and set aside an hour without interruptions so that the parents can begin to raise the issues that are particularly concerning them. Several sessions are generally needed, with later sessions perhaps held together with the local health visitor, social worker or family doctor or whoever is going to be most closely concerned with providing support when the baby goes home and the family have to cope on their own.

Quite understandably, parents tend to ask questions about the long-term future — will the child be able to marry and have children and to get a job, what will happen when they can no longer look after him? Will he have to go to hospital? But the question of what can be done in the coming weeks and months is of much more direct and immediate relevance; it is important to mobilize simple but direct and effective sources of help in the first weeks and months, and to make sure that the family is put in touch with experienced people who can support the family and work with them (see Cunningham and Sloper (1978) for further discussion of these issues).

Communication with the relevant professionals is essential here. Many hospitals involve the primary care team from the outset; the general practitioner, health visitor or social worker is brought into the hospital to provide a link between specialist and community services, and to develop the foundations for the relationship of trust and confidence which is essential to a successful partnership with the family.

In some areas, immediate contact is offered through a member of the local Society for Mentally Handicapped Children or the Spastics Society. Parents may reject these contacts at first, partly because they imply an acceptance of the 'label' that membership of such societies implies, but they should always be given a list of names and telephone numbers of people they can contact once they feel ready to do so. Short cyclostyled lists of people and organizations, showing where and how particular services can be obtained are now being produced in many areas, and kept in health clinics, GPs' surgeries, Social Services offices, public libraries and other prominent places.

Comprehensive assessment

Whether the child goes to school or not, there should be a written plan of development suited to his individual needs.

Each child needs to be carefully and systematically assessed so that he can be helped by means of careful planning to:

   (i) acquire new skills and abilities;
  (ii) compensate as far as possible for restrictions of experience and learning imposed by his disabilities;
 (iii) ensure that those around him have the means and the knowledge to provide him with those experiences and opportunities which he needs at each phase of his development.

The basis of planning for development is comprehensive assessment of the skills and abilities of the individual child and of the family's resources to meet those needs. Assessment is not a matter of a quick visit to an out-patient clinic or the administration of a formal intelligence test; it is a continuous process involving periods of observation and experimental teaching, in which the child's responses to a wide range of learning demands is carefully noted. Assessment should always result in a programme of activities which is designed to help the child to reach the next stage of his development, however small. Moreover, it is essential to take active steps to make sure that the programme drawn up in assessment or child development centres is actively carried out, whether by specific professional staff or by parents or by both in partnership.

Assessment centres need not necessarily be sited in hospitals. The medical aspects of assessment are obviously important, and visits to hospitals may be necessary for particular investigations — X-rays, electroencephalographs (EEGs) and other specialized tests. But the central aim of assessment is broadly educational. The child needs to be assessed in as natural an environment as possible; he needs to be observed at play, and in unstructured as well as structured learning situations. It is important to observe how he responds to a new situation, a change of toy or play material, or a new person coming to sit next to him. This implies that a key member of the assessment team should be a teacher, and that the setting of the service should be in a school — perhaps part of a normal nursery school, or of a special school. Other specialists should as far as possible visit the child in school: psychologists, doctors, speech therapists, physiotherapists and others can then compare their findings with the information available to the teacher on a day-to-day basis. They can also ask the teacher to make specific assessments and observations for them, so as to provide an opportunity for them to validate their own observations over a longer period. In this way it should be possible to arrive at a consensus of opinion on how the child can be helped towards the next steps of his development, whether this occurs primarily at home or in one or other type of school setting. Whatever decision is taken, the parents should play a key role in decision-making, and be helped at every stage to achieve an effective working partnership between home and school. No matter how expertly the assessment and teaching programme is designed, it will be ineffective without the full co-operation of the family. To bring this about requires at least the same level of skill and organization as is needed to teach the child in school.

Early services

District Handicap Teams

Important suggestions for the organization of services for young handicapped children have been made by the Court Committee on Child Health Services which reported at the end of 1976 (DHSS 1976); these recommendations have been accepted with some modifications by the Government and are now beginning to be introduced. Briefly, they suggest that each of the new NHS health districts, containing on average some 240,000 people, of whom 60,000 are likely to be children under 16, should have a District Handicap Team (DHT), to provide a source of expertise and advice on the assessment and development of all handicapped children and of all those whose development gives cause for concern, whether they turn out to be handicapped or not. The aim of these arrangements is to ensure that any parents who are worried about the development of their child can be referred to people with experience of normal as well as handicapped children, who know all the available local services and who are responsible for co-ordinating arrangements for developing services to meet local needs. Membership of the DHT is intended to be flexible but will generally be drawn from paediatricians, nursing officers, psychologists, social workers and teachers, all with some experience in working with handicapped children. The Court Committee also emphasized the need for a Child Development Centre, which could be located in the District General Hospital or in an appropriate community setting. These Centres would provide a focus of help for handicapped children and their families, and would provide assessment and detailed developmental programming to meet the needs of individual children.

The Court proposals for District Handicap Teams and Child Development Centres in each NHS district are certainly an improvement on present provision but there is some doubt whether they could satisfactorily meet the needs of all severely mentally handicapped children. The National Development Group (NDG 1977) has made proposals for complementary Community Mental Handicap Teams to work with those mentally handicapped children who need a more detailed programme of help and whose families need a domiciliary service, rather than a service which is likely to be based on a District General Hospital and which may be better suited to meeting the child's health needs. The Community Team will therefore start work where the District Handicap Team leaves off, either through lack of time or resources, but will in any case only deal with a very small number of mentally handicapped children presenting particularly difficult problems of assessment, planning and teaching (see Mittler and Simon (1978) and Development Team for the Mentally Handicapped (1978) for further discussion of this point).

The Warnock Committee (DES 1978) broadly endorsed the Court recommendations, and made a number of additional proposals. In particular, they suggested that educational help should be available to children from the time of birth or first identification, and that the existing minimum age limit of two years should be abolished. Educational involvement could take a variety of forms, e.g. a peripatetic teaching service which would visit families, playgroups, day nurseries and any other setting for children below school age. They also proposed a substantial expansion of nursery education for all children in the hope that more handicapped children might be able to take advantage of increased nursery provision in future.

One of their most important recommendations was for a 'Named Person' 'to provide a point of contact for the parents of every child who has been discovered to have a disability or who is showing signs of special needs or problems' (para.5.13). They suggest that the Health Visitor is probably best placed to act as Named Person during the early years, though there is no reason why other professionals should not provide this service. The important point is that parents should know that a specific person is always available to give advice, to guide them through the maze of services and to ensure that they receive all the help that is needed. In a service which is still badly fragmented between health, education, social services and a variety of voluntary agencies it is particularly important to designate a particular person to act as friend and advocate of the handicapped child and his family, and to ensure that recommendations that are made are actually carried out and regularly reviewed.

Above all, the need is for a single individual to help the family to work out its own adjustment to the child. This process takes a different form in every family. Some families take a long time to 'come to terms' with the handicap and with the child and are not ready to accept help, however expert. They must be given time and not be unduly 'pressured' to adopt a direct teaching role. Others are only too eager to begin systematic teaching with their child but may become disappointed if the results are not as dramatic as they hoped. Because no two families are alike, generalizations about families of handicapped children are suspect, just as labels imposed on particular families are best avoided — e.g. 'over-protective', 'rejecting', 'unrealistic', etc.

It is important, therefore, that services for preschool children should provide a framework within which help can be given but not imposed, a framework within which the needs and resources of families can be respected. One of the best-known services for young handicapped children and their families is the Honeylands Unit at the Royal Devon and Exeter Hospital at Exeter. This provides a range of services, largely on an informal basis. Children come to the unit on a part-time or daily basis according to need, either for short-term care for a few hours or for a period of days for more detailed assessment or programme planning; the team consists of paediatricians, child psychologists, community nurses, social workers and teachers. A useful film is available describing this project (*When the Bough Bends*). Other examples of innovative services have been brought together by Pugh and Russell (1977).

Needs of parents

Parents of handicapped children have special needs and difficulties, and society has an obligation to give them all the help and support they need to enable them to help their child to develop as well as possible. Inevitably, this involves a pooling of knowledge and experience with professional workers on a basis of equality. We owe it to them to help them to develop and maintain a sense of purpose from the very beginning if we want to help them to avoid feelings of despondency and passivity in the early years. If we can succeed in helping them to retain a positive attitude towards the possibilities of their child being helped to develop, the foundations are laid for a working collaboration with teachers once the child reaches school.

We should distinguish between needs which arise directly from the child's difficulties and needs which stem from the absence of any clear framework of guidance on how to proceed. In the first category are numerous problems which arise from having to care for a child who may be heavily dependent on the parents for the satisfaction of his basic needs; who may be physically difficult to handle or carry; apparently unresponsive to praise or stimulation; subject to severe temper tantrums, bouts of screaming or crying; multiply handicapped by visual or auditory impairment or epilepsy; impossible to take out to shops or on visits. Such a list could be extended indefinitely, but the physical problems of looking after a handicapped child are often forgotten.

The absence of a framework of help and services is in some ways even more serious. The needs of many parents tend to be neglected because it is no one's clear responsibility to provide a sense of direction. Doctors, health visitors and social workers may or may not visit the family, but none of them working in isolation can get very far. As a result, despite sympathy and advice from relatives and friends, the parents are very often isolated with their problem and do their best to live from one day to the next.

Knowledge of normal children and 'ordinary parental intuition' may not be enough. Professionals cannot assume that they have discharged their duty merely by advising the parents to treat their handicapped child as they would any other child, and to provide him with stimulating and interesting experiences. Such advice is well meaning but too vague and general to be of much value.

In the first place, the age of the child is not a good basis for planning. Not only will the child be developing very slowly but his development is likely to be patchy and uneven, so that the various aspects of his development may appear 'out of step'.

Second, normal children rush through critical periods of their development so rapidly that the parent is hardly aware of their significance and rarely stops to think whether they need to be systematically taught. But when normal development is in slow motion or distorted by additional handicaps the parent may easily settle for a particular stage of development and become insensitive to the signs and signals given by the child that he is ready to move on to the next stage.

Third, parents may become unnecessarily pessimistic and assume that because the child is handicapped in one area he is inevitably slow in all. They are easily discouraged by lack of progress and may attribute all the difficulties to the child's inherent handicaps and limitations. The family has emotional and social needs which need to be met both by the child and by a society which believes in parents caring for their handicapped children in the community but which often fails to provide the necessary practical and moral support to help them to do so.

Parents are now asking for detailed, concrete, practical help. They want guidance on how they can help their child to develop mentally as well as physically; they want help with day-to-day problems, feeding, sleeping, crying and so on. These difficulties arise in some measure with all babies, and parents may need no more than reassurance that they should deal with these problems in the way that they would for their normal children. On the other hand, they may need more than this kind of reassurance; special measures may be needed with feeding problems if the baby has a large tongue or has difficulties with swallowing. For example, Down's babies easily become obese, and advice on a diet may be needed.

But it is not enough merely to give advice to the mother, however sound the advice may be. She must also be helped to carry it out, to make suggestions on her own account and expect to be listened to as an expert, and she has the right to expect that any advice that she is given is relevant to her child and to the family situation. The parents should therefore be regarded as the key members of the interdisciplinary team.

One way of meeting parents' need at an early stage is to help them to make a developmental assessment of their own child. This can be done by giving them carefully prepared child development charts, listing specific skills and attainments of normal children at different ages. These items can be checked by the parents on the basis of their own observations of the child at home, and can then be compared with the observations of members of the professional assessment team. The aim of such assessments is to help the parents to become thoroughly familiar with the detailed sequences of normal child development, so that they are not only fully aware of the stage or skill that their child is likely to reach next, but can actively help him to attain it.

Needs of the children

A handicapped child has the same needs as other children but he has other needs as well. All children have a right to love and security, and need to live in an environment which provides experience essential to development. But an environment which is ideal for the normal child does not necessarily meet all the needs of the handicapped child. We cannot know what a child's needs are merely on the basis of experience and intuition, nor can we provide a learning environment which is geared to his specific needs until we have assessed those needs and planned systematically how to meet them.

A normal child continually seeks out experiences for himself and is active in his own development. He has a drive to explore, experiment and discover the properties of his environment — both physical and human. The handicapped child may not have the same drive or may be frustrated in his wish to explore by his handicaps or by the imposition of restrictions by others. We therefore have to find ways of bringing to the handicapped child those experiences which he cannot easily seek out for himself. At the same time, we have to strike a happy mean between doing too much and doing too little, and to realize that the delicate balance is always changing with the development of the child. This is one of the most difficult tasks for the parent, and one which should be shared with others with more experience of other families and handicaps.

We can distinguish between two kinds of restrictions on the development of a handicapped child: those imposed directly by the handicap itself (primary) and those which arise from environmental deprivations, including parental handling (secondary).

Among the more obvious examples of primary restrictions are those imposed by visual or hearing impairments which restrict or distort the means by which we learn about the world in which we live; motor impairments which result in difficulty in the use of hands and limbs and which prevent us from exploring our environment; severe mental handicap which limits the extent to which we can interpret and integrate our sense impressions with our previous knowledge and experience. Mentally handicapped children are commonly handicapped in all of these modalities.

Secondary restrictions are more difficult to describe. Adults may deliberately or unwittingly restrict a child's experiences 'for his own sake', or for the sake of others. It may be easier to feed a child oneself than to teach him to use a spoon, to dress him oneself rather than teach him to do so by himself, to ask him questions that require only a 'yes' or 'no' when he may be capable of a response that stretches his thinking or language abilities just a little bit further. It may take a child much longer to learn these things, but it is important not to deprive him of the success which learning experiences may bring, because only in this way will he enjoy a feeling of achievement.

A handicapped child may learn less about the outside world than others because it may be physically impossible, inconvenient or embarrassing to take him out. But such experiences are even more important for the handicapped child — he needs to learn about the outside world, to learn about its properties and characteristics; he needs to come into contact with many different people and to learn from repeated experience how much people differ not only in their attitude to him or his family but in other situations also. Even more than the normal child he needs to learn about the world beyond his family circle, but this takes time and patience and demands a learning experience from the public as well as from the family and the child.

Forms of early education

Although mentally handicapped children are not generally admitted to special schools before the age of 5, education authorities are increasingly aware of the need to make some form of educational provision for them before this. Now that the number of nursery school places for normal children is being slowly increased, it is fair to assume that more handicapped children will be able to attend nursery schools or nursery classes, and enjoy the benefits of an integrated education at least during these early years. Other children are attending voluntary preschool playgroups. Some of these playgroups cater for one or two handicapped children, while others are restricted to handicapped children only. A number of mothers have also formed self-help groups which meet regularly with or without professional staff and provide mutual support as well as suggestions for ways in which each child can be helped. The Toy Library movement has also mushroomed in the last few years and clearly meets a central need for parents to discuss their child's development with others.

Since the Warnock Committee has recommended that the maximum use should be made of the normal range of preschool provision, it may be useful at this point to review some of the problems of balancing the needs of handicapped children as children, with those special needs that arise from their handicap. Special education must involve a systematic attempt to meet all the learning needs of the individual child. It can never be assumed that the handicapped child is merely a child who happens to be going through the normal stages of development at a slower rate, and therefore requires only a watered-down version of a normal curriculum.

Playgroups

The main advantage of the playgroup is that it brings the child into contact with ordinary children on terms of equality. Very young children may be less aware of the handicaps of others of their own age, and even if difficulties do occur, adults are always on hand to deal with problems — which is not always the case in unsupervised play and casual social encounters. In addition, the child is presented with many opportunities for play with toys and materials that may not be available at home. The aim of the playgroup is to ensure that play is both enjoyable and successful, but that it is also developmentally appropriate, and likely to help the child to attain or consolidate physical, cognitive and social skills. A second strength of the playgroup derives from the high level of parental involvement.

The main disadvantage of the playgroup is that it may not meet the specific needs of the handicapped child. These should be determined on the basis of skilled professional assessment. If this has not been done, or if the recommendations arising from such assessments are not being implemented, the child may be deprived of the specialized teaching which he needs at the time when he most needs it. For example, a child may have specific difficulties in understanding spoken language; merely exposing him to normal children, talkative adults and a lively, stimulating but noisy environment may not achieve any educational purpose at all, and may even suggest to the child that the language spoken by others is meaningless.

Some of these problems can be circumvented if specialist advisers are associated with the playgroup. On the other hand, a child in a playgroup who, for example, is stated by a psychologist to be in need of specific language teaching will rarely be able to obtain such specialized help within the playgroup, and his parents will have to find such help somewhere else. Similar problems occur for children needing speech therapy or physiotherapy. Fortunately, the Preschool Play Groups Association is now providing some training for staff working with handicapped children.

Nursery schools

Similar advantages and disadvantages apply to the nursery school or class, the main difference with the playgroup being the presence of trained teachers, and the fact that they have easier access to the established assessment units, and also to specialists such as educational psychologists, speech therapists and remedial teachers. Many nursery schools accept a small number of handicapped children; the problem is one of reconciling the undoubted social advantages of mixing with normal children with the danger of neglecting specific educational and developmental needs which might be better met by a more specialist approach. Research carried out for the Warnock Committee (Clarke, Riach and Cheyne 1977) suggested that nursery teachers, while welcoming a small number of handicapped children, badly needed advice in methods of working with them. The problem is made even more acute by the notion of 'critical periods'; there appear to be optimum times for learning specific skills (including language); if these periods are missed, it becomes more difficult, though not necessarily impossible, to make up for lost time at a later stage. It may be true to say that it is never too late to learn, but some skills are learned much more easily at some times than at others. The skilled teacher not only knows more about these stages and critical periods; he is also likely to be quite sensitive to the smallest signs from the child that he is 'ready' to take another step forward in his development.

Special schools

Some handicapped children will benefit greatly from a playgroup or nursery school, while others have more specialized needs which perhaps can only be met in a special school. Certainly, it is increasingly common to encounter two- and three-year-old children in the new ESNS schools, apparently deriving great benefit from the opportunities offered. Here again, parental involvement is more and more in evidence in special schools, and parents and teachers are beginning to work together in a variety of ways, including weekly parent-teacher workshops.

Some ESNS schools now have nursery units which provide opportunities for specialized assessment and educational planning; the children are in contact with teachers who are more experienced and often more appropriately trained to help severely handicapped children to learn and develop their abilities. Special schools also have their disadvantages — they may separate the child from normal children, and therefore deprive him of the company of children to imitate; inevitably the child is labelled in some ways and singled out from other children. Furthermore, teachers who work with heavily handicapped children may be in danger of setting their sights too low and demanding too little. On the other hand, there are certain advantages in education in the special school and some of the disadvantages can be overcome with good planning and sensible management. A good special school also has one major advantage over the normal nursery school — it can make special provision for parental involvement and can make systematic arrangements to help parents to work in full partnership with teachers.

Such evidence as is available on mentally handicapped children who go to special schools is certainly encouraging. The Schools Council survey of the language abilities of some 1,400 children in ESNS schools (Swann and Mittler 1976, Leeming *et al.* 1979) suggested that the rate of language growth was encouraging between 3 and 6, though it cannot be established that this was due to schooling as such, since equally encouraging growth rates were shown in a different group of 150 three- and four-year-olds surveyed by McConkey and Jeffree (1975) as a preliminary to the Parental Involvement Project. Thus, 37 per cent of three-year-olds attending ESNS schools in the first study were already speaking in single words and 21 per cent had reached the two word stage. By the age of 4, 40 per cent of children in the second study were already combining two words. This study of preschool children in the Greater Manchester area revealed a surprisingly high proportion of children already attending some form of preschool provision. 65 per cent of four-year-olds and 48 per cent of three-year-olds were already attending day nurseries, nursery schools or playgroups on a part-time basis (McConkey and Jeffree 1975).

What matters, of course, is not what kind of school a child goes to, but what he does when he gets there. Placement is only the first step in planning an educational programme. Mentally handicapped children have special needs over and above their needs as young children, and we must make provision for these wherever the child happens to be.

Home teaching

Some form of special help will need to be considered for all families with a preschool handicapped child whether he goes to school or not. This may take the form of a home-visiting service, in which the mother is helped through regular visiting to work out ways of helping her child to develop. This kind of help is particularly necessary for children under 2 — the time when the mother often feels in greatest need of help and guidance.

Although very little educational help is available for children and families in the first two years, the Warnock proposals for a peripatetic teaching service to be available without any lower age limit of 2 should make it possible to enable families to be helped from the time that a child is born or identified — assuming of course that they are willing to accept help at this early stage. Whether they do so or not will largely depend on the kind of help that is offered and the extent to which it meets the needs of the family as well as those of the child.

The last ten years have certainly seen exciting and revolutionary developments in parental involvement. Parents have been helped to observe, assess and record the skills and behaviours of their child and have used these as the basis for the setting of realistic goals that could be achieved in a short period of time. Some involve programmes of behaviour modification in which parents are trained to be teachers and psychologists but are taken through a standard 'package' or 'kit' of activities derived loosely from a normal developmental approach; children are taught a range of skills and behaviours, from self-care skills to stacking bricks and threading beads, some of which are clearly more useful than others to a particular child at any given time. An example of such an approach is provided by the Portage programme, named after a small town in rural Wisconsin (Shearer and Shearer 1972). The essence of this scheme is that a single individual is assigned to work with a small group of families in their own homes, helping the parents to assess the developmental level of their child, to work out teaching targets on the basis of that assessment and to follow a series of suggestions for helping the child to reach specific goals — whether these are holding a spoon or piling up wooden blocks. These targets are reviewed every week between the home teacher and the parent.

The Portage system is being introduced experimentally into a few areas in Britain and has been evaluated by the Health Care Evaluation Research Team in Wessex (Smith *et al*. 1977). It seems to provide an effective and flexible approach to early intervention which helps the child and supports the family. It is also remarkably cheap; the training of the home visitors can be completed in about a week, but the system calls for a series of weekly control meetings between all the home teachers working in a particular area.

More recently the emphasis seems to be shifting in favour of a somewhat less prescriptive approach, and one which is based on the natural resources and priorities of the family. For example, parents can be helped by professionals to set priority objectives for their child but the methods they use to help the child to reach those objectives are largely a matter of choice for the parents themselves. Parents can be given a general understanding of the principles of systematic teaching, such as task analysis, shaping, modelling, prompting and rewarding, as well as opportunities to try these methods out under supervision. But they are then left free to determine the best methods of teaching their own child, though they are provided with opportunities for consulting professionals.

Handbooks of teaching methods, as well as detailed examples of the content of teaching, have been published specifically for parents, offering not merely general advice but detailed suggestions for teaching. These can be used by parents who are unable or unwilling to join groups but can also be productively used in small group sessions. For example, the two Souvenir Press handbooks *Let Me Speak* (Jeffree and McConkey 1976) and *Let Me Play* (Jeffree, McConkey and Hewson 1977) reflect suggestions for teaching arising from the Parental Involvement Project conducted at the Hester Adrian Research Centre and also from earlier Parent Workshops (Cunningham and Jeffree 1971). Assessment Charts developed specifically for parents (but now widely used by professionals) are designed not only to identify the skills and abilities of preschool children but also to assist in an analysis of the steps that a child needs to take to reach a particular objective. Even more detailed developmental guidelines have been produced with the needs of profoundly handicapped children in mind — e.g. the Behaviour Assessment Battery (Kiernan and Jones 1978), a handbook for parents of profoundly handicapped children (Kiernan, Jordan and Saunders 1979), as well as a further volume in the same series for parents of handicapped children in the first two years (Cunningham and Sloper 1978).

Conclusions

This Chapter reviews ways in which educational and developmental help can be provided for a handicapped child from the first weeks of life. It is based on the premise that help should be available for every child who needs it, and that plans should be made in every locality to provide it. Because the nature of the help will obviously depend on the needs of the child and the family, the range of services should meet the range of needs. Some parents may not wish to take advantage of specialist services which will commit them to the admission that their child is handicapped; others will want to be helped immediately. But it is essential that any parent who is in the slightest degree worried about the development of their child should be able to get advice and support from experienced people and not be fobbed off with vague reassurances.

Proposals made by the Court and Warnock Committees are a step in the right direction. If each of the new Health Districts had a District Handicap Team and a Child Development Centre, and if these services worked in partnership with parents, schools and community agencies to help to plan a programme of development and activities suited to the needs of each child, the outlook for parents and children would certainly be brighter than it is in many parts of the country today.

But it is also important to keep a wide range of options at local level and to plan for a variety of services. Handicapped children need help at different times from a large number of organizations and individuals. These include the primary care teams (general practitioner, health visitor, social worker), preschool services of various kinds, including playgroups, day nurseries, nursery classes and special schools and the whole range of specialist health services. Whatever services are needed, they should as far as possible be available to parents in their own homes. Too many of our services, excellent though they may be in themselves, are locked up in buildings; we have only just begun to understand the importance of providing a domiciliary service. Professionals who have been trained in a tradition where the parents were expected to come to them are now beginning to find that much can be achieved by going to the parents. Of course, this is not always practical or even desirable, but the kind of partnership with parents which is now seen as essential should be based in the home if at all possible.

5
TEACHING CHILDREN

The scope of education

If education is concerned with everything that helps an individual to learn and to develop, then education begins at birth and never comes to an end. Parents are the key figures in the educational process in the first few years; during the years when education is institutionalized in school, society delegates the major task to trained teachers. They in turn hope to entrust the pupil with responsibility for his own educational development for the rest of his life.

Such a view of education is, of course, idealistic and over-simplified. But by examining its implications for the education of the mentally handicapped, it may be possible to establish some important principles which are relevant to non-handicapped people as well.

Mental handicap is a condition which by definition involves marked difficulties in learning and in personal development. Although no two mentally handicapped children will learn or develop in the same way, we know that they will all experience severe difficulties in thinking and learning to develop the skills necessary to live as members of the community.

But we also know enough to be confident that much more can be done to help mentally handicapped people to become more skilled in learning and to stretch their abilities to the utmost. This challenge is fundamentally an educational one, whether it is met at home, in school or in hospital. We also know something of the dangers of failing to provide an educational environment. Mentally handicapped people are especially vulnerable to neglect of all kinds, particularly educational neglect. If we fail to teach them, they are unlikely to learn. Some people even go as far as to say that everything that we want a mentally handicapped person to learn will have to be taught. Mentally handicapped people are often less competent than others in learning incidentally, and in observing and imitating others, and many of them are also poorly endowed with a 'natural' curiosity to experiment and to explore their environment.

The challenge to professionals, therefore, is to find ways of assisting and accelerating processes of development which we ordinarily take for granted, and which in normal people require little in the way of formal instruction. If we fail in meeting this challenge, the development of the handicapped person is likely to be slower than it need be — in other words, he is more likely to be 'under-functioning' — an unnecessary but all too common secondary handicap in disabled people generally. We might almost say that, within certain limits, we get out what we put in.

But neither our experience of parenthood nor our training as professionals normally equips us with the need or the skills necessary, for example, to teach a baby to become interested in his environment, to reach out and grasp objects, to learn that objects continue to exist even when they can no longer be seen. Nor do we normally have to think very hard about teaching a young child the elements of his own language. Yet mentally handicapped children often have to be taught to do these things and much more; they may have to be taught to play, and to use play as a tool for language and for learning about the environment of things and people.

If education is concerned with all those forces which help an individual to learn and develop, it follows that the 'treatment' of mental handicap must be primarily educational. Interpreted in this broad sense, everyone who comes into contact with a mentally handicapped person is working as an educationalist, whether he is a parent, teacher, nurse, doctor, psychologist or speech therapist. Even architects, administrators and politicians have an educational role to play in the treatment of mental handicap, since their task is to create environments which are favourable to learning and development. But because it is not enough to merely create appropriate opportunities and environments for learning, we entrust to skilled teachers the task of helping the child to make the best use of such abilities as he possesses. This task requires detailed assessment and observation, and the formulation of a specific programme of teaching suited to the unique needs of the individual learner.

Education in school

Since 1 April 1971 when the Department of Education and Science assumed responsibility for the education of mentally handicapped children, no child, however severely handicapped, is regarded as 'ineducable' or 'unsuitable for education in school'. Education authorities are also responsible for the education of all children in hospitals for the mentally handicapped, whether they are attending the hospital school or not.

The transfer of responsibility brought into the education system some 30,000 children who were previously the responsibility of local and hospital health authorities. It came about because it was increasingly clear that mentally handicapped children had been considerably underestimated in their ability to learn and to respond to educational influences and because it was no longer considered justifiable to cut them off from the mainstream of education or to deprive them of educational resources. Indeed, there is growing acceptance of the view that the more handicapped the child, the greater the skills of the teacher need to be, and that handicapped children require positive discrimination in their favour.

Before considering some of these achievements and problems, we can briefly note a major parallel development in the USA. The passing of Public Law 94-142 in 1975 mandates the nationwide provision of special education and other relevant services for all handicapped children, regardless of the severity of their handicap. An individualized instruction must be written down for each child which specifies:

   (i) the child's present levels of educational performance;
  (ii) annual goals, including short-term objectives;
 (iii) educational services to be provided;
 (iv) dates for initiation and duration of services;
  (v) appropriate objective criteria and evaluation procedures for determining whether instructional objectives are being achieved.

These goals are somewhat more specific than those to which we are accustomed in the British system. Nevertheless, they are an example of the kind of direct accountability and programming auditing systems which are discussed in Chapters 1 and 9 of this book.

Progress made in Britain since 1971 has been emphasized in the report of the Warnock Committee (DES 1978) which extends the concept of special education from the 2 per cent or so of handicapped children now in special schools to about 20 per cent of the school population who will have some form of special educational need in their school lives. The Warnock report stresses that the aims of education are the same for all children, no matter how severely handicapped, but that the methods of realizing these aims must necessarily differ with the needs of the child. As far as mentally handicapped children are concerned, they state:

It is now recognised that the tasks and skills to be learned by these children have to be analysed precisely and that the setting of small, clearly defined incremental objectives for individual children is a necessary part of programme planning (para 11.57).

It is this approach which is summarized in this Chapter, and illustrated in much greater detail in the book summarizing the work of the Schools Council project (Leeming *et al.* 1979).

How successful has the transfer been? How have education authorities at both local and national levels responded to the challenge? What achievements have been recorded, what are the main shortcomings, and what remains to be done?

It has to be admitted that we have very little factual information on the work of special schools for the mentally handicapped. But there would probably be a wide measure of agreement that the transfer of responsibility from health to education has been largely successful. Education authorities at national and local level have made considerable progress since 1971 in bringing the schools, the teachers and the children into special education; much has been done to shield special schools and in particular the 30,000 who were 'the last to come in' from the economic blizzard which has been raging with increasing ferocity and which has severely affected every sector of the education and other public services.

But there are many fundamental and practical problems surrounding the education of mentally handicapped children. We can do little more than pose these questions here.

(1) What is the rationale for providing education for these children?

(2) What should be the aims of education, and are they in any sense different from the aims of education for ordinary children?

(3) How useful is normal child development as a guide to the education of the handicapped?

(4) How relevant are existing teaching methods developed from work with young normal children?

(5) How early should education begin, and how long and in what form can it continue? How can educational provision be made for adolescents and adults?

(6) What kind of teachers do we need, and how should they be trained?

(7) How can parents be more directly involved in the educational development of their children, both in and out of school?

Cunningham (1974) poses four basic questions, to which we might add a fifth.

(1) What *should* we teach?
(2) What *could* be taught?
(3) *How* shall we teach?
(4) What *is* actually being taught and how?
(5) *Where* shall we teach?

Although we cannot in the present state of knowledge go very far in answering such questions, we may begin by reviewing what little factual information is available on the children, schools and teachers.

Children

We have very little information about the children in the new special (ESNS)* schools though a number of surveys now in progress should provide useful information. We do know, however, that the majority of mentally handicapped children of school age are now attending school, though it should be added that this is not the case in all parts of the country. All children of school age should either be attending school or be receiving home teaching or some other form of education. Education authorities are statutorily charged with this responsibility, and cannot claim that any child is too handicapped to benefit from education.

Numbers
Numbers attending have risen rapidly over the past fifteen years. Thus, there were less than 10,000 children attending Junior Training Centres in 1958, compared with about 30,000 in ESNS schools in 1976 of whom some 3,000 are in hospital schools, and the remainder living in the community and attending day schools, mostly from their own homes; mentally handicapped children are now the second biggest group in special schools, second only to the mildly handicapped (ESNM), of whom there are approximately 60,000.

The age range of the children in ESNS schools is between 2 and 19, with about 1,800 pupils nationally in each of the main year bands between 5 and 16. An increasing number of under-fives is being admitted to special schools, but the total in 1976 was still

*The Warnock Committee have proposed the substitution of 'children with severe learning difficulties' in place of 'educationally subnormal (severe)'. We shall continue to use the abbreviation ESNS here, as the Warnock recommendations have not been officially adopted at the time of going to press.

only 1,213 (5.8 per cent). Similarly, only 1.4 per cent of the total ESNS population in day schools was over 16, though the proportion is higher in hospital schools.

How do these numbers compare with the school age population generally? For practical purposes, we can estimate that 4 out of every 1,000 children in schools between 5 and 16 are likely to be mentally handicapped (ESNS). This is equivalent to about seventy-five places in ESNS schools for a *total* population unit of 100,000 people: the DES estimate that for a total *school* population of 50,000 children, somewhere between 130 and 160 places will be needed in ESNS schools. Compared to a total population of nearly ten million children, 30,000 mentally handicapped children seems a small proportion.

Clinical characteristics
The range of handicaps and disabilities in ESNS schools is very great. At one extreme there are profoundly multiply handicapped children whose level of development corresponds to that of a child of a few months or even weeks in comparison with a normal child. We shall also find children who can walk and talk without difficulty, and whose intellectual and learning difficulties only become apparent when an attempt is made to teach them or to observe and analyse their ability to think and solve problems. In addition, children described as autistic are sometimes characterized by their normal appearance, and even extraordinary grace and agility, but also by severe cognitive impairments and exceptional difficulties in understanding language.

The clinical and medical characteristics of ESNS children have not been adequately investigated. All that we know for certain is that about one third of the children have Down's Syndrome (mongolism), but even this condition is far from uniform in its effects. The stereotype of the 'happy, smiling, musical mongol', delightful to know and easy to teach, is fortunately not entirely without foundation, but hides a great deal of individual variation. Few Down's children are profoundly handicapped (IQ less than 25), but their personalities and cognitive abilities vary widely, as does their physique. About 97 per cent of cases of Down's Syndrome are 'classical' trisomy 21 — i.e. they carry an extra chromosome 21 — but other forms of Down's Syndrome are also known, especially 'mosaics', in whom a proportion of the cells is normal. Although there are important genetic and biological differences between trisomy 21s and other Down's children there is a suggestion from large-scale studies in American institutions that mosaic children show only marginally higher IQ scores (Belmont 1971).

If there is some doubt whether even the Down's children can be regarded as a homogenous group, the remaining 65 per cent are even more heterogenous and range enormously both clinically, behaviourally and educationally. For this reason alone, attempts to compare Down's Syndrome children with 'the rest' are of little value. Nearly all the children can be described as multiply handicapped; indeed, the previous concept of multiple handicap has been transformed by the incorporation of mentally handicapped children into the educational system. The term multiple handicap used to be reserved for obvious overlap of handicaps — e.g. the child with both visual and auditory handicap (the 'deaf-blind'). We now see that the multiple handicap is the rule rather than the exception in ESNS children. Thus, a significant proportion of the children have auditory or visual handicaps of varying degrees of severity, many are physically handicapped, while a considerable number show evidence of disturbed behaviour or overt psychiatric disorders. The majority have severe speech and language difficulties. It will be apparent therefore that all ten of the existing categories of handicap are fully represented in ESNS schools, and that nowhere else is the concept of multiple handicap so challengingly illustrated. Such a challenge obviously calls for teachers with outstanding skills and training.

Surveys of school populations are beset by severe difficulties because the children have not always been adequately investigated. Such attempts have also foundered on the extreme poverty of the record systems available in most schools, and by the lack of comparability in record keeping between one school and another and between different authorities. Local government reorganization, a new DES initiative on record systems introduced in their circular 2/75 and the Warnock recommendations may bring about some measure of improvement, but at the present time only the most approximate classifications can be attempted.

Nevertheless, it may be useful to summarize the findings from the recent Schools Council survey of nineteen ESNS schools in the North West of England. (See *Table 5.1* overleaf.)

A survey of ESNS children attending schools in sixty-five hospitals for the mentally handicapped has recently been completed by Bland (1979). These children are very much more severely handicapped than those attending day special schools, though they represent only a small minority of all mentally handicapped children. Bland's survey does however cover the majority of children in hospital at the present time. Estimates supplied by the

Table 5.1 *Number and percentage of children in major diagnostic classifications in 19 schools*
(N = 1,381)

Category	N	%
Down's Syndrome	393	34.3
Cerebral palsy	104	9.1
Hydrocephaly	65	5.7
Microcephaly	54	4.7
Autism/psychosis	28	2.4
Phenylketonuria	14	1.2
Other categories	26	2.3
Undefined or unknown	461	40.3
Total	1,145	100.0
Missing information	236	17.1

Taken from Leeming *et al.* (1979).

headteachers in the hospital schools suggest that just under half (45 per cent) are profoundly handicapped and function at a level corresponding to IQ levels of under 25. About 12 per cent of pupils had serious defects of vision, including 3.5 per cent who were totally blind. Similarly 7.5 per cent had serious hearing losses, and 79 per cent had serious speech defects, including total lack of speech. About one third were suffering from severe physical handicaps.

Abilities and disabilities
We are also dependent on local surveys for a more detailed picture of the abilities of the children and the work of the schools. Two recent studies can be quoted: the survey of Hughes (1975) of eighty-eight schools and the Schools Council survey of language abilities of some 1,400 children in nineteen schools in the Manchester and Cheshire areas.

Hughes (1975) devised an assessment scale modelled on Gunzburg's *Progress Assessment Charts* (1975) in which the teachers themselves assessed the abilities of a sample of 151 pupils of all ages from forty-four schools on items grouped into four main areas — self-help, communication, occupation and socialization. He concludes that many children are lacking in a large number of skills necessary to function in the community. Examples of the findings include the following:

(i) 29 per cent can walk about neighbourhood and cross streets unsupervised;
(ii) 7 per cent use public transport independently;
(iii) 23 per cent go on simple errands outside home and school;
(iv) 21 per cent make minor purchases.

The Schools Council survey (Swann and Mittler 1976; Leeming *et al*. 1979) concentrates on language and communication abilities, using teachers' ratings on specially developed questionnaires. The striking feature of this survey relates to the remarkably slow growth of language abilities over the school age period.

(1) The proportion of children reaching three critical levels of spoken language abilities increased very little between 6 and 14, though there were signs of improvement at about 14 or 15.
(2) Of those leaving school at 16, 22 per cent were unable to form simple two word sentences, 18 per cent had not yet reached the one word stage and 43 per cent could not form grammatical sentences.
(3) 23 per cent were unable to respond reliably to their own name.
(4) On an objective and standardized measure of receptive vocabulary (English Picture Vocabulary Test) the level of vocabulary development rose by an equivalent of less than one year's development between the ages of 10 and 16.
(5) These somewhat negative findings are offset by the relatively rapid language growth shown by the youngest children in the schools i.e. those between 3 and 6 years of age.

The very slow rate of development shown by children in ESNS schools is considerably slower than that which would be predicted on the basis of their intelligence alone. The lack of skills of many of the school leavers again raises fundamental questions about the whole nature of the educational process for mentally handicapped children. What are our aims for this group of children? To what extent should our aims derive from normal educational theory and practice? Do mentally handicapped children have special needs over and above their needs as children? How appropriate are our methods of teaching? Before discussing these questions, we briefly review some of the available information about the schools themselves and the staff who work in them.

Schools

The total number of special schools for ESNS children was just under 400 in 1976. Although many of these former JTCs were 'purpose-built' in the 1960s, the modern appearance of the schools can be deceptive, and they contain many features which make them less than ideal. Indeed, the term 'purpose-built' is something of a misnomer. Most are far too small and the amount of space per pupil is less than half of what it should be, according to DES standards of special schools. The classrooms tend to be cramped and do not provide the scope or flexibility which is required. There is little provision for individual teaching or therapy, no room for visiting specialists to work with individual children or for a secretary (health authorities rarely provided them). Playgrounds are often unimaginative and not related to the play needs or physical handicaps of the children.

In his survey of eighty-eight ESNS schools, Hughes (1975) notes the following facts supplied by the headteachers:

(i) 61 per cent of the schools were described as purpose built; 14 per cent were in old school buildings and 25 per cent were in converted buildings;

(ii) 73 per cent of the schools had adequate playground facilities;

(iii) 18 per cent had a gymnasium, 68 per cent had gymnastic equipment, 64 per cent had use of a swimming pool;

(iv) 39 per cent had adequate storage facilities.

In 1972 the Department of Education prepared a guidance document on designing schools for ESNS children (*Design Note 10*). The amount of space per pupil is doubled, and many useful and far-reaching suggestions are offered. A number of schools designed along these lines have now been completed. The design has been described as 'modified open plan', and has its critics.

The average ESNS school now contains about seventy pupils. Although it is being increasingly accepted that junior secondary age children should be taught in separate schools, nearly all the schools contain the entire age range from 2 to 19, though in practice the majority of pupils are between 5 and 16. Schools are generally organized into six or seven classes of about eight to ten children, each with a teacher and most with a second adult acting as classroom assistant. The children are roughly divided by age, though the age range in any one classroom is likely to be very wide — certainly much wider than in an ordinary school.

The main exception is the 'Special Care Unit' which tends to contain children of all ages with the most severe handicaps, perhaps 20 to 25 per cent of the ESNS school population. Many of them are unable to walk, and some cannot even sit; very few of them can use or understand language; all of them require individual intensive attention and a systematic approach to their development. Although the term 'special care' is widely used, it is falling out of favour mainly because it suggests that the most severely handicapped children are in some way removed from the main stream of the special school, and require a predominantly nursing approach rather than an educational one. This would now be disputed by many teachers, who are taking an increasing interest in ways in which the development of even the most profoundly handicapped child can be actively fostered.

Some schools have renamed their Special Care classes as Special Needs Units or Development Units; others have virtually abolished them and tried to integrate every child into the other classes in the school for part of the day while withdrawing them for special treatment sessions with speech therapists or physiotherapists or with other specialist staff for short periods. In other words, they have retained special needs provision but done away with special classes. Similar suggestions for a variety of approaches to the integration of the most severely handicapped have also been made for Adult Training Centres by the National Development Group (1977b), though the proportion of severely handicapped students in ATCs is still very small (see Chapter 7).

Similar problems are posed by a small minority of severely disturbed children who are sometimes placed in special needs units. These children may disrupt the work of other classrooms and take up a disproportionate amount of the teacher's time at the expense of other activities and other children's needs. Some schools are therefore trying to organize their work in such a way that these children receive individual treatment for their disturbed behaviour from a teacher specially appointed for the purpose but not necessarily in a special class set aside for disturbed children. Instead, the teacher may work in the ordinary classroom helping the child to build up positive behaviours but dealing with disruptive behaviour in a systematic and planned manner.

Teachers

Only about one third of the staff of the former Junior Training Centres had any form of appropriate basic qualification, but the proportion had risen by 1975 to approximately 80 per cent (2,460 out of 3,135). In the early 1960s the number of qualified staff had been only about 12 per cent, the improvement in the 1960s being due largely to the work of specialized two-year training courses for teachers of the mentally handicapped established by the National

Association of Mental Health and by a small number of colleges, under the auspices of the Training Council for Teachers of the Mentally Handicapped (DHSS 1974). This Council was set up by the Ministry of Health in 1964, following the publication of the Scott report on the training of teachers of the mentally handicapped. The Training Council achieved considerable success in developing training courses for teachers of adults and children. Its work came to an end in respect of the training of teachers in 1971, but it continued to work in the field of training Adult Training Centre staff until its work was taken over by the Central Council for Education and Training in Social Work in 1974.

The training courses that were running in the 1960s produced many teachers of outstanding ability. It is these teachers and their tutors who more than any other group convinced the education authorities that the children were capable of responding to learning, provided they were taught by carefully chosen methods suited to their particular abilities and disabilities. Mildred Stevens, who was tutor to one such course for ten years, has described some of the teaching practices and principles; her books are still virtually the only accounts of the education of mentally handicapped children published in Britain (Stevens 1976, 1978), and provide a unique insight into the development of professional skills and confidence among this group of teachers, as well as a vivid picture of conditions in schools at this time.

Trained teachers have been recruited in a variety of ways since 1971. In the first place, a large number of teachers achieved recognition as qualified Burnham teachers after five years teaching experience following their two years specialist training for work with the mentally handicapped. Second, a number of teachers who were working in ordinary or special schools have transferred to schools for the mentally handicapped since 1971. No figures are available on the number of teachers who have come into the new special schools by these routes. Third, teachers are being recruited following specialist initial training which is available in about twenty colleges of education. Some of these have developed from former Training Council courses, and have been absorbed by colleges of education; others have been established since 1971.

The initial training of teachers in aspects of mental handicap has met with some criticism. Students have complained that far too little time is devoted to mental handicap on the syllabus, and that more time and more opportunity to specialize were available on the former courses. These problems arise because in the three or four years available the colleges are trying to train teachers who will be competent to teach ordinary as well as handicapped children; it is difficult to arrange a timetable and a curriculum to meet both these aims (Stevens 1978). As we shall see, the specialist teacher requires much more than a knowledge of normal children and 'normal' education methods. Furthermore, tutors in colleges of education do not always possess practical experience of teaching mentally handicapped children, and are themselves handicapped by the lack of books, materials and curriculum for ESNS schools. There is also little in the way of a sound theoretical rationale in this field, though the foundations have been ably laid by McMaster (1973) and Cunningham (1974), and the DES (1975) have themselves issued important curriculum guidelines.

The Warnock Committee has now expressed its own reservations about the adequacy of existing courses of initial training in the ESNS field and has recommended that they should be monitored and evaluated by Her Majesty's Inspectorate; no new courses of initial specialist training are to be developed. The Committee clearly preferred to concentrate on providing a variety of one-year advanced courses in special education for all teachers working with handicapped children, either full time or an equivalent period of part-time study, as well as a range of in-service courses, some of which would need to be general, others quite detailed and specific. They suggest that special financial incentives should be linked to the recognized qualification in special education and that this should replace the additional allowance which is now payable for teaching handicapped children.

Teachers of ESNS children have a special claim to the training resources which will hopefully be released by the Warnock proposals. Although they are teaching the second biggest group of children in special schools, only a very small minority (7 per cent) have a special educational qualification. There are teachers who have taken mental handicap as a main subject or option in their initial training, those who are qualified by virtue of the former Training Council qualification in addition to five years subsequent experience, and those who have taken one of the advanced diploma courses in universities or colleges. Only one of these specializes in the teaching of ESNS children (Westhill College, Birmingham). In addition, a number of teachers have taken a variety of in-service courses, some designed to lead to awards, such as Certificates, Diplomas, B.Eds or M.Eds in special education.

The need for a range of specialist courses in mental handicap is overwhelming. Not only are relatively few teachers specifically qualified for work in this field, but the range of knowledge is expanding so rapidly that even those who qualified some years ago need opportunities to attend advanced and refresher courses.

Striking developments are taking place in the education of this group of children both in this country and overseas; new ideas and methods are being pioneered both in the schools and in research and development centres. For example, advances are being made in basic assessment of the skills and abilities of children, in goal setting and methods of programme planning, record keeping and evaluation and in curriculum development generally. There is a growing interest in the education of the most severely handicapped children as well as in methods of preparing school leavers to live and work in the community. To this end teachers need to study the kind of skills handicapped young people need in the community, and to work in closer partnership with the whole range of community agencies, including not only ATCs but FE colleges and employment and rehabilitation services. The Warnock proposals for joint training between teachers and other professionals (e.g. social workers, speech therapists and health visitors) are particularly relevant in this connection. Joint courses with FE and ATC teachers are also likely to be developed in future.

Proposals for staff training in the mental handicap service as a whole are more fully discussed in Chapter 10 but one of the most pressing needs is to end the isolation of ESNS schools and the staff who work in them from their colleagues in the rest of special and ordinary education. To this end, much more use might be made of the 500 or so Teachers' Centres. These centres have an important part to play in providing specialist short courses and workshops, where practical problems of assessment and teaching are discussed and evaluated, and where teachers and other specialists can meet to discuss and tackle their difficulties. The Manchester Teachers' Centre, for example, appointed a curriculum development officer for ESNS children, set up a working party consisting of teachers, a speech therapist and a research worker and conducted a survey of the language abilities of ESNS pupils in Manchester schools (Kellett 1976).

Curriculum

The concept of curriculum may at first sight appear both awesome and inappropriate for mentally handicapped children. Although it has come to acquire somewhat formal overtones in the theory of education, and has in some countries been interpreted as a prescribed set of activities tied to a timetable, its importance to the educational development of mentally handicapped children cannot be sufficiently emphasized. It will only be discussed in broad outline here, since detailed discussion of this whole area has been attempted in the report of the Schools Council project on the education of ESNS children (Leeming *et al.* 1979).

A curriculum may be defined as a set of organized experiences provided by an educational system to realize the goals of education (Cunningham 1974). The DES (1975) pamphlet defines it as 'a school's plan for facilitating a child's growth and for developing selected skills, ideas, attitudes and values.' These definitions raise further questions about the goals of education, and whether these apply equally to mentally handicapped and to non-handicapped children. Such questions are basically philosophical in nature but none the less relevant, provided they do not remain at this level, but are given practical expression in the day-to-day activities of the classroom. What is involved here is a relationship between general aims on the one hand and specific objectives on the other.

The aims of education
The general aims of education are the same for the mentally handicapped as for anyone else. General aims are necessarily expressed in global terms; for example, philosophers who write about the goals of education tend to speak in terms of personal autonomy and independence; specialists in the education of handicapped children are fond of saying that children should be able to 'achieve the maximum of their potential', be helped to 'adjust to the demands of the community and to take their place in society'.

Such statements of aims are useful enough but they are necessarily too general and vague. How will we know whether or not a child has 'fulfilled his potential', especially now that we no longer believe that we know how to measure potential by means of intelligence tests? How can we estimate the extent to which a child is not fulfilling his potential, and do we know how to narrow the gap between his potential and his performance?

Terms like autonomy and independence can be useful and need not be vague; a child increases his independence by learning to walk, and by learning to speak, just as much as by learning to read. The fact that some skills are at a more advanced level than others does not make the teaching of basic skills any less educationally important.

Sources of the curriculum
Given the vagueness of the general aims of education for the mentally handicapped, what should be the source of the curriculum, and how shall we decide what we are going to teach?

Many workers in this field are content to base their work on the framework provided by our knowledge of normal child development.

But how far does a detailed knowledge of normal child development provide a useful guide to determining the curriculum of the severely handicapped child? In the 1960s, teachers working with mentally handicapped children were strongly influenced by the movements in British infant and nursery education; these placed a strong emphasis on providing a rich and stimulating environment, and encouraging the child to take advantage of a wide range of materials and learning opportunities. The choice of materials was influenced by the overall developmental level of the child; there was therefore an emphasis on nursery school materials and methods, since the developmental level of many of the children corresponded to the 'mental age' encountered in nursery schools — i.e. between 2½ and 5 years.

But it could not be assumed that toys and play materials for young normal children were necessarily suitable for much older mentally handicapped children, even though their levels of mental development might be comparable. The fact that a fifteen-year-old young person has a mental age of 3 years does not mean that he should be educated only according to the methods and principles suitable for normal three-year-olds.

These methods were themselves a reaction against the rather formal 'sense training' methods which had been used in many schools, based loosely on influences deriving from the work of Seguin, Itard and others. But the methods were applied to groups of children and were not sufficiently related to the needs of the individual. Thus it was not uncommon to see rows of children sitting in desks, each child engaged in the same task of threading beads or completing identical form boards.

During the late 1960s, psychological research began to raise questions about the validity of approaches based exclusively on free activity and on 'learning by doing'. These studies suggested that mentally handicapped children had specific difficulties in spontaneous and incidental learning and that it could not be assumed that the child would learn merely by exposing him to the conditions for learning which were suitable for other children (Clarke and Clarke 1974).

Here again, a balance needs to be struck between the advantages and disadvantages of using our knowledge of normal development. It is certainly useful as a general framework, because it provides signposts for the teacher in search of a curriculum. But the signposts are sometimes few and far between and do not provide enough detailed or specific guidance to help one to travel from one landmark to another.

Teaching methods

An attempt is now being made in many schools to achieve a balance between stimulation and structure; this involves retaining the lively, child-centred, stimulating environment as a background, while at the same time using structured methods as a foreground. The need for more structured methods has undoubtedly been more widely recognized in the past five years or so, not only because of the findings of research but because teachers themselves felt dissatisfied with the results of existing methods and seemed to be actively seeking for a more systematic approach without at the same time abandoning what they regarded as the most valuable elements of the infant and nursery school approach.

The essence of this approach lies in the identification of short-term teaching objectives. An objective is a statement of what it is that the child will be able to do that he could not do before. It must be specific, and it must be attainable in a very short time — perhaps as little as a few minutes.

This contrasts with the rather general long-term aims which are often stated by teachers and others concerned with special educa-tion. It is not enough to say that we are aiming to teach a child to communicate, or to dress himself or to learn to become independent. These general aims have to be broken down into small steps which can easily be defined and therefore measured. In this way, we shall be able to evaluate whether or not we have reached our objectives. If we have succeeded, we move on to the next objective; if not, we carry out a more detailed analysis to try to make the task simpler, and begin to teach again. In other words, if the child fails to learn, we re-examine our own teaching methods; we do not blame the child for being too handicapped to learn.

What, then, are these methods? Baldly summarized, such a systematic approach contains a number of essential components.

(1) Assessment
(2) Selection and analysis of task
(3) Presentation of task
(4) Evaluation

(1) *Assessment*

Assessment defines the entry point to the curriculum. Teachers should not therefore think of assessment as a highly specialized set of rituals which can only be performed by psychologists. Assessment is essentially a task for those who are going to teach the child, whether they are teachers or parents. It is not only a matter of administering specialized intelligence tests, but involves an attempt to establish what the child can and cannot do, with the aim of setting a teaching target that is related to his immediate needs.

In carrying out assessments, the class teacher can make use of fairly simple and straightforward checklists. These lists help to pinpoint the stage that a child has reached in critical areas of his development — for example in physical development, self-care skills, play, social maturity, language and communication abilities and so on. But charts and assessment scales are obviously not enough. They should be supplemented by detailed observations of the child's behaviour in a variety of structured and unstructured situations. The teacher will need to devise a simple system of recording which can be used to plan her teaching and as a means of evaluating progress.

A welcome development in special education is the blurring of the distinction between assessment and teaching. One expression of this is the so-called mini-learning experiment. This takes the form of defining a teaching objective that can be taught in a very short period of time, and recording the child's response to this teaching. This can even be done within the course of a conventional testing situation; after completing the test in a normal manner, and according to the rules and conventions of the test, the tester tries to teach a child to carry out a very small task. For example, he might try to devise a means of teaching him to complete a form board, or to learn a simple discrimination between two objects. In this way, he is not only recording the child's response to a standardized test, but is using this response as a basis for teaching the child to do something that he could not do before. The child's response to the learning situation is then measured objectively, and changes in the strategy of teaching can be introduced and evaluated. In this way, testing and teaching become part of an ongoing experimental approach to meeting the child's needs.

(2) *Selection and analysis of the task to be taught*
The assessment process should always lead to the formulation of a plan of development which is related to the needs of the individual child. Deciding on priorities is not always an easy or obvious task. On the basis of their detailed knowledge of the child, teachers will need to make certain decisions and to choose between different priorities. It is not always a matter of teaching the child to take the next step in his development in, say, self-care or language or motor skills. It is often necessary to try to isolate and identify the nature of the difficulties that the child may be experiencing in reaching the

next stage; there may be a problem in acquiring an essential component or sub-skill. For example, in teaching a child to learn to use a spoon, it may be necessary to teach him to look at the spoon, or, if he is physically handicapped, to retain his grip on the handle.

It may also be necessary on occasion to try to deal with a severe behaviour problem before teaching new skills; for example, head banging or a marked mannerism such as rocking, may need to be brought under control before developmental teaching can begin.

(3) *Presentation of the task*
Having analysed the task and identified the steps needed to teach it, the task can then be taught one step at a time. Various methods have been developed to help the child to learn. For example, the systematic use of prompting may involve the teacher doing the whole task for the child at first, and then gradually fading the prompt in very small stages over a number of trials, the speed of fading depending on the child's response. In teaching a child to use a spoon without spilling, the child may be physically guided through all but the last of the sequence of actions, and then taught to complete more and more of the actions for himself, with as much help as is necessary.

The use of systematic reward has been found to be highly effective in teaching mentally handicapped children, and the principles of reward training are now better understood. But reward training is only a means to an end; before we begin to use rewards, we need to have selected a teaching objective that is relevant to the needs of the child we are teaching. Reward training can easily be misused to teach children to do the things that we want, and that are convenient to us, rather than meeting the needs of the child. The very effectiveness of reward training makes it necessary to be cautious about the uses to which it is put.

(4) *Evaluation*
If the teacher has set a specific and definable objective, it should be possible to evaluate whether or not it has been achieved. This can be done by means of a simple record system or by special short test sessions in the form of 'probes'. These enable changes to be made in the course of the teaching; for example if teaching is not successful, then the task to be taught may need to be broken down into even smaller steps, or the method of reinforcement may need to be modified.

But the most important test is not whether the child learns but whether he uses what he has learned. This is perhaps the most difficult challenge of all. It is one thing to learn a skill in the classroom;

quite another to use it outside the teaching situation. Teachers are therefore very concerned at the present time with methods of teaching the child to generalize his learning from one setting to another.

The teaching of language and communication skills

It may be useful to try to illustrate how these general principles might be translated into action, taking language and communication teaching as an example. A fuller account of language teaching, with many 'worked examples' can be found in Leeming *et al.* (1979).

Recent work clearly shows that mentally handicapped children can be taught to develop language and communication skills, but that systematic and structured methods are necessary if they are to learn, and above all if they are to learn to use language in ordinary life. During the 1960s and up till quite recently there were many reports in which language was largely taught in rather artificial one-to-one 'clinical' sessions; the results were often good, in so far as children learnt to understand and use a wider range of language structures in the training situation. But it is only very recently that more emphasis has been placed on the teaching of language in ordinary, natural settings, such as the home, in shops, on public transport and in the playground. In order to learn to speak, children need to have something to say, and someone to talk to. This is why it is both more natural and more effective to involve families from the outset in systematic attempts to teach language skills.

It is now accepted that language can be taught long before the child begins to speak. The roots of language lie in the child's first attempt to communicate; we have to build on these foundations in the case of mentally handicapped children, and try to help them to learn that any form of communication is rewarding. Communication may begin with no more than a look or a smile, and then gradually develop towards gesture.

One of the most dramatic educational developments in the past few years has been the gradually increasing use of systematic sign languages with mentally handicapped people. (Kiernan 1977). Some of these are modifications of sign languages used by deaf people; others are no more than a few basic signs, such as signs for me, you, give, yes, no, eat, drink, toilet, signs for certain objects or activities. But these signs build bridges between the silent child and those around him; and it is on such foundations and communication can be built.

We also find increasing interest in teaching children to learn to listen, to learn that certain sounds are associated with certain activities, and to learn that listening can be enjoyable. A number of studies have shown that even profoundly handicapped children are able to express choice for one type of sound rather than another — for example, by moving a large switch they can choose to listen to one type of music rather than another (Friedlander 1970).

Learning to play is also recognized as one of the essential foundations of language development; children are therefore being taught to play symbolically and representationally — for example, pretend games, games with dolls — indeed, any game in which one thing is made to stand for or symbolize another (Jeffree, McConkey and Hewson 1977).

The goal of language teaching is, of course, to teach a child to speak in words, phrases and sentences and finally to use words to communicate meaning and intention. Here again, techniques are being developed to do this, using principles of assessment and task analysis. The teacher may begin with a programme of imitation training, in which the child is trained to imitate large movements of the body; these are then localized to the head, mouth or tongue; finally the child is taught to imitate sounds.

Some language teaching programmes have also become available on the commercial market — e.g. the *Peabody Language Development Kit, Goal, Distar, Jim's People, First Words Language Programme* (see Leeming *et al.* (1979) for a critical discussion). These methods are slow and time consuming; staff in schools and residential establishments may not have the time to carry them out. But partnership with parents can achieve a great deal.

Creative activities

Although the approach to education outlined here is broadly behavioural, and relies to a large extent on assessment, developmental planning, task analysis and prescription, there is no reason why educational experiences for these children should necessarily be sterile or lacking in enjoyment. Of course, success in learning and in the attainment of goals is a reward in itself, but it is important to allow plenty of time for creative activities, for enjoyment and for free activity, since these bring their own reward and are as important to the total development of the child as the attainment of formal learning goals (Stevens 1976, 1978).

It is therefore important to provide opportunities for children to benefit from creative activities, such as drama, music, physical education, swimming, games, sports and a wide range of recreational activities. In fact, virtually all activities open to normal children should also be available to the mentally handicapped. These are an essential part of their education and of their personal development, since such activities can often provide the means of self-expression and a source of satisfaction.

Experiments in integration

The vexed question of where children are to be taught has been left till last because this issue is best seen in the context of what and how they are to be taught. The essence of recent approaches to teaching lies in the attempt to find a balance between stimulation and structure, between general aims and activities on the one hand and precise objectives on the other. This balance needs to be maintained no matter where the children are — whether in a special school, in a special class attached to an ordinary school or even alongside non-handicapped pupils for some or the whole of the school day.

There is a great deal of interest at the present time in proposals to end or at least modify the exclusive use of special schools for handicapped children. Unfortunately, the issues are sometimes put far too crudely and even too sentimentally as a straight choice between segregation and integration; the assumption is made that special schools 'segregate' and normal schools 'integrate'. But the issues are far more complex than this. Not only is there a whole range of provision from extreme segregation to total integration, but a school which may at first sight appear to fall at one extreme or the other in terms of its 'label', may in fact be operating very differently in real terms. For example, a class of handicapped children attached to an infant school may in practice never work or play with normal children and lead a segregated existence in all but name; similarly, even when a special school is on the same campus as a normal school, there need not necessarily be any contact between staff or children. A residential special school in a remote rural area may become fully part of the community, and its pupils accepted as local children. A handicapped child may even be in an ordinary classroom every day but may be isolated socially and educationally from other children and from the activities of the class. It all depends on the extent to which integration is planned and worked for, and also on the willingness of both sides to make it work. Merely placing handicapped children in a normal school does not guarantee that any social or educational integration will take place. Indeed, there is evidence from experiments in the integration of deaf and partially hearing children of the 'glass wall' problem — i.e. integration in name only (Mittler 1975).

The problem is partly one of reconciling the undoubted *social*

advantages of integration with the *educational* needs of the
children. Special education wherever it is provided is a form of
positive discrimination in favour of the handicapped child. It
makes available on his behalf a favourable pupil-teacher ratio,
teachers with special training, classroom assistants, specially
adapted physical conditions, and a concentration in one building of
specialists such as speech therapists, physiotherapists, occupational
therapists, and sometimes also physicians, social workers and
psychologists. If handicapped children are to be educated in
ordinary schools, this element of positive discrimination must be
preserved.

There can be no doubt that handicapped children should not be
unnecessarily segregated from other children, and that a greater
degree of integration is an excellent long-term aim. But there is
some danger that the specific educational and learning difficulties
and needs of mentally handicapped children may not be adequately
catered for in ordinary schools, especially at a time when educational spending is having to suffer severe cut-backs and shrinking
resources. We can only hope that local authorities who are considering this question will not opt exclusively for an integration or
segregation policy, but will try to plan a range of provision, so that
rational decisions can be made and implemented on the basis of the
child's assessed needs, and not merely on the tide of a concern for
integration for integration's sake.

The debate about integration has been partially overtaken by
events — by Section 10 of the 1976 Education Act, by the Warnock
Report and by the period of consultation which will help the
government of the day to reach its own conclusions about the
report's recommendations, presumably some time in 1979.

Section 10 of the 1976 Education Act states that on a day to be
appointed by the Secretary of State, handicapped pupils in England
and Wales are to be educated in ordinary schools in preference to
special schools 'except where it is impracticable or incompatible
with the provision of efficient instruction in schools or where it
would involve unreasonable public expenditure'. No date has yet
been fixed, nor have the qualifying phrases been satisfactorily
defined. But Section 10 merely restates what has in fact been
official policy for many years; Ministry of Education Circular 276,
published in 1954, said 'no handicapped child should be sent to a
special school who can be satisfactorily educated in an ordinary
school'. The Secretary of State stated in 1977 that Section 10 has
given a new impetus towards integrated provision, 'in which special
schools would continue to have an important place'.

The view that special schools will undoubtedly continue to be needed, especially for 'children with severe or complex disabilities — physical, sensory or intellectual', is reinforced in the Warnock Report. The report includes a lengthy discussion of the wide range of provision which should be available and illustrates three different but overlapping types of integration. They distinguish between:

(i) locational integration, where special classes are set up in ordinary schools;

(ii) social integration, where children attending such special classes or units eat, play and consort with other children and possibly share out-of-classroom activities with them;

(iii) functional integration where there is also joint participation in educational programmes.

The report provides examples of four types of integrated provision:

(i) full time education in an ordinary class with any necessary help and support;

(ii) education in an ordinary class with periods of withdrawal to a special class or unit or other supporting base;

(iii) education in a special class or unit with periods of attendance at an ordinary class and full involvement in the general community life and extra-curricular activities of the ordinary school;

(iv) full time education in a special class or unit with social contact with the main school.

The Warnock Report also provides a useful discussion of the kinds of steps that will need to be taken by LEAs to meet the three qualifications — practicality, efficiency and cost. But it also emphasizes that integration in ordinary schools is not a cheap alternative to provision in separate special schools. 'Parliament having willed the ends, we would expect the government to will the means' (para 19.17). Success depends on:

(i) special training for teachers with responsibilities for children with special needs;

(ii) sustained support at a high level from the various services;

(iii) suitable facilities.

Implications for ESNS children
Although the Warnock Committee were careful to spell out the conditions necessary for progress towards more integrated provision, and indicated that special schools would continue to cater for

the majority of children currently categorized as ESNS, it seems likely that LEAs will increasingly be experimenting with a variety of provision for ESNS children in the coming decade.

So far, however, less than 2 per cent of these children (475) are in special classes (DES 1978). In reply to a Campaign for the Mentally Handicapped (1974) enquiry, the DES indicated that only 2 out of 103 projects for new schools, or replacements or extensions of existing schools, for ESNS children approved since 1971 involved the provision of special classes in ordinary schools. The number of new or replacement school places involved in this reply was about 6,000.

Among the few published reports of integration projects for the ESNS is one from the London borough of Bromley, written by one of the participating teachers (Pierse 1973). Classes for junior ESNS children were attached to six infant schools, each with a maximum of nine children, one teacher and two welfare assistants. Some of the children joined classes in the main school for certain activities; similarly normal children joined the special classes for short periods, e.g. for story-telling. In addition, a comprehensive school in Derbyshire has a class for ESNS children as well as a class for more mildly handicapped children.

A major research project now under way at the National Foundation for Educational Research is looking at a variety of integration projects for different kinds of handicapped children in several parts of the country; this should provide useful information for the development of sound educational policies. Although little information is available at the present time on the integration of ESNS children, we do have important studies on physically handicapped (Anderson 1973; Cope and Anderson 1977) and visually handicapped children (Jamieson, Partlett and Pocklington 1977).

Although there are few signs of moves to establish classes for ESNS children in ordinary schools, the Warnock suggestions for the more effective use of special schools are particularly important for ESNS schools. Many of these schools have still not been fully absorbed into either special or ordinary education and both the children and the staff who teach them are often isolated from other schools and other children. Not enough is known about the work of ESNS schools; few teachers from special or ordinary schools seem to visit them, nor do teachers from ESNS schools visit other schools as much as they might.

There is too little appreciation of the developments in teaching that have taken place in the last few years, and not enough knowledge of what can be achieved both by the children and staff. The Warnock proposals for in-service training for all teachers are therefore likely to lead to a growing awareness of the work of ESNS schools and this in turn should lead to the building of bridges between schools. Similarly, the designation of some special schools as resource centres may lead to a larger number of the younger ESNS children being retained in infant and junior schools, with strong support from specialist teachers.

Special schools for ESNS children are undoubtedly going to be needed for a long time, even if there are moves towards experimenting with special classes. They will continue to be needed as a base not only for skilled teaching but also for the team approach which is agreed to be essential but which it is going to be much more difficult to provide if children are too dispersed, e.g. speech therapy and physiotherapy, occupational therapy, psychology, social work and medical support.

Special schools will really need to become specialized centres of excellence rather than isolated havens of care if they are to continue to justify their existence in the face of the mounting pressures towards more integrated forms of provision. This in turn calls for a massive programme of training and in-service education for teachers and other staff working in the schools. LEAs will need to ensure that teachers and other staff are helped to update their knowledge and skills. Some schools can already claim to have reached very high levels of skill and professional competence. Others still have some way to go. But all schools need high-level help from the education service, in particular from local advisers in special education and from HMIs, if schools, teachers and pupils are to receive the positive discrimination which is their due.

Conclusions: ten principles

(1) Education is concerned with everything that helps an individual to learn and to develop new skills and abilities. It therefore begins at birth and is much broader than the curriculum of the school.
(2) Parents are at the heart of the educational process, and need to be helped to play a much more central part in helping the learning and development of their handicapped children. This detailed involvement should begin as soon as the handicap is identified, and be actively supported by professional workers, including health visitors, physicians, social workers and teachers. It should be even more strongly developed when the child reaches school. Parents and teachers should work in full partnership, to assess the child's present level and needs, and to plan on a day-to-day basis to help him to reach the next step in his development.

(3) Each child should receive regular comprehensive assessment by a multidisciplinary team. The emphasis in comprehensive assessment should be on what steps can be taken to help the child to reach the next stage of his development, a decision on who is to be responsible for implementing the plan or programme of teaching, and the criteria by which it is to be evaluated.

(4) It is impossible to generalize on where the educational and personal needs of young handicapped children are best met; the decision must rest on the assessment process and on the needs of the child. Among possible alternatives are special school, special class, nursery school, play group, day nursery, or any combination of these. It may also be preferable for the child to remain at home and for the parents to receive help from a visiting teacher or other specialist.

(5) The question of whether mentally handicapped pupils should be taught in special or ordinary schools should be seen as one of reconciling the child's educational and learning needs with the need to maintain contact with ordinary children in the community. But in our concern to avoid isolation of handicapped children from their peers, we should not lose sight of the evidence from research that mentally handicapped children do not automatically benefit merely from exposure to a rich and stimulating environment, to the challenge of normal children and normal experiences, and to the presence of well-intentioned but inexperienced staff. The education of mentally handicapped children demands the highest level of training, competence and skill.

(6) Once the child goes to school, teachers should make a thorough assessment of the child, by studying his abilities and disabilities, carrying out regular developmental assessments and bringing in specialists such as speech therapists and physiotherapists, physicians and psychologists as appropriate.

(7) The school will need to find and develop a balance between general activities which are broadly related to the aims of education and specific objectives which are based on the results of formulating the needs of the child as an individual and which arise from the assessment process.

(8) The content of education for mentally handicapped children will vary for each individual child, but is likely to comprise a wider range of teaching than is normally found in other schools for normal or handicapped children.

(9) The content of the curriculum for older children should consider the skills needed by young people in the community. Pupils should be placed in situations of increasing demand and

complexity and helped by small degrees to become more competent in meeting the demands of their local community — e.g. in shopping, using public transport, meeting people in a wide range of formal and informal situations.

(10) It is clear that we have only just begun to explore the possibilities of providing an educational environment for mentally handicapped children, and that there is still much to be learned and more to be achieved. It would be foolish to be over-optimistic because there must be limitations to what can be achieved. But whereas we used to stress the limitations imposed by the nature of the child's handicap, we are now more inclined to examine the limitations of our own abilities to design and implement an appropriate teaching programme. We are also aware that underestimation of abilities — to which the mentally handicapped are particularly prone — can lead to poor performance, and that children respond well to challenges and demands made on them. If these are just within their reach and if the teaching is carefully designed to help the child to attain a particular skill, then the chances of success are correspondingly greater.

It now seems obvious to us that education of the mentally handicapped is not only worthwhile on humanitarian grounds but is technically possible to a greater extent than we have previously thought. We need to convey this to the general public, to teachers in the normal sector, and to educational administrators who determine the resources that are to be given to special education.

6

LEAVING SCHOOL

Continuing education

It is fashionable nowadays to speak of life-long or continuing education for all, and to make provision for everyone to have access to educational opportunities for the whole of their lives. The Workers Educational Association and Extra Mural Departments have for many years been providing adult education facilities for those who were willing to take advantage of them; more recently there has been a vast expansion in further education colleges catering for the 16 to 19 group, and a substantial increase in the number of adults enrolling in evening classes of all kinds. The success of the Open University in attracting many thousands of previously unqualified part-time students to demanding courses of study after a hard day's work, but at a level entirely comparable to that reached by undergraduates studying under somewhat more favourable conditions, confirms once again the existence of a pool of ability in the population, consisting of people who have left school early without formal qualifications but who have the ability and the drive to benefit from a course of university studies.

The time has now come for these opportunities to be extended to those disabled people who for one reason or another have been excluded from them. Physically handicapped people of normal intelligence have been gaining access to further and higher education but even their needs have not always been understood. Problems tended to be discussed in terms of access and wheelchairs, but not enough attention was paid to the physical and psychological problems of learning; it is one thing to get a student in a wheelchair into a college by building ramps, and to modify toilet facilities for him, but quite another to help him cope with problems such as turning pages over, taking notes from a blackboard or following a lecture delivered at a speed faster than he can manage to follow.

Handicapped school leavers are disadvantaged in so far as their needs for continuing education have generally been badly neglected.

The extent of the need can be gauged by a follow-up of handicapped school leavers conducted by the National Children's Bureau. Tuckey, Parfit and Tuckey (1973) obtained information on 1,700 of the 9,000 pupils who left special schools of all kinds in 1968-9, and personally interviewed half of them. Although more than four out of every five were thought by their head teachers to be suitable for a period of further education or training, less than a quarter were receiving it. These figures exclude the mentally handicapped who were not at that time within the educational system. As far as the mildly ESN children were concerned, fewer than one in ten were receiving further education or training, though over three-quarters were thought to be suitable by their head teachers.

The educational needs of disadvantaged and disabled adults were fully discussed for the first time in the Russell Report on Adult Education (1973) — a report which has still to be implemented by the Government. This report highlights the need for continuing education of handicapped and disabled people in general, and also considers provision for severely mentally handicapped people who, despite being now regarded as 'educable' as children, are still not gaining access to opportunities for continuing education.

It is no exaggeration to single out the mentally handicapped as the most disadvantaged group of all in this respect. Perhaps the most damaging form of deprivation arises from the consistent underestimation of their abilities. Authorities have on the whole taken the view that education stops at 16; Social Services Departments have not always done as much as they might have done to secure further educational opportunities for people attending ATCs.

But what do we mean by education and educational opportunities? Certainly something broader than the provisions made in schools or indeed by institutions of any kind; we have argued that education for the handicapped is concerned with everything that systematically helps an individual to learn and to develop new skills and abilities, and that viewed in this sense, education begins at birth and never ends. Education is not concerned merely with what is taught, but with how it is taught. In this sense also everything that we do is educational in the broadest sense — whether we call it work training, industrial therapy, social education, craft work or literacy and numeracy projects. An educational approach is also based on a thorough assessment of an individual's learning needs and difficulties and leads to the design of a programme to help him to use and extend his abilities and to acquire new skills. Furthermore, an educational approach is never static. It is always concerned with the next step, and the means of helping the student to reach it. It involves experimenting with different methods of teaching a task, analysing and breaking down the task into constituent components and using rewards and incentives systematically.

It follows from this also that an educational approach is common to all who work with the mentally handicapped, whether they are called nurses, instructors, managers, social workers, therapists or care staff. In discussing continuing education, we are not therefore concerned with education in any narrow sense, as involving only literacy or numeracy or what is often taught in schools, but with the adoption of an educational approach in the widest sense. But educational skills have to be learned and cannot be merely acquired by intuition or experience. For this reason alone, ATC staff, nurses and social workers need to establish a working partnership with educationalists, learn their skills and work with them to adapt and modify these skills in the light of what is known about the needs and difficulties of mentally handicapped students.

Meeting needs

What then are the needs of these young people? In a fundamental sense, their needs are no different and no less heterogenous than those of other young people. But these needs and rights are often ignored and are therefore worth restating. We reviewed general statements of the rights of the mentally handicapped in Chapter 1 and concluded that useful though these were as a charter of rights, they needed to be translated into specific service objectives. The NDG (1977b) also formulated the needs of young people at the beginning of its pamphlet on ATCs. The present discussion therefore emphasizes the educational and personal needs of younger people and then examines ways in which these might be met.

Educational needs

Educational needs can be interpreted both broadly and narrowly. In an earlier chapter, we defined education as being concerned with all those forces which contribute to an individual's learning and development, and concluded that, looked at in this universal and comprehensive sense, the process of education begins at birth and never ends. We might also argue that the more handicapped the individual, the more strongly this truism should be translated into reality. Many people have commented on the sheer absurdity of a fixed school-leaving age for mentally handicapped children, whether this age is fixed at 16, 19 or 21, and on the irrelevance of the policy adopted in some Adult Training Centres that 'education classes' should not be provided for those over 26. Such arrangements reflect a narrow, administrative and institution-orientated view of education as something provided exclusively by schools and other designated institutions. We could view it instead as a continuing process by which handicapped people have a right as citizens to demand of the society in which they live that they should be given not only all the opportunities for personal development open to any other citizen but any additional specialist help that may be required to help them to take advantage of those opportunities.

If this is a broad and possibly utopian interpretation of educational need, we can take a narrower view by reminding ourselves that the average school leaver from an ESNS school scores on a variety of developmental and attainment tests at a level corresponding to that of a normal child between 5 and 6 years of age (Marshall 1967). In other words, the mentally handicapped child leaves school with a level of intellectual development and educational attainment comparable to that with which the normal child enters school at 5. It is precisely at this moment that formal education is supposed to end.

Many mentally handicapped youngsters are just beginning to be able to respond to attempts to help them to acquire basic educational skills, including literacy and numeracy. We have already reported some suggestive evidence from the Schools Council survey of language abilities which appears to reflect a sudden 'spurt' in language skills in the last year before school leaving (Swann and Mittler 1976). Whether or not such a spurt might be demonstrated for other abilities as well, it is clearly vital to capitalize on the growing interest of these school leavers in learning new skills and to help them by every possible means to extend the range of their competence. To deprive them of educational opportunities at the very time when they seem to be able to benefit from them is the antithesis both of common sense and of sound social policy. How and where to provide for these educational needs, however, is a more complex question, to which there is no simple answer. We will examine a number of possibilities shortly.

The need for adult experiences

In addition to the need for educational skills and for optimum competence in basic skills of numeracy and literacy, young people also have the right to demand experiences appropriate to their age, whatever their stage of mental development might be. The tendency in the past has been to treat mentally handicapped adolescents and adults as perpetual children, and to deny their status and rights as adults and as citizens. There are still institutions where adults of all ages are referred to as 'boys' and 'girls', and where paternalistic or authoritarian attitudes are adopted by staff who are convinced that they know best what is good for the mentally handicapped. Many ordinary people who come into contact with them 'talk down' to them in an indulgent and patronizing way, and find it difficult or impossible to understand or to accept that in all essentials except one they deserve to be treated as adults.

The denial of adult status and rights to the mentally handicapped is reflected in a variety of ways, but perhaps nowhere more dramatically than in our attitudes to their sexuality. It is only comparatively recently that the sexual development and sexual needs of disabled people has been discussed at all, and it will be many years before either the general public or professional staff begin to understand their own attitudes or to develop a coherent policy in these matters. Although a number of conferences and discussion papers have been devoted to this subject, these are often characterized by little more than the expression of liberal, enlightened attitudes and goodwill, rather than by illustrations of what might be done by staff and families to help handicapped people to express their need for mature sexual relationships. We prefer to regard the mentally handicapped as asexual for as long as possible until there is definite indication to the contrary. Fortunately a number of direct and more practical discussions are now becoming available (e.g. Greengross 1976; Craft and Craft 1978).

Sexual development is perhaps the most drastic example of the tendency of our society to deny the need for adult experiences to the mentally handicapped but more obvious and pervasive examples can be seen in our attitudes to providing employment and training for employment. This subject will be discussed more fully in a later chapter but can be illustrated by examples of underexpectation in both teachers and Adult Training Centre staff.

In Nesbitt's (1976) survey of the curriculum available to leavers in twenty-nine ESNS schools, twenty-five out of twenty-nine teachers considered that the Adult Training Centre was the only possible placement both in the short term and the long term. Nothing appears to have been done to introduce children to some of the jobs for which they might be trained, and the only contact they had with 'vocational representatives' was with firemen and policemen. Six schools had no contacts of any kind with people in specific trades or occupations.

It is not surprising, therefore, that young people in Adult Training Centres have wildly erroneous and inappropriate conceptions of what kind of jobs are done by people, what they do and what they earn. This was brought out in a study by Reiter and Whelan (1975) who devised an *Inventory of Vocational Interests* in which trainees were asked to describe and discuss photographs of people engaged in a wide variety of trades and occupations. This study also revealed a disquieting degree of incompetence in knowledge of money and earnings — it was rare for trainees to credit anyone with more than about £2 as a week's earnings (i.e. the maximum level of their own income at the time). The low level of knowledge about money values seems to reflect lack of teaching in both school and Adult Training Centre, possibly based on the view that it was not worthwhile to attempt to teach money concepts or values.

A third example of underexpectation is taken from a study by Grant (1971) who asked experienced Adult Training Centre staff to first, rank a series of eight industrial assembly tasks in order of difficulty and second, to predict whether individual trainees would be able to learn the task after training. The results showed that although staff were good at ranking the tasks in order of difficulty, they were quite inaccurate at predicting whether individual trainees would master it. Females were particularly badly underestimated.

Despite these rather depressing examples of underexpectation and lack of demand, we really have far too little information at our disposal to enable any reliable or valid generalizations to be made about the extent to which we provide mentally handicapped young people with adult experiences. But it seems likely on the strength of the available evidence that we tend to underestimate their abilities and to adopt a somewhat protective attitude which leads us to restrict opportunities for growth, for the learning of new skills and for the kind of personal development that comes from meeting the challenge of a task that is slightly beyond our existing level of competence or achievement.

The need for preparation and guidance

This right to be exposed to the challenge of demand can only be met gradually, and by a series of carefully planned small steps. Young people have to be prepared for any change in their environment, however small, and cannot be expected to adapt easily to new demands and new environments. Two examples will illustrate this obvious but often neglected point.

(1) A twelve-year-old boy was making such good progress in his ESNS school that it was decided after much discussion and case conferencing to 'promote' him to a school for mildly ESN children.

Unfortunately, although he was told about his change of school, and had visited it, no attempt was made to introduce him to his new school life or routine by gradual stages. Instead, he was left at a different bus collection point one Monday morning, picked up by a different bus full of children he had never met, and deposited in a much bigger school where despite the best efforts of staff he became first confused and later disturbed. He 'lost' his toilet training skills and began to handle and smear faeces. After several weeks of increasingly disturbed behaviour during which he took no part in the life of the school and learned nothing, he was eventually returned to his ESNS school, where he immediately resumed his former routine and became a 'model' pupil.

(2) An Adult Training Centre with an excellent record of training and achievement in a range of 'own product work' was located in the middle of a trading estate, but did not provide opportunities for trainees to become familiar with the kind of skills and operations available in local industry. When one employer took a small group of the ablest trainees on a trial basis, they were so distressed and tearful that they had to be brought back to the Adult Training Centre.

Both examples illustrate the paramount need for preparation and for a gradual change from one environment to another. The nature and speed of such preparation will obviously vary from one individual to another, but no plan for change, however small, can afford to neglect discussion of this vital point. It is only fair to point out, however, that even when staff take great pains to adopt a step-by-step approach to rehabilitation, success is by no means assured. Gunzburg (1975) reports a careful programme of this kind in which hospital residents were trained and prepared with great care for a more independent life in the community. Nevertheless, some of the residents were themselves quite resistant to rehabilitation and began to develop subtle evasive tactics and 'disappearing acts' when the next step seemed inevitable. Gunzburg remarks that at one time an unspoken agreement seemed to have arisen that the word 'hostel' would not be mentioned by him or by them.

Whatever the speed of transition from one environment to another, it is certain that full co-ordination between staff working in both settings will help to ease the process of adjustment for the young person. The process of preparation must begin to be discussed and planned long before the actual move takes place, so that the young person can be accustomed by small stages to the new environment, the new people he will meet and work with, and above all, the new demands that will be made on him.

The needs of families

The families of mentally handicapped young people should also be regarded as a vulnerable group who will need special consideration and help at the time when a son or daughter is preparing to leave school. Above all, they should be consulted and involved as full partners in the process of assessing the needs of the child and in deciding how those needs can best be met. No amount of co-ordination between professionals, no amount of assessment and decision making, however competent or thorough, can compensate for the damage that may be done by the exclusion of parents at this stage.

Most families will have adjusted to some extent to the problems presented by their child, and will have developed a day-to-day routine over the years. But as the time for school leaving approaches, they are bound to become increasingly apprehensive about the future, and to revive all the basic problems and anxieties of any family with a handicapped child. What is to happen to him when he leaves school? What will happen to him when the family can no longer look after him? Will he have to go into some form of residential care, perhaps spend most of his adult life in a hospital for the mentally handicapped? More immediate and pressing questions concern the extent to which the local ATC is suitable to meet his needs, whether there are local alternatives to the ATC and what kind of help they can expect as a family.

It is not hard to justify the special claims of these families for help at this time. The stress and anxiety surrounding the transition from school can easily be imagined. The sudden disruption of the daily routine of school and of the structured framework of day-to-day life may cause stress both to the young person and to his family. The family may have to make a major readjustment at this time; the mother may have to give up her job in order to look after her handicapped youngster, with repercussions on the family's finances as well as on her own morale. The youngster may begin to produce behaviour problems partly out of sheer boredom and partly as a reaction to the lack of training in the use of leisure and recreational opportunities. The situation at home may then become increasingly tense and explosive, especially if no obvious solution is in sight.

Services for school leavers

Provision for school leavers and young people is now one of the most inadequate features of all our social, educational or health services for handicapped people. The more we improve our services for children at school, the more glaring is the contrast between what is provided at school and what is available when they leave.

Even at a time of economic stringency, it should be possible for each area to make some improvements in its services for this group of young people. The numbers of children leaving all ESNS schools is now less than 2,000 per year, corresponding to an average of around five children per school per year. What seems to be required is a framework within which the pupil's needs can be assessed, and a decision made on how these needs can best be met with local resources. No pupil should leave school without such assessment of his needs, and without a co-ordinated plan to meet them.

The evidence available indicates that this rarely happens at the present time. The majority of pupils leave school at 16, with little or no assessment and no plan for what is to happen to them after they leave. Few head teachers take the initiative in calling in other specialists to the school, and few LEAs have established any form of co-ordinating machinery with Social Services Departments or with other agencies such as Careers Officers, Employment Rehabilitation Centres, Young Persons' Work Preparation Courses and Colleges of Further Education. The fault does not solely lie with the head teachers, since they have seldom been given the encouragement or authority to act on their own initiative in this matter. In any case, decisions made by the head teachers as a result of a joint assessment process could only be implemented if there was a fully agreed framework within the authority as a whole, agreed by the relevant chief officers.

As a result, most ESNS pupils leave school at 16 and proceed straight to the local Adult Training Centre, assuming that a vacancy can be found. Although it is quite possible that the Adult Training Centre is in fact the placement best suited to the needs of the pupil, this cannot be assumed without detailed assessment of the pupil himself or without a full consideration of all the alternatives available locally. Even so, most head teachers seem to assume that their pupils will go to Adult Training Centres, presumably because they have little experience of their leavers going anywhere else. But other possibilities should not be neglected.

Abilities of school leavers

The range of abilities of ESNS school leavers is so wide that few useful generalizations can be made. A small minority will leave school with few obvious or outstanding indications of the severe learning difficulties which have handicapped their school lives.

Free of physical disability, quite competent in the use of language, apparently able to cope with many of the demands of everyday living, they may be able to cope with a job and require relatively little help from the helping agencies. These young people closely resemble the majority of pupils who leave schools for the mildly educationally subnormal (ESNM), many of whom cope as well as those from other secondary schools with similar backgrounds. They have the same problems in finding and keeping a job, in maintaining their interest in work that is often dull and unrewarding, and in getting help when they need it.

No one knows how many children from ESNS schools come into this category, but we do know that a proportion — perhaps 10 per cent — of children were transferred from ESNM schools, not only on account of their learning difficulties, but also in many cases because of behaviour problems. Anne Marshall (1967) who studied 165 fourteen- and fifteen-year-old children in nineteen former Junior Training Centres in the mid 1960s reported that these children constituted something of an 'A stream elite' and that many of them had begun to learn to read, although they were also rated as more maladjusted on the Bristol Social Adjustment Guides. It is not surprising therefore that these more competent children should adjust somewhat better to the demands of the community on leaving school.

At the other end of the scale, however, there are children who are heavily handicapped, and who are likely to remain dependent, even with special help, for the rest of their lives. About a quarter of the children in ESNS schools are in 'Special Care Units', and suffer from multiple handicaps of various kinds. They pose severe problems to their families, and to staff who are concerned with their training, education and care, particularly at the age of 16 when they have to leave school. Because of the shortage of ATC places, many of the most severely handicapped young people, having become accustomed to the daily routine of school, have then to stay at home all day with families, who may not receive any help themselves in teaching and occupying their son or daughter. Eventually, most of these young people are admitted to hospitals for the mentally handicapped.

Between these two extremes, however, the majority of young people have a wide range of abilities and disabilities. To characterize such a large and heterogeneous group of young people by IQ or clinical type explains very little, and may be positively harmful in helping the person concerned to obtain access to services. Even if we assume, for example, that this 'middle group' has an IQ range somewhere between 35 and 55, those with an IQ of 50 would not necessarily 'do better' in terms of almost any criterion of adult competence than those with an IQ of 40. If the IQ tells us little about a person's relative strengths and weaknesses even in the kind of problem-solving tasks conventionally measured by the tests, far less can it provide useful prediction on career guidance (see Cobb (1972) for a full discussion of prediction).

Suggestions for better services

A number of suggestions for improvements in existing services for school leavers have been made and there are signs that some of these are being implemented in some areas. The essence of all suggestions for better practice lies in a framework within which the needs of school leavers can be assessed and met through co-operative and multidisciplinary teamwork.

The NDG (1977a) published a short pamphlet specifically devoted to mentally handicapped school leavers; the Warnock report has also made a number of important recommendations for all handicapped school leavers. Common to both reports is the suggestion that the process of assessment of need should begin between one and two years before the young person is due to leave school, and that the initiative for carrying out not only educational assessment but for inviting other key professional people into the school should normally lie with the head teacher. His task is to begin to draw up a profile of abilities and disabilities and to identify the young person's strengths and weaknesses for coping with the next stage of more independent living in the community. The family has to be involved in this process from the beginning and not merely be brought in at the end in order to be told what it is that the professionals have decided is in the interests of their child.

The need for multidisciplinary assessment is widely agreed; the fact that it is still not available in many parts of the country is related in part to the lack of clearly stated policy which has been agreed by all the relevant agencies and which results in the alloca-tion of specific responsibilities to named individuals. The newly established Joint Care Planning Team and Joint Consultative Committee have a particularly important bridging function in ensuring an adequate and better co-ordinated service for school leavers, instead of the current situation where everyone waits for everyone else to make the first move.

Although the initiative lies with the head teacher, there will have to be a commitment by people outside the education service to contribute to the process of assessment. We have already noted that the number of young people involved is comparatively small —

probably not more than five per year from every ESNS school —
but other handicapped young people will also need help and will be
making increasing demands on the services of scarce staff. The
particular claim of the mentally handicapped however lies in the
fact that they will nearly all continue to need full-time services after
they leave school, and that unless such help is given in the form of
services that best meet their needs, inappropriate admission to
hospital becomes much more likely.

Apart from the ongoing assessments carried out by school staff
and the continuous involvement of the family, specialist input will
be needed from an educational psychologist, a social worker, and
the manager of the local ATC. Both NDG and Warnock strongly
emphasize the need for a Careers Officer to be involved. Indeed the
Warnock Report goes further by suggesting that the Careers
Officer should become the Named Person and have called for the
appointment of at least one full-time specialist Careers Officer for
every 50,000 of the school population, to work closely with a
greatly expanded and more appropriately trained force of careers
teachers in schools. But although there are signs that the Careers
Service is developing specialist interests in handicapped school
leavers, relatively few of them are now involved in the assessment
of children from ESNS schools. In a recent survey of fifty-three
ESNS schools in NW England, only around 10 per cent of leavers
had been seen by a specialist Careers Officer (Preddy and Mittler
1979).

In contrast, there is evidence from the same survey that social
workers are now beginning to make a bigger contribution. Well
over half the schools reported social work involvement in the
process of assessment of school leavers, whereas a contribution
from educational psychologists was reported by less than a third of
the schools. Little information is available on the extent to which
families are involved, nor are there any accounts of ways in which
professionals try to involve the young people themselves in choice
and decision making by helping them to express their own prefer-
ences and to contribute to their own assessment.

Unfortunately, most youngsters still leave school without even
an IQ assessment, not to mention a comprehensive assessment. The
information that accompanies a young person from school to an
Adult Training Centre is regarded as totally inadequate by most
ATC staff, who have to make do with scrappy, out-of-date and
sometimes inaccurate information.

From the point of view of the young people, therefore, the first
need is for a long process of careful assessment, not only of intelligence but of many other qualities and characteristics, including

social, self-care and language skills, competence in literacy and numeracy, and qualities of personality and temperament. Assessment of the needs of the pupil should be followed by a decision on how these needs can best be met by the resources of the community in which he lives. It is essential, therefore, that those concerned with the assessment are fully aware of the whole range of resources and facilities that are actually available. This seems obvious enough, but recent surveys and interviews with staff from a wide variety of agencies concerned with handicapped people have reflected an alarming ignorance of potential sources of outside help and of the work of other professionals and organizations, as well as an apparent unwillingness or inability to call in existing community resources. For example, a survey of the curriculum and facilities offered by twenty-nine ESNS schools to their final year pupils, only ten reported any contact with a Careers Officer, and only one with a Disablement Resettlement Officer. Furthermore, only one school conducted any kind of follow-up of their leavers (Nesbitt 1976).

The picture that emerges from these and other surveys is one of isolation of these schools and Adult Training Centres from other agencies, possibly due to lack of awareness of what might be offered, or to a belief that these services were not available to them.

Local possibilities

We can now consider some of the possibilities which might be available locally to meet the needs of the mentally handicapped school leaver. Because these will obviously vary from area to area, it will be useful for whichever body is co-ordinating service provision to draw up a comprehensive list of these alternatives, and to revise the list in the light of experience. This group is likely to be well placed to influence the growth of provision in the area, and also to make better use of existing resources.

The possibilities being listed are obviously neither comprehensive nor mutually exclusive, but are intended mainly as a checklist and an aide-memoire.

(1) *Special schools*

Although it is DES policy to encourage all young people to remain at school up to the age of 19, only a very small proportion of handicapped children currently remain at school beyond the age of 16. In January 1976 only 1.4 per cent of pupils in ESNS schools were over 16, though the proportion was around 10 per cent in schools situated in mental handicap hospitals (DES 1978).

One reason why most pupils do not remain in school relates

simply to lack of buildings and classroom space. Because, by current DES standards, the former JTCs allowed only about half the amount of space per pupil which is now considered essential for ESNS children, these schools became overcrowded overnight. Unfortunately, many of them do not have the land for the extra classrooms that would be needed if pupils were to remain at school longer. For obvious practical reasons, therefore, the older pupils must make way for the younger ones who are moving up the school. Finally, priority is understandably given to making the special school available to the under-fives.

Although it is unlikely that the school-leaving age will be compulsorily raised for handicapped children, the Warnock Report makes recommendations designed to ensure that pupils who would benefit by a longer period at school are not forced to leave simply because there is no longer room for them. We have already argued that the notion of a fixed leaving age is somewhat arbitrary for severely handicapped children; we can now consider ways in which educational provision can continue to be made even though the young person is no longer attending school full time, and may even be in full-time employment. All of us have rights of access to further and adult education, and there is no reason in principle why these rights should not also be made available to the mentally handicapped.

(2) *Senior schools*

One of the arguments sometimes advanced against the policy of encouraging young people to remain at school till 19 is based on the need to provide more demanding and more adult experiences to young people who have spent many years in all-age schools. Most special ESNS schools contain children as young as 2 or 3; it is hardly surprising therefore to find that some of the older, more able children are keen to leave and that their parents too may feel the need for their children to be exposed to a new environment. Some special schools are still too protective and too undemanding, and may have built up unduly low expectations of what their older pupils may be able to achieve. Nesbitt's survey of twenty-nine schools certainly suggests that this is the case.

Partly for these reasons, some local authorities have begun to consider alternative ways of helping young people to build a bridge between school and the community. One suggestion that has been made takes the form of a senior school. Such a school would aim to prepare the pupil to cope with increasingly difficult and demanding learning and social situations. It would forge working links with community agencies, such as ATCs and FE colleges, and also explore the possibility of sheltered employment or work experience schemes. It would work closely with social workers and Careers Officers, and generally plan to expose the youngster to situations of gradually increasing demand and expectation. There need be no fixed age for entry, but many pupils might be able to benefit from the age of about 12 to 14, and stay until 19 or beyond. Continued and systematic attempts might be made to help pupils to acquire as much proficiency as possible in basic skills of literacy and numeracy, using specialist methods and appropriate educational technology.

A number of LEAs are now building or planning separate secondary schools for ESNS children, with flexible ages of entry and leaving. An account of one of the first of these schools (Oaklands School, Isleworth) has been provided by its head teacher (Early 1975); in this school an additional continuation class is available for the over-sixteens who also attend classes at a Polytechnic and an Agricultural College. Secondary schools for ESNS children are likely to be small, especially in view of the falling birthrate and lower incidence of mental handicap, but they can be linked both with comprehensive schools and with other special schools and share some of their facilities.

(3) *Further and adult education*
There has been a growing interest in the last few years in the possibility of extending further and adult education facilities to the mentally handicapped. A small number of FE colleges have begun to make special provision for disabled students in general, including the mentally handicapped, and many more FE, Technical and Adult Education Colleges have expressed interest in the possibility of providing courses of various kinds (Mittler and Gittins 1974; King's Fund Centre 1975; Baranyay 1976; Kedney and Whelan 1976).

The Warnock Committee have now recommended a major expansion of further education facilities for all disabled students and regard this as one of their priorities. But they recognize that only a small minority of FE colleges accept or cater adequately for the needs of the more severely disabled students, including the mentally handicapped, and that the staff of the colleges will require a great deal of support as well as major modifications in their own training to help them to meet the needs of these students. Although there is growing enthusiasm and interest among FE staff, it is important that they should have opportunities to learn about the day-to-day problems of working with the mentally handicapped. Experience of mentally handicapped people and of their learning problems and needs can be gained by sustained contact with special schools or ATCs; one can only hope that colleges will create opportunities for their staff to share their planning with teachers and ATC and school staff, and develop a framework of mutual collaboration to help the young mentally handicapped school leaver to derive full benefit from further and adult education facilities.

The Warnock Committee made a number of crucial recommendations for the expansion of FE facilities for disabled students.

(i) Some FE establishments should experiment with modified versions of ordinary FE courses for young people with special needs, including vocational courses at operative level and courses in social competence and independence;

(ii) At least one college in each region should provide courses for the most severely handicapped students;

(iii) Every FE establishment should designate one member of staff as responsible for the welfare of students with special needs, and for briefing other members of staff on their special needs.

FE and Adult Education facilities for the mentally handicapped are beginning to be provided in a variety of ways:

(i) Evening classes and activities for students from ATCs, schools or from the community. Evening classes can also be held in the school or ATC;

(ii) Day classes for groups of handicapped students attending singly or in groups for either a full day or a half-day each week;

(iii) Full courses for four or five days a week catering for most of the FE needs of students (e.g. the course in Park Lane FE College, Leeds (Sanders 1974);

(iv) Teachers based on FE colleges visiting ATCs and hospitals daily (McAllister 1974).

Content of courses

More important than the organizational aspects is the content of what is provided. This obviously varies greatly at the present time; we simply do not know whether the courses or subject matter taught are based on assumption of what staff think would be useful, whether it is preceded by any form of survey of analysis of need and whether the students themselves are consulted. Nor do we know about the extent to which 'special' provision was made for mentally handicapped students in the colleges, and whether this involved partial or total segregation from their fellow students.

The balance between integration and segregation is difficult to strike, both for the individual and for the group, since it is necessary to meet both the special needs of the student for teaching geared to his particular needs and difficulties as well as his social and personal needs to be treated 'as far as possible' as any other student.

Among the content of courses or activities that are or might be provided, whether in colleges or elsewhere, are the following:

(i) Opportunities to acquire or develop basic educational skills, including literacy and numeracy. (It is still policy in many ESNS schools not to teach reading.) The modification of adult literacy programmes and the use of simple aids and materials as well as the design of reading schemes which cater for adult interests are likely to be beneficial. But the teaching of basic reading and number skills to the mentally handicapped requires not only considerable skill and ingenuity, but also familiarity with recent developments in teaching methods involving educational technology, including programmed learning and simple teaching machines. People who have not learned by traditional methods may respond well to a programmed learning approach, since this is not only novel but also depends on the presentation of the teaching task by small and graded steps.

(ii) Both reading and number skills can be taught or practised in practical situations involving shopping and the actual use of these skills and abilities in 'real' rather than simulated situations. This is already done in many schools and ATCs.

(iii) Home-making skills, including simple and more advanced cooking, bedmaking and housecleaning, as well as budgeting, saving, shopping, choice and care of clothes.

(iv) A wide range of practical subjects, including woodwork, metalwork, dressmaking, car maintenance and general repair and do-it-yourself skills.

(v) Art and craft work, including pottery, painting, jewellery making.

(vi) Sport and recreational facilities.

The importance of sport and recreational activities cannot be over-emphasized. Not only can mentally handicapped people often become very proficient in this field, and thereby gain a real sense of satisfaction and achievement, but these activities often bring them into contact with non-handicapped people on more or less equal terms. Furthermore, even limited ability in sport or recreational skills ensures that mentally handicapped people have a life of their own outside the day-to-day routine of their work, whether they live at home, in hospital or in residential homes.

For this reason, it is important to ensure that mentally handicapped people have access to all the community leisure and recreational facilities. The recently established sports and leisure centres are a case in point; in some places, mentally handicapped people receive special help and teaching in physical education, in swimming and in a very wide range of sports. The more able ones may be able to compete with other people, but even if this is not possible they often derive immeasurable satisfaction from merely taking part in or in using the community's facilities in much the same way as any other citizen. The staff of these centres often welcome the challenge presented by disabled people who need to be helped to make the most of what is available, unlike the general public who are often fairly competent in the first place, and may need little direct help in learning the skills that disabled people can only master after a great deal of effort, both on their own part and on the part of those who are trying to help them. Their reward lies in the all too obvious sense of achievement of a mentally handicapped person in mastering a skill or even a small component of a skill or in competing in a sports tournament.

A number of organizations are now seriously examining the possibilities of providing such opportunities even for the most severely disabled people (e.g. the Disabled Living Foundation, Gateway Clubs). It may not always be possible for such people to attend community recreational facilities, though this should always be the ultimate aim; but a great deal can be done to help them to enlarge their experiences and obtain pleasure from simple activities. Even the opportunity to dip one's hands into water, run sand through one's fingers or watch a slowly changing mobile is a form of recreation, in strong contrast to the lack of anything to do or look at which is often all that is thought to be suitable for a profoundly handicapped person (see Stuart 1975 and Solly 1975 for further suggestions).

The possible content of courses is intended to be merely illustrative rather than comprehensive. Wider questions of training content will be more fully considered in a later chapter, but it seems appropriate to indicate — if only in brief outline — some of the possibilities which might be made available to young people after leaving school, though of course there is no reason why access to most of the resources listed should not be made available to mentally handicapped people of any age.

(4) *Adolescent assessment unit*
The first adolescent assessment unit has been opened at Sheffield, run by the Social Services Department. The unit accepts mentally handicapped school leavers at about 16, and carries out an intensive assessment of their needs, using a wide range of assessment methods. The unit is directed by a psychologist, and is run in close association with local ATCs. The intention is that young people should only remain in the Assessment Unit for a few months, and that at the end of this period of comprehensive assessment the staff, in consultation with the family and with the young person himself, should draw up a plan designed to meet his needs, and set in motion the means of carrying it out.

The Sheffield unit appears to be the first of its kind. But what matters is not whether a special building is put up or set aside for assessment purposes. It is important to think of assessment and decision making as a continuous process, requiring certain objectives, techniques, procedures and materials; looked at in this light, it can take place in a variety of settings and contexts, and is not necessarily limited to a building or facility known as an assessment centre. Assessment should provide the foundations for any programme of training or teaching, no matter whether it is carried out in school, ATC or college.

Preparation for work
Among the local facilities which should be better known to people working in mental handicap services is the increasing range of services provided by the Manpower Services Commission (MSC). A useful summary of existing services can be found in the Warnock Report. Although the MSC and related agencies have been greatly expanding their facilities for disabled people, the extent to which they are being or can be used by mentally handicapped people is not yet clear. But even though mentally handicapped people have made only limited use of employment and rehabilitation facilities so far, there is no reason in principle why at least the more able should not do so, though staff working in these services may require time and training to adapt their methods to the needs of mentally handicapped people.

The Disablement Resettlements Officer is the main source of advice and can act as the link between mentally handicapped people and the whole range of employment and rehabilitation services. These include Employment Rehabilitation Centres, Young Persons' Work Preparation Courses, Training Opportunities Schemes (TOPS), Remploy factories and other forms of sheltered employment, as well as enclave sheltered work groups in open industry. Since the range of facilities is likely to increase under the impetus of the Holland report (*Young People and Work*, MSC 1977); and the MSC's policy statement (MSC 1978) it is obviously important that mentally handicapped people should not miss out on one of the few public services that is expanding.

Severity of handicap

It is important not to draw arbitrary lines between the least and the most severely handicapped, whether in terms of IQ or physical disability, since it is unjustified to predict in advance that any given individual will derive no benefit from any of the facilities and resources that have been considered. This can only be decided on the basis of a systematic and comprehensive assessment of an individual's needs, leading in turn to a determined attempt to expose him to the challenge of demand and high expectation. If we decide in advance that a heavily handicapped person will not benefit from a particular training or recreational programme, without giving him the benefit of at least trying, then we are in danger of merely perpetuating the vicious circle of the self-fulfilling prophecy which has handicapped disabled people for so long. We do not, for example, have the knowledge to take full responsibility for denying people their right of access to, say, recreational and leisure activities on the ground that they are unlikely to 'appreciate' them. It was this kind of reasoning that led us in the past to deny handicapped people the right to learn to count with real money: bolder experiments soon established that more people could appreciate and use money than had previously been thought possible.

Nevertheless, there must be limits in the extent to which the most severely handicapped people can benefit from facilities now being made available, though the argument being advanced here is that we do not know what is or is not 'realistic' for an individual handicapped person, or how far he might respond to a demanding situation that stretches his skills and abilities to the utmost. This is particularly true when young people first leave the comparatively sheltered environment of the school and find themselves for the first time in a more demanding and a more adult environment. Parents, professionals and the young person himself are sometimes surprised by the effect of such a change in general outlook and willingness to try to respond to new challenges and experiences.

Even if the first results are not encouraging, and a severely handicapped person fails to respond to such a challenge, it may be unjustified to conclude that the attempt was not worthwile. The challenge may be presented again at another time, possibly by smaller or more gradual stages, ensuring that the experience brings opportunities for success and enjoyment rather than exposure to failure. For example, if an attempt is being made to teach a severely handicapped person to swim, few people would give up all attempts to take him to water merely because he was unsuccessful or even visibly distressed the first time. If this was our attitude to the teaching of swimming to normal children, very few would make much progress. Instead, we go about reaching our goals by a different route and gradually try to help the person to acquire more confidence in the water and to achieve some success, however limited. Similarly, some handicapped people seem to make little or no progress at first when it comes to learning a new skill, so that staff and parents may become discouraged and conclude that the attempt was not worthwhile because the skill is obviously 'beyond' him, and because it would be cruel and unkind to persist.

In reality, of course, staff are busy, resources are scarce and decisions about priorities need to be made. In an ideal world, everyone, no matter how heavily handicapped, would be given every opportunity to try to learn new skills and abilities, but in practice this does not and cannot happen. Questions relating to the most severely handicapped people will be discussed in greater detail in a later chapter, but it seems appropriate at this stage to refer to their needs in the context of leaving school and gaining access to community facilities right from the start. The alternative is to deny them opportunities for stimulation and challenge, and to put them at risk of being labelled as 'unresponsive' or 'unable to benefit'.

Conclusions

(1) The aim of this chapter has been to make a case for helping mentally handicapped young people to gain access to continuing education, whether they remain at school, or attend ATCs, and whether they live at home, in residential homes or in hospitals.

(2) Education is interpreted broadly, as concerned with all those factors which systematically help an individual to learn and to develop new skills. It is not therefore confined to the content of what is normally provided in special schools by teachers employed by LEAs.

(3) Although access to education can thus take a variety of forms, and need not be limited to educational agencies, it does involve full collaboration between professional staff working in schools, ATCs and colleges.

(4) The needs of each handicapped pupil should be fully assessed by a team of officers, including the young person's teachers, a member of staff of the local ATC, a psychologist, a medical specialist, a social worker and wherever possible a specialist Careers Officer. The family and the young person himself should be involved at every stage. No one should leave a special school without such an assessment of need, and without a written plan on how those needs are to be met within local resources. A named officer should be appointed as co-ordinator to ensure that the plan is carried out, and to help the young person and his family both in the immediate school-leaving period and for as long as possible. The number of pupils involved is not large — about five per school per year, less than 2,000 a year nationally.

(5) The needs of the young person can be considered not only in relation to where he should go next, but also in terms of his personal needs for adult experiences and status, and his need to be helped to acclimatize himself gradually to a more demanding and a more adult environment.

(6) The needs of the family also deserve full consideration at this time. Not only should they be fully involved in discussions at every stage, but allowance should be made for the adjustment they will need to make to the implications of their son or daughter leaving school. For example, one of the parents may need to give up work and there may be severe tensions in the home unless an appropriate place can be found. The four years following school leaving are often times of family crisis, which frequently finish with a request for hospital admission.

(7) It is also suggested that each area might draw up a list of all its education, training and recreational resources that might be made available to the mentally handicapped. In addition to the obvious agencies such as ATCs, further and adult education facilities have much to offer, and should be much more fully used in future.

7
TEACHING ADULTS

Introduction

Although we rightly pay a great deal of attention to children, this concern should not obscure the needs of adults who are far more numerous and whose need for services is just as great, if not greater. While the vast majority of children live with their parents and all children of school age now attend special schools, there is no corresponding statutory obligation to provide services for all adults. As a result, some people have to spend all their time at home, with little or no training. Their families are often under severe strain at a time when they are becoming older and perhaps less able to meet the needs of their adult sons and daughters. These increasing difficulties and stresses frequently result in a reluctant demand for residential care, which can generally only be provided in distant hospitals.

Adult Training Centres

The main form of community provision for mentally handicapped adults is the Adult Training Centre (ATC). About 38,000 adults now attend ATCs every day, most of whom live at home with their families; the government plans to double the number of places by about 1990.

Nevertheless the work of ATCs is not as well known as it should be, considering their central place in the provision of community care both now and even more in the future. The general public hardly know they exist; television programmes and newspaper reports about mental handicap services always seem to concentrate on the hospital services; the staff themselves are often isolated not only from their local communities, but from parents, and from their colleagues working in both general and mental handicap services.

As a result of this isolation, much criticism of the work of ATCs is based on an outdated notion of what Centres used to be like, rather than on an informed and up-to-date knowledge of the extent to which Centres have changed in the recent past. The image of the ATC held by many people is of a soulless, monotonous sweatshop where sterile, meaningless and unpaid work activities are provided in the name of 'therapy' and where the emphasis is all on production and contract work rather than on training and rehabilitation.

No one would deny that such Centres are still to be found, but they are in a minority. Many changes have taken place in the last few years, and staff are trying in most places to provide an active regime of training in which mentally handicapped people are being helped by positive means to become more competent not only to work but to live more independently in the community.

But the staff of the Centres are working against heavy odds. They have, until very recently, been given next to no guidance on the aims of the service by either central or local government; they have become professionally isolated from their colleagues in the education and health services and from community agencies as a whole. Responsibility for their work was transferred from Health to Social Service Departments in 1971, following the recommendations of the Seebohm Report, and many were again involved in the major reorganization of local government which took place in 1974. Many of the new Social Service Departments were, quite understandably, preoccupied with the problems of creating a single new local government department out of many different agencies and were often so thankful that the ATC at least existed, and seemed to be providing some sort of service, that mental handicap in general and ATCs in particular were often low down on the priority list. Furthermore, when many Social Service Departments did eventually consider how the service might be improved and better related to other local services, the deteriorating financial situation made it difficult or impossible to put better ideas into practice.

There is also much uncertainty at the present time about the most appropriate form of training for staff. In 1974 responsibility for staff training was devolved to the Central Council for Education and Training in Social Work, following the winding up of the work of the Training Council for Teachers of the Mentally Handicapped, first set up by the former Ministry of Health in 1964. This Council had pioneered and developed a one-year college-based course leading to the award of the Diploma in the Training of Mentally Handicapped Adults (DTMHA), but this Diploma is due to be phased out in 1980. After this, it is proposed that staff should take the new Certificate in Social Service. Staff have expressed strong reservations about the relevance of this new form of training. This is not the place to enter into a detailed discussion of these issues; but the key to a better service undoubtedly lies in better staff training and depends on staff morale; the problems will therefore need to be resolved if the Centres are to develop their work in the light of new ideas and methods.

Recent developments

Although many Adult Training Centres have been somewhat isolated and neglected in the past, there have been a number of recent developments which have brought them much more to the forefront of discussion. These will first be briefly summarized; specific suggestions for change will then be considered in greater detail.

(1) *Government policy.* The Government has repeatedly re-affirmed the very high priority attached to the development of day services for mentally handicapped adults. In the consultative document *Priorities for Health and Social Services* (DHSS 1976a) issued in March 1976, it was suggested that targets for the growth of ATC places first spelled out in Table 5 of the 1971 White Paper *Better Services for the Mentally Handicapped* should be fully maintained.

These targets indicate that by 1991 there should be 150 ATC places for each total population unit of 100,000 people, a total of some 73,000 places in all. Local Authorities as a whole have, in fact, already reached a halfway stage in achieving these targets — on average, there were some 82 places per 100,000 population in 1977, though this hides the usual vast local variations, a few already having around 150 places, others providing for less than a third of that number. The Government estimated that about 2,400 new places would be needed each year in England alone, with corresponding increases in the number of staff; this calls for an average annual revenue expenditure increase of 6.5 per cent over a five-year period, and a capital outlay of about £6 million a year over the same period, at 1975 prices.

This degree of government priority is most welcome; after all, a suggested growth rate of 6.5 per cent is much above the average for health and personal social services as a whole, and is second only to the elderly. The priority was reaffirmed in *The Way Forward* (DHSS 1977) in which the importance of maintaining White Paper targets was again stressed. The early signs are that local authorities are responding to this initiative. In particular, they are beginning to try to provide for the most severely handicapped people in Special

Care Units. Joint funding has been widely used, and represents a particularly good use of NHS money, since it should ultimately prevent unnecessary hospital admission for long-term care. Nevertheless, the severe restrictions on public expenditure are bound to have an adverse effect on progress.

(2) *The publication of the first National Survey of ATCs in England and Wales.* This survey was carried out in 1974 by Dr Whelan and Dr Speake from the Hester Adrian Research Centre, with the help of a DHSS grant, and the results published in full in a booklet *Adult Training Centres in England and Wales* (Whelan and Speake 1977). The survey contains a wealth of information about the work of the Centres, based on a 78 per cent sample of 305 ATCs, catering for nearly 25,000 trainees. The survey is paralleled by a survey of Scottish Centres, with results in many respects similar to those obtained in England and Wales (Jackson and Struthers 1975).

(3) The publication by the National Development Group of their pamphlet *Day Services for Mentally Handicapped Adults* (1977b), making a large number of recommendations for the development of day services. These include changing the name of Adult Training Centres to *Social Education Centres* (SECs), and describing those who attend them as *students*. The pamphlet is now the subject of formal consultation by the Government. Without wishing to anticipate any national decisions that might be made, I shall adopt the proposed nomenclature for the remainder of this discussion.

(4) The National Association of Teachers of the Mentally Handicapped, the main professional association representing the staffs of SECs, has itself made suggestions for ways in which day services for adults can be developed, by revising the 'Model of Good Practice' for ATCs, issued by the then Ministry of Health in 1968. Their recommendations, as well as those arising from the National Survey, have been largely incorporated in the National Development Group's pamphlet, which supersedes the 1968 guidelines.

Social Education Centres: basic information

Before discussing the work of Social Education Centres, we should first look at the users of the services, whom we shall call students, though others may prefer the more usual designation of trainees. Most of the information is taken from the National Survey (Whelan and Speake 1977), and therefore represents a sample of about three-quarters of all ATCs and students, but we begin with information taken from official DHSS statistics, (DHSS 1977a).

Table 7.1   *Basic data*

Total number of ATCs (England only) (March 1977)	423
Total number of students (England only)	37,800
Number of managers and instructors	3,100
Other staff	2,018
Number of places per 100,000	82
Target for 1991 per 100,000	150

Where do the students come from?

It is generally thought that most of the students attending SECs come from ESNS schools, but in fact only 40 per cent are recorded as entering from this source. A further 11 per cent come from ESNM schools, and as many as 15 per cent are referred by community agencies — which suggests that they did not come straight from school. The full details are given below:

Table 7.2   *Preadmission base of SEC students*

	N	%
ESNS school or Junior Training Centre	9,469	40.5
ESNM school	2,651	11.3
Community or social agency	3,586	15.3
Other ATC	3,238	13.9
Subnormality hospital	1,784	7.6
Mental illness hospital	735	3.1
Sheltered workshop	222	0.9
Other source	1,693	7.2
Total	23,378	100.0

Since the survey was conducted, it seems likely that the rising unemployment figures for school leavers has increased numbers of admissions of young people from ESNM and other special schools. This strengthens the case for a positive rehabilitation approach, since many of these young people should be able to respond to an active regime and to take their place in the community.

Age of students

The age distribution of 23,888 SEC students in 1974 is outlined in *Table 7.3* overleaf.

Table 7.3　*Age of students*

Age	N	%
16-19	4,361	18.2
20-24	6,167	25.8
25-29	4,623	19.4
30-39	4,555	19.1
40-49	2,235	9.4
50-59	1,490	6.2
60+	457	1.9
Total	23,888	100.0

It is clear from these figures that the population of students is predominantly a young one — 44 per cent are under the age of 25 and 63 per cent are under 30. Perhaps this provides some justification for the emphasis on a broadly educational approach, and for the change of name suggested by the NDG. More important than the name of the Centre is the implication for the need for throughput — people as young as this should be actively prepared for life in the community, and should not be expected to spend the rest of their lives in the Centre.

Types of handicap

The National Survey also provides information on the number of people who were rated as having various combinations of mental, physical and psychiatric disabilities. These are summarized in *Table 7.4*. The incidence of specific clinical conditions is summarized in *Table 7.5*; once again, we note the very large number of people whose clinical condition is not known or not recorded (61 per cent).

Table 7.4　*Types of handicap*

	N	%
Mental handicap only	19,037	79.69
Mental and physical handicap	2,615	10.35
Physical handicap only	253	1.06
Mental handicap and mental illness	812	3.40
Mental illness only	911	3.81
Unknown or other	260	1.09
Total	23,888	100.00

We can see from *Table 7.4* that four out of five students are rated by staff as having 'mental handicap only' and that the number with additional handicaps is still fairly small, though there are signs that this may be increasing, and that SECs are beginning to admit a proportion of people whose primary disability is not mental handicap.

Table 7.5   *Incidence of specific clinical conditions*

	N	%
Down's Syndrome	5,357	22.09
Epilepsy	2,236	9.22
Cerebral palsy	959	3.95
Other	925	3.81
Not known or recorded	14,774	60.92
Total	24,251	100.00

Abilities and disabilities

General experience indicates that no two Centres are alike, whether in respect of the students as a whole or of a single year's admissions. Some Centres seem to contain a very large number of people whose abilities — by any measure — would be greatly superior to those of many other Centres. For example, there are Centres where the majority of people seem to have considerable educational attainments and are competent in literacy and numeracy. Their problems are largely due to difficulty in finding employment, which may be related to the economic situation in the area. In other Centres, however, we find a very large number of people who are undoubtedly severely mentally handicapped.

No generalizations can be offered about the 'average' Centre; moreover, the survey data available from the National Survey and the Scottish survey is expressed in proportions and percentages of people who have acquired particular skills, and therefore fails to provide a detailed picture of the distribution of abilities in any or all of the Centres.

Nevertheless, the National Survey provides a useful snapshot of the educational, social and vocational abilities and disabilities of some 24,000 SEC students in 1974. This information is summarized in *Tables 7.6* (educational and social attainments) and *7.7*, a similar table reflecting staff ratings on a variety of skills relevant to work and occupation.

Table 7.6 *Summary of educational and social attainments of SEC students, as rated by staff*

Percentages rounded   N = 24,251

	able %	not able %	not known %
Talks in sentences	69	14	17
Counting and measuring	38	41	22
Reading	26	53	21
Recognition of colours	59	20	21
Telling time	34	43	23
Use of money, incl. budgeting	28	54	18
Use of telephone	23	55	23
Writing	29	48	23
Signature.	41	37	22
Public transport	28	50	22
Post Office procedures	21	53	26
Prepares basic meal, incl. shopping	24	51	26
Personal hygiene	52	23	26
Health hazards	28	38	34
Honesty	53	11	37
Normal courtesies	62	12	26
Use of medical, dental, social services	17	49	34
Sexual responsibility	19	28	54
Could live on own	6	63	31
Can take own medicine	18	46	36

Taken from Whelan and Speake (1977).

These figures have been presented in some detail, because the work of SECs and the characteristics and needs of their students and staff are little known or understood even by other practitioners in the mental handicap service. As a result, they have become rather isolated not only from the general public but from their colleagues in other sectors of both general and special services.

The extent of this isolation can be summarized by listing the number of Centres (out of 305) that had been visited at least once during the year prior to the National Survey by outside staff (see *Table 7.8*). Figures in brackets refer to the number of such visits that were requested by the staff: the remainder were initiated by the visitors themselves.

These figures do not include a number of other key members of staff in relevant services — e.g. nursing staff concerned with training functions very similar to those being carried out in day services, and teachers working in special schools, either ESNS or ESNM.

Table 7.7   *Summary of work attainments*

Percentages rounded   N = 24,251

	able %	not able %	not known %
Has appropriate work attitude	50	32	19
Works without close supervision	40	44	15
Recognizes tools	48	30	22
Uses hand tools only	50	29	21
Uses powered machinery	20	54	26
Can show sustained effort	38	40	22
Can adapt readily to a different task	41	38	21
Able to work accurately with few mistakes	35	46	19
Works at acceptable speed	38	39	23
Checks own work	20	56	24
Works co-operatively with others	61	17	22
Expresses work preferences	34	40	27
Contributes to own product design	4	44	52

Adapted from Whelan and Speake (1977).

Table 7.8   *Visits by outside staff*

Speech therapist	27	(18)
Psychologist	79	(42)
Doctor	192	(120)
Social worker	285	(246)
Disablement resettlement officer	142	(84)
Careers officer	115	(49)
Physiotherapist	17	(11)
Chiropodist	68	(37)
Industrial rehab. unit rep.	24	(15)
Education dept.	110	(76)
Local industry	221	(138)
Director of Social Services	223	(44)
Asst. Director	237	(67)
Local sheltered workshop	41	(21)
Officer i/c day care	244	(122)
Warden of hostel	148	(72)

Taken from Whelan and Speake (1977).

Detailed suggestions are made by the NDG for ways in which staff of SECs can forge closer working links with their colleagues in other agencies.

These figures are worrying, particularly in the light of the abilities and needs of students summarized in *Tables 7.6* and *7.7*. For example, hardly any centres reported a visit from a speech therapist or physiotherapist in the previous year, despite the severe handicaps of the students; similarly, only a minority of the Centres had even a single visit from Disablement Resettlement Officers, Career Officers or staff connected with sheltered employment services.

Prospects for Social Education Centre students

This brings us to the prospects of rehabilitation for the SECs' students. The only figures available are taken from the National Survey, and concern numbers of students leaving the Centres during the previous years either for open or for sheltered employment. Out of a total of 24,252 students, only 934 (less than 4 per cent) entered open employment, and only 97 (0.4 per cent) entered sheltered employment. It is a strange comment on our current conceptions of rehabilitation that it seems to be ten times harder for a mentally handicapped person to enter sheltered employment than open employment (Whelan and Speake 1977). Even so, the throughput of the Centres is extremely low, especially when one adds that some 18 per cent returned to the Centres within one year. The total numbers of students leaving the Centres for any reason was under 3,000 (some 12 per cent). Some of these transferred to hospital, some to other Centres, and a considerable number just stopped attending, for 'reasons unknown'.

The information on low throughput is particularly depressing in the light of estimates of rehabilitation potential made by the staff themselves. These are summarized in *Table 7.9* below.

Thus, well over a third of the people now attending SECs are thought by the staff to be capable of open or sheltered employment now or after a further period of training. The number of students entering open or sheltered employment would need to be increased tenfold if these statistics were to be realized. But this demands a major commitment not only from employers but also from the staff of the employment and rehabilitation services.

Table 7.9 *Staff estimates of employment potential*

N = 23,378

Ready for	now		with further training		total	
	N	%	N	%	N	%
Open employment	958	(4.1)	1,728	(7.4)	2,686	(11.5)
Sheltered employment	2,880	(12.3)	3,155	(13.5)	6,035	(25.8)
Total	3,838	(16.4)	4,883	(20.9)	8,721	(37.3)

Adapted from Whelan and Speake (1977).

The work of Social Education Centres

We can now turn to the question, 'what goes on in the Centres?' This question cannot be answered comprehensively, on the basis of the National Survey alone, because the work of the Centres is changing rapidly, partly as a result of changing attitudes, particularly to sub-contract work, and partly because the fluctuating economic and employment situation has immediate as well as long-term effects on the work of Centres. Furthermore, it is now difficult to generalize about Centres, since some are operating along entirely different lines from other Centres even in the same area. It seems that managers have considerable autonomy and freedom, though they are all obviously directly affected by the economic situation.

Work training

Looking at SECs nationally, it is probably true to say that while some Centres are still very work-orientated, and devote much of their time to the fulfilment of own product or sub-contract work, and others are concentrating increasingly on social and further education in the broadest sense, the majority of Centres are trying to achieve a curriculum that provides both social and further education as well as work training, and trying to interrelate them into an overall cohesive programme of activities. The attempt to provide such a balance, however, has led to criticisms that the Centres are 'all things to all men' and that it is impossible in practice to attempt to meet all the needs of mentally handicapped adults without some attempt at a differentiation of functions.

Many Centres have been trying during the last few years to achieve clearer differentiation of functions, but there has until now been little central guidance, and little evidence of local interest in the development of a coherent day services policy on the part of Social Service Departments. This is the conclusion reached by Whelan and Speake (1977) who recommend that a specialized advisory service should be available for staff working in SECs similar to the system of special education advisers available at both national and local levels to teachers working in special schools.

Before examining proposals for clearer differentiation of functions, we can look again at the snapshot of work activities provided by the National Survey. To quote Whelan and Speake (1977):

> Over 63% of trainees were said to be engaged in work which did not require tools, for example: packing, sorting or labelling, or work which required only non-powered hand tools. We might conclude from this that most trainees were engaged in basic and general pre-vocational training. However there are also indications ... that more specialised training is available in some ATCs in such areas as laundry work, horticulture and industrial sewing.

There is also more evidence of Centres rejecting sub-contract work if it deprives them of training opportunities, or forces the staff and students to work to inflexible timetables. Some Centres are turning increasingly to their own product work — including concrete-block making, ornamental concrete work, toy manufacture, 'inflatables', boat building, industrial ceramics, jewellery and pottery, candle-making, shrinkwrapping, paint spraying, car washing. Wherever possible, these activities should be related to the work opportunities outside the Centre, as only a third of those who did enter open employment had any experience of similar work while attending the Centres. However, many jobs done in the Centre have considerable training potential and there is no reason why every job done should necessarily be available outside the Centre, provided that such training opportunities are properly exploited.

Some Centres are also beginning to find paid work for groups of students outside the Centre; for example, local authorities have employed groups of mentally handicapped people to work on public amenities such as parks and gardens, and clearing canals. Some have used the Job Creation scheme for this purpose, so giving opportunities to demonstrate the ability of mentally handicapped people to do a useful job.

One of the best-known schemes is that reported by Peter Lowman, the manager of a food preparation factory in Great

Yarmouth. Working in close partnership with the local Centre, he successfully employed a large number of mentally handicapped workers in food preparation, and reported that his workers were able to accept the mentally handicapped as co-workers, provided great care was taken to provide detailed training not only in the job itself but in the social and personal demands that went with it. This may involve a member of the SEC staff working as a peripatetic instructor in the factory, and providing a bridge between the mentally handicapped workers and the rest of the factory. He may only be needed at the transitional stage but his help should be freely available at other times also. Lowman's (1975) recommendations to other employers include the suggestion that a named individual in the factory should be responsible for the handicapped workers on a day-to-day basis, and should ensure that they are familiar with the layout and routine of the factory, including clocking in, whereabouts of the toilets, canteen etc. Trial periods of part-time or full-time employment are also useful.

Social education

It has long been appreciated that the ability of mentally handicapped people to enter open employment is determined as much by their social competence as by their ability to do the actual work demanded of them. For this reason hospitals and Centres have always tried to pay particular attention to social education and training.

Social education is a wide term and can be interpreted at various levels. At one level, it is important for the student to be able to use public transport, know his way around shops and post offices, and have some general awareness of local services and where to get help. At another level, he may also need to learn 'how to behave' on public transport, not to push his way to the front of queues, to wait his turn in the post office, and not to interrupt other people's conversations. The 'interpersonal' social skills sometimes need to be actively taught, with the help of specific methods and techniques that have been developed for this purpose both in hospitals for the mentally ill as well as in hospitals and day services for the mentally handicapped. By no means all mentally handicapped people will need help at this level of 'social skills training', but for those who do, a favourable response to such help may make all the difference between acceptance and rejection by those with whom they come into contact.

Social skills training methods include 'modelling' of the appropriate behaviour either by another student or by a member of staff;

role-play situations where someone makes either large or small deliberate 'mistakes' in social situations, so as to lead to discussion and demonstration by other students of how they would have behaved in the identical situation. The methods can be applied to mock interviews and simulated work situations, and provide a useful rehearsal for the kind of problems that may be encountered in work and other social encounters. It is likely that videorecording will be increasingly used in future, once such equipment becomes more widely available and is seen to be a key resource for training.

Social education also includes a strong emphasis on helping students to become more competent in a wide range of language and communication skills. It is well known that many mentally handicapped people are seriously handicapped in this field, some-times by difficulties of articulation which make it difficult for them to be understood, sometimes by having very limited language skills, and often by underfunctioning — i.e. by failing to use the language skills that they do possess, for example, limiting themselves to one or two words when they are in fact capable of longer and more complex sentences.

Staff are increasingly using a more systematic and structured approach to teaching language and communication skills than was formerly the case; it is becoming increasingly clear that reliance cannot be placed on the use of general language stimulation, or on just 'encouraging conversation'. The help of speech therapists and psychologists is being sought to try to determine the language abilities of students and to work out ways in which both general and individual language programmes can be developed, but there is much that staff can do even if they cannot get such advice. Simple assessments of language ability can be carried out by staff in association with parents, along the lines already developed by teachers (see Kellett (1976) for an example of a group of teachers developing a survey of language abilities for a group of ESNS schools). There is also an increasing interest in the use of basic sign and gesture 'languages' as an aid to communication for those who have not yet developed speech, particularly in Special Care Units.

Also included in education performances are programmes con-cerned with competence in basic number skills — including count-ing, weighing, measuring, telling the time, use of money and budgeting. These skills can be taught systematically and by the use of structured methods, perhaps including a programmed learning approach and involving the use of specially prepared audio-visual aids, or even simple teaching machines.

Although there is much scope for a systematic and structured approach to teaching, it is just as important to create and take advantage of ordinary opportunities to allow students to use what they have learned in ordinary situations. There is a wealth of evidence from research to indicate that mentally handicapped people have particular problems in using what they have learned in other settings: it is one thing to teach coin discrimination in the Centre's classroom, quite another to ensure that students will be able to select the right coins from their pockets when standing in a cafeteria queue.

One of the most difficult tasks for the teacher, therefore, is to find a balance between structured teaching and the need to practice and use what has been learned in ordinary situations inside and outside the Centre. This is one of the reasons why it is essential to develop an active working partnership with parents. The recent BBC series *Let's Go*, made specifically for mentally handicapped people, provided a useful opportunity for such a partnership.

Many Centres are also experimenting with teaching basic literacy skills. Although more ESNS schools are now beginning to teach reading to those pupils who show evidence of being able to benefit, many students are leaving special schools at the very time that they are beginning to be responsive to the teaching of reading. Some Centres are using the Adult Literacy programmes, and enlisting the help of specialists in this field, as well as using the BBC programmes specially developed for the purpose of developing literacy skills.

Some of these activities might easily be described as further education rather than as social education. Strictly speaking, the term Further Education is used in educational parlance generally to refer to facilities outside schools for the 16-19 age group; these are usually provided in Colleges of Further Education, in contrast to facilities in Colleges of Adult Education which cater for people above this age. In practice, this distinction is not rigidly adhered to for non-handicapped people, but the term further education is used quite broadly to describe the extension of educational opportunities to the handicapped.

In the previous chapter we considered a number of ways in which the FE sector was beginning to make a contribution to the education of mentally handicapped adults, and indicated that it was becoming increasingly common for staff of SECs and FE colleges to work in closer partnership. This can take a variety of forms, and no single pattern seems to be developing.

As this chapter is particularly concerned with the work of SECs, it is only fair to point out that the work of further education teachers is not always as fully appreciated by SEC staff as it might be, and is indeed sometimes regarded with some suspicion. This is partly based on the relative lack of knowledge and experience of handicapped students on the part of FE teachers in general, and also on their lack of qualifications for this work, and partly springs from a general sense of insecurity among SEC staff at the present time, arising out of the phasing out of the Diploma in the Teaching of Mentally Handicapped Adults and its replacement by the Certificate in Social Service. This has now been reinforced by the Warnock Committee's recommendations that the 'educational element' of the work of ATCs should be provided by LEAs. The Committee did not define the nature of this educational element very clearly, nor did the report clarify exactly what changes would be involved in the proposal. Nevertheless, although staff are in general favourable to a more educational approach to the work of the Centres, there is a considerable sense of professional depression among staff at the present time, sometimes expressed in the fear that FE staff will 'take over' the Centres.

Two points might be made in this connection. First, the fact that SEC staff in general welcome a more educational approach is reflected in the express wish of members of the NATMH that responsibility for SECs should be removed from Social Services and transferred to Education Departments. Although there is little likelihood that the DES will accept this responsibility, the policy in most parts of the country is to try to develop active working links between SECs and the FE sector. Certainly, this is the policy recommended in the NDG's pamphlet on day services, which spells out various ways in which such working links can be built up.

Second, it should be emphasized that any FE teacher who works part-time or even full-time in an SEC is responsible to the manager of that SEC, just as anyone working in a special school is responsible to the head teacher.

Despite these transitional problems, there seems to be wide agreement in the field that more collaboration between the FE sector and SECs is highly desirable, and will benefit the mentally handicapped. Although it is true that few FE teachers have very much experience with handicapped students, the same could have been said of teachers in ordinary schools who began to work with ESNS children after 1971, who seem to have adapted very well to the different needs and conditions of the new special schools and who are working successfully with their pupils. Furthermore, the resources of the colleges are considerable, and inevitably exceed what can be provided within most SECs which were designed primarily for work training, with some provision for education, usually in the form of a single 'classroom'.

Although many colleges are well equipped to provide facilities for mentally handicapped students, the key to success is obviously planned collaboration. It seems sensible, for example, for colleges to consult SEC staff and other mental handicap specialists before embarking on courses or providing facilities for the mentally handicapped, to avoid any element of competition for students, and to ensure that whatever is done is on a basis of local partnership. Despite superior facilities, FE colleges should draw on the experience of special schools and SEC staff on questions of course content, on the special learning difficulties and on ways in which they might be overcome. College staff on the other hand will, at the end of the day, need to form their own professional judgement about how their particular skills and their equipment and human resources can best be deployed with this new group of students. Experience has shown that mentally handicapped students do respond to the challenge of demand, and that it may be better to overestimate than underestimate what can be achieved.

Proposals for change

We turn now to proposals which have been made for the development of SECs; these come from a variety of sources, not least from the staff of SECs themselves, partly in their revision of the former official guidelines contained in the Model of Good Practice (Ministry of Health 1968). Many of these revisions were incorporated in the NDG's own recommendations, contained in their fifth pamphlet 'Day Services for Mentally Handicapped Adults'*. There is some degree of consistency in the various recommendations which have been made, and a fair measure of agreement in the field as a whole about directions in which progress is possible. Furthermore, the National Society for Mentally Handicapped Children has also published a number of minimum standards which can be used by their members at local level to evaluate and monitor both special schools and SECs (NSMHC 1977).

The NDG's suggestions are pivoted on a number of basic principles.

(i) Using the SEC as a key resource for mental handicap in the community, with both staff and students making the fullest possible use of the whole range of local agencies and resources.

(ii) A differentiation of functions and management structure within the SEC, which involves the establishment of

---

*Published in July 1977. This, and all other NDG publications, are available free from DHSS, Alexander Fleming House, Elephant and Castle, London SE1 6BY.

four functional sections — Admission and Assessment, Development and Activities, Special Care and Advanced Work.

(iii) The adoption of a broadly educational programme which involves a full assessment of the needs of each individual, leading to the design of a programme of activities which is organically related to those needs, making it possible for students to develop their skills, abilities and interests and to have systematic and structured teaching to enable them to do so.

(iv) A systematic programme of staff development, allowing staff to develop specialist skills inside and outside the Centres, to take part in in-service training schemes and to play a full professional role in the work of the Centres.

We will briefly summarize some of the main suggestions for change; a fuller discussion can be found in NDG Pamphlet 5 (1977b).

Pushing the walls aside

If an SEC is to be the chief resource for mentally handicapped adults in the community, it will need to develop working links with a wide range of community agencies and to ensure that there is no possibility of the Centre being isolated from the resources of the community. This has implications for both staff and students.

Students should be helped to use the SEC as a base from which they make increasing use of community facilities — e.g. FE colleges, sports and leisure centres, clubs and societies — as well as the main statutory agencies to which they have full rights of access — e.g. housing, employment and health, social services and social security. For some students this will mean dividing their week between the SEC and community facilities.

The extent to which students can make full use of community facilities depends on the availability of staff time to create and develop such links, and encouraging their colleagues in these agencies, as well as the general public, to develop a better understanding of the needs of mentally handicapped people. Many people are still quite unfamiliar with mentally handicapped people, and may therefore have quite erroneous ideas about their characteristics and limitations. Some people still have stereotypes of the mentally handicapped as dangerous, violent, promiscuous or sexually irresponsible, and need to be helped to understand the 'ordinariness' of mentally handicapped people.

This is why it is important to make it possible for SEC staff to work outside the Centres, and to be seen by their colleagues in other agencies as people with special knowledge and experience. For example, specialist staff might be helped to develop liaison roles with schools, FE colleges, sports and leisure facilities and above all with those concerned with employment. Hopefully such staff will not be limited to liaison functions, but will also be able to spend some of their time working with mentally handicapped people in other agencies; the most obvious example here is the peripatetic instructor who works with a full-time group of SEC students in a work enclave but who may gradually spend less time with them as they become more accustomed to a work environment and as their workmates become more accustomed to them.

The NDG pamphlet makes many other detailed suggestions for ways in which better working relationships can be established and developed between SEC staff and their colleagues in other agencies, including those in the health, education and social services, as well as with parents and voluntary societies.

Working with families

One of the most urgent tasks for SEC staff is to work more productively in partnership with parents and families. Their colleagues in special schools have shown that much more can be achieved by parents and teachers working in partnership than by working alone. Indeed, there is a danger that valuable training opportunities may otherwise be squandered.

Partnership between families and staff of SECs is not quite the same as the partnership which has been established between ESNS teachers and parents of younger children. For one thing, mentally handicapped people in SECs are not children but individuals with rights and responsibilities of their own and a status as adults which must be respected. This means that programmes of training cannot simply be imposed from above by people who 'know better', whether they are parents or SEC staff. It is no use parents and staff agreeing that the student should achieve a certain objective if the student himself has not been fully brought into the process of consultation and has altogether different ideas. More problematic still is the genuine conflict of interest which sometimes arises when staff and parents have different perceptions about what the student should and should not attempt. Staff occasionally report that parents are reluctant to allow their sons and daughters to attempt new skills, such as learning to use public transport or to use electrical tools and appliances. Problems also arise over relationships with the opposite sex and over sex education programmes.

It is precisely because of these problems that a working relationship between the staff and families is essential. If parents are brought into partnership with staff, they will have an opportunity of discussing the aims of the Centre and can then relate particular aspects of the Centre's teaching programme to the aims of the Centre as a whole. Furthermore, parents who are in regular contact with staff are more likely to be able to discuss their feelings and anxieties with staff. In turn, staff who meet the families regularly are more likely to be able to discuss their own needs and problems on a basis of equality and trust. Of course, many problems will remain, and cannot be resolved merely by talking and goodwill alone, but they are more likely to be resolved if parents are in partnership with staff than if both are working, as they often are, in isolation from one another.

Differentiation of functions within the SEC

One of the problems facing SEC staff is that they have been asked to tackle an impossibly wide task. The needs and abilities of students in most Centres vary so much that it is virtually impossible to devise a programme to meet all of them satisfactorily. On the one hand, there will be students who are only mildly handicapped, and whose needs are for a short intensive period of social education and work preparation to enable them to compete more successfully for jobs on the open market. On the other hand there will be others with severe physical and mental handicaps who will require intensive training for many years to come. Because it is obviously impossible for SECs to be 'all things to all men', recent reports have recommended that there should be much greater differentiation of function within SECs. The NDG's recommendations are for four functions or processes: Admission and Assessment; Advanced Work; Special Care; and Development and Activities.

These sections need not necessarily take place in different buildings, though some Social Service Departments do prefer different Centres to have different emphases; the intention is to encourage Centres to develop different types of programmes. The aims of the four sections are briefly summarized below:

(1) *Admission and assessment.* The National Survey indicated that the needs of many students in SECs are inadequately assessed; they are often merely observed 'on the job', but are not exposed to systematic assessment procedures which lead directly to the design of a programme of work and training activities which are related to their individual needs. The suggestion, therefore, is that every new

entrant to the SEC, whatever his age, should spend a period in the Admission and Assessment Section; during this time, his basic skills and abilities will be assessed not just by tests but by observing how he responds to a wide range of carefully designed demands. The many skills that will be assessed will probably include his ability to use a variety of tools; his social independence in such areas as using public transport, shopping, budgeting; his leisure interests and skills; relationships with other people; self-help skills, such as ability to dress, feed and toilet himself, as well as table habits, care of clothes and health and hygiene needs; basic educational skills, such as language and communication, literacy and numeracy and understanding of time and money.

It goes without saying that the family should be involved in detail at this stage, and should be encouraged in every way possible to contribute their unique knowledge not only to the drawing up of a profile of abilities and needs but to the design of a programme of activities which is designed to meet those needs. The family may also have special needs at this time, and may benefit from the opportunity to talk to staff about their own problems, particularly those relating to the more adult needs of their son or daughter.

(2) *Special care.* One of the most serious deficiencies of the present system is the lack of provision made for the most severely handicapped young people leaving school. Although ESNS schools cater for virtually every child, no matter how severely or profoundly handicapped, ATCs are not legally bound to make similar provision. Indeed, the Model of Good Practice for ATCs issued by the former Ministry of Health in 1968 specifically discouraged ATCs from taking 'special care cases'. As a result, only 13 per cent of ATCs had identifiable Special Care Units in 1974 and only 60 per cent of ATCs had any trainees whom they regarded as special care cases.

NDG Pamphlet 5 (1977b) strongly recommends that this policy should be reversed, that SECs should in future make provision for all students, no matter how severely handicapped, and makes a number of suggestions for ways in which the abilities of this group of students can be actively developed, and how the students themselves can be actively integrated with the work of the rest of the Centre. This recommendation is long overdue, partly on humanitarian grounds and partly in the spirit of the 1971 White Paper and subsequent government policy of preventing all but the most essential hospital admissions. This group of students is a cause of great concern to parents who are faced with a sudden withdrawal of services if their son or daughter has been attending the Special Care Unit of an ESNS school for ten or more years and faces the prospect of having to remain at home indefinitely if their nearest SEC is unable to make provision for the most severely handicapped young people leaving special school. Many families have suffered real hardship and undergone great stress at this time, and many more are worried about the prospects of having to face this problem in the future.

Fortunately, there have been some signs of improvement since 1976, mainly due to the use of joint funding money to build, equip and run Special Care Units. Joint funding involves a transfer of funds from the National Health Service to Social Service Departments for schemes which are in the interests of the service as a whole. Special care certainly comes into this category, and can also be regarded as value for money, since it prevents unnecessary admission for permament care in a mental handicap hospital, at much greater overall cost. A number of new Special Care Units have been set up, some attached to SECs, others housed in separate accommodation, and run by a separate manager, though still responsible to the Social Services Department. It remains to be seen at the time of writing (1978) whether the recommendations made in NDG Pamphlet 5 will become official policy, and whether Social Service Departments will be able to make provision for this group of students, as their colleagues in the education services have done since 1971.

(3) *Advanced work*. SECs have not only failed to provide adequately for the least able, but have also achieved less than might have been possible for the most able. Despite the work and productivity orientation of many SECs in the past, and despite the fact that many students came from ESNM schools, the number who have entered open employment was under 4 per cent in 1974, and is probably even fewer today. This is due to a variety of causes, including the increasing number of unemployed people in the community, and the shortage of unskilled jobs even in times of fuller employment, but it must be related in part to the absence of a systematic policy of training for work and linking with the whole range of statutory and voluntary agencies concerned with employment and training for work.

It is against this background that Pamphlet 5 recommends the setting up of an Advanced Work Section in each SEC. This section will concentrate on providing realistic pre-work training and experience where working tasks done will approximate much more to those of ordinary work. There will still be some emphasis on social and educational training, but this will be related more closely to the demands of work — e.g. time keeping, understanding pay slips, deductions, savings, independent travel, job hunting, being interviewed for a job, coping with social and personal problems arising from the work situation, and so on.

The social demands arising directly or indirectly from work require as much training and attention as training for work itself. Experience has shown that mentally handicapped people frequently fail not because of inability to do the work as such but because of lack of training and familiarity with all the social demands of a job. This is not just a matter of teaching obvious skills such as time keeping and clocking in, but the more subtle aspects of the social demands of a job, such as how to cope with being teased, sent on impossible errands, ways of talking to the foreman, the shop steward, how to manage in the works canteen and so on. Of course, these skills cannot be directly trained in advance, since no two jobs will be alike in their demands, but staff in SECs and hospitals realize that preparation for work should include active attention to these matters if there is to be any hope of the person not just getting a job but keeping it both to his own satisfaction and that of those who work with him.

The Advanced Work Section will also need to forge close relationships with the whole range of organizations and agencies concerned with employment in the local community. These include officials of the Department of Employment, such as the Disablement Resettlement Officer and the staff of local Job Centres; the Employment Rehabilitation Centres; local Remploy or sheltered employment facilities; specialist Careers Officers and Young Persons Work Preparation Courses; specialist vocational training schemes; representatives of local employers such as Chambers of Commerce and other relevant organizations, such as local Trades Union Officers. These contacts are all important; it is more than possible that the low rate of employment is at least in part due to the isolation of SECs and to the absence of guidelines to staff on ways in which they can set about increasing work opportunities for mentally handicapped people.

Before leaving the subject of training for work, it is only fair to raise the question of whether it is justifiable to try to argue the case for employing mentally handicapped people when so many non-handicapped people are unemployed.

The argument is finely balanced and in the end depends largely on one's personal philosophies and on the perspective from which the argument is being conducted. Those who consider themselves advocates for the mentally handicapped will argue that some have shown themselves to be capable of sheltered or open employment after a carefully designed and intensive period of training and that even more could be trained to this end if resources were made available. They will also argue that the unemployment argument is not really valid, since mentally handicapped people were no better off when there was full employment. Furthermore, the Manpower Services Commission has recently greatly extended the scope and quality of its services for disabled people in general, despite the economic and unemployment crisis, and mentally handicapped people have a right to their share of these new resources.

A number of innovative experiments have shown that employment opportunities can be provided even now. Perhaps the Pathway Experiment which began in South Wales, but is now being extended to a few other areas, is the most important. This scheme is currently organized by the NSMHC and takes the form of a training grant which is paid to the employer for every trainee accepted under the scheme. Trainees who are considered suitable for a period of trial employment are referred by hospitals, SECs and other agencies; each trainee is allocated to a 'foster worker' who helps to train them not only in the requirements of the job but also in the wide range of social and personal demands that go with it. The scheme has been a marked success in South Wales and was able to place twice as many trainees as were expected, mainly because most of the employers and foster workers refused to accept the training grants offered, so that funds were available to extend the scheme (see Cooper (1978) and Huckman (1978) for a brief account of Pathway and related schemes).

Schemes such as Pathway and those described by Lowman have shown that a number of mentally handicapped people can enter even open employment, provided that systematic attempts are made to prepare them for all the demands of work, and provided that government and other agencies responsible for finding work for disabled people are reminded that mentally handicapped people should be included in their efforts. Similarly, employers who have not previously encountered mentally handicapped people as workers may assume that they are by definition unsuitable, without further investigation or discussion with those who work with them. The onus is therefore on mental handicap practitioners and agencies to help employers to realize that some are not only able to work but can become successful and highly motivated employees.

(4) *Development and Activities*. The Development and Activities Section (DAS) constitutes the core of the SEC, and is similar in some respects to the existing ATC. It will be largely concerned with an active programme of training which is geared to the needs of each individual; this programme will arise from the analysis of needs resulting from the findings of the assessment

process. The programme of the DAS is seen as wide ranging and comprehensive; that is, it should include work training as well as social and further education. The aim should always be to explore ways in which the students can be helped to make progress and to learn new skills. Some of these skills will be concerned with activities for daily living, so that the foundations are being laid for more independence in such areas as self-care, budgeting, domestic skills and use of public transport. There should also be a strong emphasis on helping people to develop leisure interests and to make maximum use of community facilities for this purpose. A separate chapter of Pamplet 5 is devoted to this important area. Although the DAS will contain a number of people who may need to remain in the SEC for some time, the aim should always be to provide training which will increase the ability of students to cope with increasingly demanding situations. Many of these students who have ageing parents may well be able to manage quite well in hostels or in other forms of sheltered residential accommodation, and some could even be trained to live successfully in group homes. Here again, training schemes will succeed only to the extent that they manage to involve the parents in full partnership with staff. It is of little use if students are being trained to use public transport or to cook a meal if parents feel their son or daughter is not 'ready' to undertake these tasks, or if they feel that they are being exposed to too much danger in the process. Similarly, it sometimes happens that students are doing much more for themselves at home than in the Centres, and that staff are simply not aware of the discrepancy.

The Development and Activities Section therefore provides a firm base for the main training activities of the Centre. It should not be seen as a place where nothing but diversionary activities take place; every activity should have training potential. This does not mean that there should be no fun or relaxation; only that the overall aims and objectives should be seen as leading to the acquisition or consolidation of skills and interests. There is no place for a return to the philosophy of just keeping people occupied, and calling it therapy.

Training methods

How can these improvements be brought about? What changes will be needed to move from where we are now to where we want to be? How can a start be made? The basis of an educational approach lies in a detailed assessment of the abilities of each individual, followed by the design of a programme of training and activities which is organically related to his needs. Assessment is now seen as the responsibility of the staff themselves, and not as the prerogative of specialists such as psychologists. While they should certainly be available as consultants and advisers, those who actually do the teaching are obviously much better placed to assess and observe.

A wide range of assessment methods has been developed which are designed to be used by those who know the student best — including the parents. The Progress Assessment Charts (Gunzburg 1975) are probably the best known; they provide a fairly detailed breakdown of a range of abilities under the broad headings of Self-Help, Socialisation, Communication, and Occupation, each of which is further broken down into four more detailed subheadings. Charts are now available for relevant levels of development, ranging from those corresponding to the preschool level to the more advanced abilities required to live independently in the community. Gunzburg has also produced a series of Progress Evaluation Indices which provide a measure of average performance levels according to age and intelligence. These charts are not merely for assessment — they are designed to lead directly from assessment to programme planning, though it must be admitted that they are not always used as such. A wide variety of other assessment methods is also available; some of these are listed in various publications, including Pamphlet 5 (NDG 1977b), and Clarke and Clarke (1974).

The basis of systematic teaching lies in the definition of precise teaching objectives, and in the use of systematic methods of helping students to achieve them. The essence of this approach has already been summarized in Chapter 5; the principles and methods are equally applicable to adults, even though the content and objectives may vary. Here again, the emphasis lies on methods and procedures which have been well researched, and which are described in a number of easily accessible publications — e.g. Perkins, Taylor and Capie (1976). They include task analysis, fading and prompting, modelling, chaining and the use of systematic reinforcement. Precise record keeping is also essential for purposes of evaluation.

Although these methods are quite systematic, they cannot be simply identified with behaviour modification. A knowledge of behavioural methods is essential to such a systematic approach to teaching, but it should not be assumed that behaviour modification is simply concerned with the use of reinforcement. It is in fact much broader than this — what matters in an educational context is the identification of what it is that is to be taught, and the selection of the most appropriate methods of helping the student to reach a clearly defined goal.

These are powerful and effective teaching methods but they are only just beginning to be introduced, and do not feature as strongly as they should on staff training or in-service courses. One of the most important needs, therefore, is to provide staff with opportunities not only to learn about these and similar methods, but to be able to use them in their own work settings. It is one thing to read about teaching methods in books or to listen to lectures by experts; it is quite another to try them out at first hand. This is why staff training is at the heart of all new developments, and is more fully discussed in Chapter 10.

Conclusions

This chapter is based on the proposition that a great deal more can be done to develop the abilities of mentally handicapped adults. Research and practice have shown that they are able to continue to learn and to develop their skills and abilities, provided they are given time to learn and are taught by systematic and structured teaching methods.

The main community resource for this purpose at the present time are the 400 or so Adult Training Centres, hopefully to be renamed Social Education Centres, containing some 38,000 students, but which should more than double their numbers by 1991. This therefore seems an opportune time to review the work and achievements of the Centres, and to consider how they can most usefully develop in the next ten years and beyond.

This chapter reviews some of the main findings of recent surveys, and discusses the main recommendations for adult training services made by the staff associations, by parents and by the National Development Group for the Mentally Handicapped. There is much room for optimism about what can be achieved in the field of adult training if we can learn to put into practice the knowledge and experience derived from research and practice in this country and abroad. The key to progress lies in staff training and development.

8

A PLACE TO LIVE

Introduction

Where do mentally handicapped people live? How adequately are their needs met by the kind of residential accommodation that is provided for them and how could we make better provision in future to ensure a better quality of life?

Questions concerned with housing must be at the heart of any mental handicap service. It is essential to develop a coherent housing policy for each community that takes account of the needs of its mentally handicapped citizens for a place to live. And yet we have made very little progress towards working out a national strategy for meeting the housing needs of mentally handicapped people. People still assume far too readily that these needs can be met only in hospitals or in special purpose-built hostels. Very little attempt has been made so far to provide a wide range of housing accommodation, which is consistent with the enormous variations in the range of need, or to work out the kind of support services required. We have sadly underestimated the ability of mentally handicapped people to live in ordinary housing or to be trained to do so. We have not planned for a sufficiently wide range of housing accommodation.

Levels of need

We can consider needs at a variety of levels — the needs of the individual, of his family, of his immediate neighbourhood, of his local community, including voluntary organizations — and the responsibilities of the statutory agencies at local and central government to meet these needs.

The individual

We start with the individual because, characteristically, he is often the last person to be consulted about where he is to live. Although his wishes will obviously have to be balanced against the needs of others, much more needs to be done to devise ways of involving mentally handicapped people in decisions about where they are to live. This is not merely a matter of asking them questions but of presenting them with a sufficiently wide range of opportunities for choice. It is no use asking a hospital resident if he would rather live in a hostel if he has never seen a hostel or has no conception of what it is like. It may take a number of visits or even trial periods for him to be able to make any kind of informed choice on the basis of real knowledge. It is for the policy makers to provide him with a sufficiently wide range of options within which to choose.

Although it is normal in our society for young people to leave the family home at some stage, it is often assumed all too readily that community care means family care. We therefore plan alternative residential accommodation only for those people whose families can no longer manage to contain them for one reason or another. It is probably inevitable that at a time when resources are so tight and when so little progress has been made towards providing housing for disabled people in general, that we should be trying to cope with crises rather than with meeting needs long before a crisis point has been reached. But if we are trying to meet the needs of individuals, we should be thinking of how young people can, in the normal course of their development, be helped to achieve a greater degree of independence by living outside the parental home. It will inevitably be many years before we can reach such an ideal state, but application of the principle of normalization certainly suggests that this should be the aim.

The family

The policy of waiting for a family crisis before providing residential accommodation inevitably places intolerable burdens on the family. But even before the family are anywhere near such a crisis point, the problem of future housing is one that provides much cause for concern even from the earliest months of the child's life. One of the first questions that parents ask, and continue to ask as the child gets older is, 'what will happen to our child when we can no longer look after him?' The absence of a housing policy is reflected in our inability to provide a satisfactory answer to such a question at the present time. We need to be able to discuss a range of housing alternatives with families long before they have reached a crisis point so that they can plan their own lives in the knowledge that they will not be expected to shoulder the entire burden of their growing child for the rest of their lives.

Most families naturally want to keep their child at home. However, of the 80 per cent of families who keep their child at home at the present time, there are undoubtedly many who are under a great strain. Some of these families are actively seeking residential care but are unable to obtain it; others refuse to consider it because, to them, residential care means care in hospital and no-where else.

Despite the high priority given to children, and despite a most encouraging reduction in the number of children living in long-stay hospitals, it is a sad fact that local authority residential accommodation for mentally handicapped children has been at a virtual standstill since 1969. At that time, there were only some 1,800 residential places either provided directly by the local authorities or made available to them in other ways. In 1976 the numbers had not yet reached the 2,000 mark, though the most recent estimates suggest that there has been an encouraging increase in the number of children's places since 1976, partly as a result of the high degree of priority placed on this need by central and local government and also as a result of joint financing which provided the funds to make it possible. Even so, the number of places per 100,000 total population has stood still at around 4, in contrast to the target of 10 residential places per 100,000 set out in the 1971 White Paper *Better Services for the Mentally Handicapped*.

On the other hand, accommodation need not only be provided in local authority hostels: it seems likely that more use will be made in future of ordinary children's homes, small family-type group homes for four to five children, and of fostering and adoption.

Despite the unsatisfactory economic situation, there are encouraging signs of a wider range of residential accommodation being planned. Children are seen as a priority not only for humanitarian reasons but because the problem is relatively small, given the fact that most families are willing and able to keep their child at home. It seems likely that many of those families who now seek long-term residential care for their child would not need to do so if they had much more direct help from professional staff, and occasional support in the form of home helps and baby sitting, as well as access to frequent short-term periods of relief care. The demand for long-term residential care often arises because of the absence of any form of continuing support for parents who are left to struggle on in almost complete isolation from any source of help. Even with good supportive services, however, families who, for whatever reasons, can no longer manage to look after their child should have access to residential care in the community rather than in a distant hospital.

Some children are now being looked after in small-group homes in ordinary housing, containing six to eight children looked after by house parents. Others are accommodated in community homes for non-handicapped children in residential care; a number are being fostered and a few are even being adopted. A variety of day fostering schemes are being developed (e.g. in Somerset) which allow parents to leave their child with a known foster parent for periods of hours, a week-end or a few days without going through any formalities but simply by making direct contact with the foster parents. Leeds have reported a similarly flexible fostering scheme providing a short course of training for foster parents. This widening range of support services for families should result in a significant reduction in the demand for admissions for long-term care. As a result, for example, of the wide range of services provided by the Honeylands unit in Exeter, the demand for long-term admissions is reported to have dropped from 13 per 100,000 population to about 2 (see Pugh and Russell (1977) for further examples of support services).

These services will, however, also be needed by the children who are currently in hospital but who could be satisfactorily looked after in residential accommodation in the community. Most of the children now in hospital are severely handicapped, either physically, behaviourally or both, and undoubtedly require residential care, but such care does not have to be provided in a hospital. Here again, however, the numbers are encouragingly small — less than 4,000 children in long-stay hospitals in England; this is something like 8 children per 100,000 population.

The total demand for residential care for children in a population unit of 100,000 people is very difficult to estimate and will vary considerably from area to area, depending not only on the nature of the population but on the services already available. It is now doubtful whether any single national norm, of the kind provided in the 1971 White Paper, is appropriate. It is already apparent that the authors of the White Paper greatly overestimated the need for residential care in hospital in planning for as many as 13 beds per 100,000 population by 1991 when, in fact, the ratio has already been reduced to about 8 per 100,000 population by 1978. However, as we have seen, there has been no corresponding growth in places on the local authority side, with numbers at a virtual standstill around the 2,000 mark until recently. The first target, therefore, is to launch an all-out drive to provide at least 10 residential places per 100,000 population well before 1991. This would correct the gross imbalance in residential care which has developed over the past ten years between the health and local authority sectors.

Government guidance on this question is now in the course of preparation.

Crisis periods
Most families with a mentally handicapped member go through certain periods of crisis when their resources are stretched beyond breaking point. Such crises do not always necessarily result in a demand for long-term residential care; they may be connected with a bereavement, unemployment, financial problems or marital difficulties. The family may be under severe stress but the stress may not be directly related to the handicapped person himself although he is, of course, likely to be affected in a variety of ways.

One of the aims of a community service, therefore, is to prepare contingency plans to provide residential care, either short term or long term, for every family, long before any particular need arises. Every family has the right to know that their child will receive residential care if the need for it should arise for any reason at all; they should know where such care is likely to be given and should have opportunities long in advance to see the facility for themselves, to meet the staff and, above all, to allow the child himself to learn from the experience of living away from home for a short period. Nothing is more important for the welfare of the handicapped person himself than to be gradually prepared for any change of accommodation; nothing is worse than a sudden and traumatic removal from one environment to another at a time when he is already experiencing massive disruptions as a result of the family's problems.

This kind of forward planning is an essential hallmark of a good service. It stands in strong contrast to the requests for emergency admissions which are made every day and for which the family, social workers, the staff of residential units and above all the handicapped person himself are totally unprepared.

Although no one can predict when such crises will occur, there are certain key stages in the development of a handicapped person during which we know that demand for residential care is particularly acute. One of these occurs at the school-leaving stage. The age group between 16 and 20 is by far the most vulnerable of any age group for hospital admission irrespective of degree of handicap — a rate of 69 per 100,000 population as against 28 for all ages combined (DHSS 1978, Table B1.1). If we want to tackle the problem of inappropriate admissions to long-term hospital care, the 16 plus age group should certainly receive high priority, as suggested in the Government's five-year plan for Health and Personal Social Services *The Way Forward* (DHSS 1977).

There are a number of reasons for the vulnerability of this particular age group. First, a number of people leaving school at 16 and who are unable to get a place in an Adult Training (Social Education) Centre are simply having to stay at home with nothing to do. Quite frequently one parent (usually the mother) then has to give up work in order to remain at home. The young person himself, having been accustomed to ten years of structured daily activities at school, is suddenly thrown back onto his own resources and tends to become bored, restless and quite possibly disturbed. Tensions develop within the family which lead to further behaviour disturbances which finally result in the kind of crisis that leads to an emergency request for hospital admission.

A particularly vulnerable group consists of the most severely handicapped young people, who formerly attended Special Care Units of ESNS schools. Very little provision is available for these young people in Adult Training (Social Education) Centres, largely because of the former Ministry of Health policy of restricting admissions to Adult Training Centres to people of higher levels of ability and encouraging the use of hospitals, either on a day or a residential basis, for the most severely handicapped adults. Fortunately, there are now signs of this policy being reversed. Largely due to initiatives taken by Joint Care Planning Teams and the use of joint financing, some Special Care Units have been provided since 1976 (see DHSS Planning Guidelines 1978/1979, Local Authority Circular (78)6, para. 2.13.6); these are either attached to Social Education Centres or are provided as autonomous units run by their own staff appointed by Social Service Departments but run in collaboration with Health authorities, and sometimes with Education authorities as well. But this policy is only just beginning so that many young people are still leaving ESNS schools every year for whom no appropriate provision has been made. Here again, the essential of a good service is forward planning. As suggested in NDG Pamphlet 3 (1977a), there should be a long period of assessment of needs while the young person is still at school, with full family participation, so that the family can know in advance the kind of services that they can expect to receive once their child leaves school.

It is obvious, then, that residential options need to be available in each community for young people at this most vulnerable period of their lives. Not only is there a paucity of services for school leavers, particularly for the most severely handicapped, but the young person as well as his family are going through the normal difficulties associated with growing up. These are not, of course, inevitable in every case but those concerned with the planning of local services will certainly need to try to anticipate a demand for residential services at this time.

Unfortunately, adolescents are singularly badly placed where residential accommodation is concerned. They are often too old for children's accommodation and too young for adult accommodation. The children's accommodation, even if it exists, is not geared to cope with adolescents, particularly those with behaviour disorders or severe physical disabilities, and generally has an upper age limit of 16. Such adult accommodation as is available tends to be for a fairly able elite who present few outstanding problems. Many of them are in their thirties or forties so that neither they nor the staff take kindly to the arrival of boisterous and possibly disruptive teenagers. There is then no alternative to hospital admission. But it is precisely because of the absence of appropriate community provision that the young people have to remain in hospital far longer than is necessary. They continue to require residential care because their families can no longer cope, but such residential care as is available in the community is not geared to their particular needs. This quickly creates a new institutionalized generation.

Even where the young person himself remains relatively stable and is attending a Social Education Centre or other community provision, and is presenting no particular problems, the family are inevitably getting older and increasingly anxious about the future. Many parents with mentally handicapped adolescents or young adults are already looking after their own aged parents. Such a mixture of age and disability produces stresses all its own, over and above the ordinary difficulties of family life brought about by the increasing age and infirmities of the parents themselves. If each family with a mentally handicapped person were known to a social worker or to a small locally based community mental handicap team, whether or not the family were reporting stresses or difficulties, intelligent planning for future residential accommodation could be made in a calmer and more constructive atmosphere rather than as a last-minute crisis service.

Immediate neighbourhood

Community care is not just a matter of remaining with one's family but being accepted as a resident of a local community. Where the young person has been living with his own family for all his childhood, this generally presents few problems. Even where the behaviour of the young person may provide cause for embarrassment or inconvenience to neighbours and to people living nearby, such behaviour is quite often accepted with varying degrees of equanimity by local people. There are, however, occasions where a family may feel able to cope with a disturbed young person but where the people living in the immediate vicinity make a complaint and put pressure on the parents to have their son or daughter removed, e.g. when families have moved to a new district. In these cases, it is often helpful for a social worker or community worker to visit the homes of the people involved, and to try to arrange discussions between them and the family. Such meetings often result in offers of help of various kinds and a much more understanding attitude, though this is by no means always the case.

Much more common, and therefore more serious, is the situation that arises when there is a proposal for housing a group of mentally handicapped people where none have lived previously. Whether the proposal is for a newly built or converted hostel or for a group home, suspicion and hostility is still encountered though perhaps less frequently than formerly. This should be a matter neither of surprise nor of blame. The general public cannot be expected, as a matter of course, to accept mentally handicapped people in their midst, merely because community care has been government policy for many years. Most members of the general public have very little experience of mental handicap and are largely unaware of the developments that have taken place in recent years. They cannot be expected to know that many mentally handicapped people do lead quite peaceful and ordinary lives as local citizens.

It has been a general experience that opposition to providing housing for mentally handicapped people is very much less if great care is taken to involve local people as fully as possible and at the earliest possible stage. It is understandable that they should become anxious when confronted by a decision that has apparently already been made. On the other hand, the response is likely to be much more favourable if they are given a chance to meet the mentally handicapped people beforehand and if they have opportunities to discuss their anxieties with people who are knowledgeable about mental handicap and who, preferably, are already acquainted with the proposed new neighbours.

Many people are still very confused about the differences between mental illness and mental handicap; they imagine that mentally handicapped people are likely to be violent, sexually irresponsible or otherwise unpredictable and disturbing in their behaviour. There is also a widespread fear that property values will suffer, although there is in fact no evidence that this has happened so far. There needs to be full discussion about the nature and extent of professional support and supervision, what will happen in case of difficulties, how local people can call for help and support if problems arise and how the residents themselves can obtain help if they need it. In other words, one can never take enough trouble to prepare local residents beforehand for the arrival of a group of mentally handicapped people in their midst. Where this has been done, local people have often gone out of their way to be friendly and supportive and have provided help in a variety of ways.

Much depends also on the size of the unit. Little difficulty has been experienced with ordinary three-bedroomed houses; indeed the chances of mentally handicapped people being not only 'accepted' but welcomed are probably in direct proportion to the ordinariness of the houses they live in. A twenty-four-bedded hostel, on the other hand, or any other accommodation which stands out in some way from the surrounding houses is more likely to induce anxiety or hostility on the part of neighbours. Much also depends on simple but important decisions about special sign-posting and labelling. E.g. a large notice board, even if it only says 'Blankshire County Council', may undo any advantages from finding an ordinary name for the house, or dispensing with the word 'hostel' on the notice board. Similarly, neighbours will need to know whether staff will be living in or nearby and how accessible they are, how they (and the residents) can get help and where responsibility for the service lies. These and related questions are discussed in CMH Enquiry Paper 7 *Looking at Life* (Tyne 1978).

Local community and voluntary organizations

The success of a local housing scheme depends as much on the wider local community as on the immediate neighbourhood in which the residents are living. A group of people can be 'in the community' but still living in almost total isolation from community services and facilities. They may not be attending local clubs or pubs, know next to nothing about local sports and leisure or recreational facilities and be in touch with none of the voluntary organizations that are specifically concerned with mental handicap or other organizations which might meet their needs in a variety of ways.

Putting mentally handicapped people in touch with the local community and its various organizations and agencies calls for someone who not only knows where the organizations are and how they can be contacted but also about how these organizations might welcome mentally handicapped people as members. Decisions also need to be made about the extent to which mentally handicapped people should be left largely to their own devices in making use of community facilities or whether more conscious and deliberate efforts need to be made. No guidelines can be given on this point, as this will depend very much on the needs and skills of the residents themselves. But decisions will need to be made one way or the other.

On a general level, a balance will also need to be struck between leaving residents to themselves to integrate as best they can into the ordinary community or making special efforts to ensure that they make full use of community facilities. The risk involved in the first course is isolation and inactivity; one result of the second strategy is that residents might be unwittingly pushed into one activity after another when they might in fact prefer to remain at home. There is the added danger of drawing special attention to a group of mentally handicapped people by setting up all kinds of special facilities for them and thereby highlighting differences rather than similarities with the rest of the neighbourhood.

At the very minimum, however, it seems useful to suggest that amongst those who should at least know of the existence of a group of mentally handicapped people in a local community are the local secretary of the National Society for Mentally Handicapped Children, the Secretary of the local Gateway Club, members of the Area Social Work Team and any community workers who are working in the area. The residents will presumably be in some form of work during the day, attending Social Education Centres or involved in some regular programme of work or activity. It is comparatively infrequent for mentally handicapped people to be housed in local communities with nothing to do all day, though it is possible that one or two may remain behind to keep an eye on the house and to carry out routine domestic work.

Statutory agencies

The division of responsibilities between Housing and Social Service Departments is undoubtedly one of the many reasons why there has been such slow progress in providing residential accommodation in the community. From an administrative point of view the distinction is clear enough: Social Services Departments are responsible for residential accommodation in which there is an element of care and direct supervision, whereas housing authorities are responsible for providing accommodation to people without such need for direct supervision or support. Traditionally, therefore, Social Service Departments have been given the responsibility of providing hostels while Housing Departments have tried to use or adapt ordinary housing stock for disabled people of all kinds.

This division of responsibility has not been particularly serious until comparatively recently — i.e. only when it became increasingly clear that hostels were by no means the only solution to the problem of providing residential accommodation in the community and that it was important to try to provide ordinary or only slightly adapted housing for many mentally handicapped people who might otherwise live in hostels or even hospitals.

Fortunately, the operation of the 1977 Housing Act promises to blur the previously rigid distinctions between the responsibilities of Housing and Social Service Departments. For example, Housing Departments are now responsible for providing accommodation for homeless people. This might include those people now living in hospital who could be discharged to ordinary housing if it was available. The hospital would need to notify the housing authorities that a particular person was now fully ready to leave hospital but had no home to go to; at the same time they would obviously make arrangements for social work or community nursing support and ensure that full services were available to meet the needs of the people concerned. Similarly, Housing Departments at local level and Department of the Environment at national level are beginning to consider housing subsidies and Housing Association grants even where there is an element of care. (See speech by Minister of State (Health) to NSMHC, June 21st 1977. Copies available from NSMHC.)

Hostels and Beyond

But too many planners and officials still think in terms of the traditional twenty-four-bedded hostel as the only suitable form of housing for mentally handicapped people in the community. Because these hostels are generally purpose built, they tend to be extremely expensive both to build and to run. The capital costs now average £10,000 per place, and debt charges range between £20,000 to £30,000 a year.

It is hardly surprising, therefore, that hostel accommodation is extremely patchy. Nevertheless, provision for adults has grown at a substantially faster rate than that for children. Most local authorities now have some hostel accommodation, though none are anywhere near the 1991 White Paper targets of 60 places per 100,000 total population. The average number of places provided in 1975 was only around 12. Eleven authorities appeared to have no provision of their own; a further thirty-five were providing fewer than 10 places; five were already providing over 30 places per 100,000 total population (Tyne 1977). There are many problems of interpretation about the figures currently collected and published but there can be no doubt about the enormous variability in the provision of residential accommodation for mentally handicapped adults from one part of the country to another. Tyne's conclusion is as follows: 'Many Authorities are making very little provision; there is continued heavy reliance on the private and voluntary sector; there is very wide variation between Authorities and their level of provision.'

The local authority residential hostel is now being increasingly seen as the hub of a network of residential accommodation rather than as its sole expression. Some authorities (e.g. Northumberland, Gloucestershire) are beginning to think in terms of the hostel as the central resource and support for a series of satellite units, consisting of a wide range of group homes and other residential accommodation. The staff of the hostel provide essential support and back-up services for people living in more independent accommodation elsewhere who can look to the hostel and its staff not only for support in case of difficulty but also for sources of companionship and recreational and leisure interests which can be more easily provided in a larger hostel.

This idea stems from an influential experiment in Eastern Nebraska (ENCOR) in which an attempt was made to provide what were known as 'alternative living units' to all mentally handicapped people in the community and eventually for many of those in the existing State institutions. The range of alternative accommodation was as wide as can be found in any community. For example, the satellite units might consist of an ordinary council flat, with a married couple, both going out to work and requiring virtually no support or supervision; a group home containing six people with living-in residential staff; group homes without residential staff but with regular visits from specific social workers or community workers; group homes requiring only an occasional visit (see Thomas, Firth and Kendall (1978) for a recent account of ENCOR). As far as England is concerned, the residential hostel can provide a source of support for such satellite units, though this will obviously require a considerable modification of present staffing patterns.

All this, however, is very much in the future. At the present time very few mentally handicapped people live in group homes. A CMH enquiry conducted in 1975 was only able to locate about seventy-five group homes with approximately 400 residents.

The official figures for community residential accommodation that have been quoted above refer to those that are primarily a local authority responsibility. In addition to these, there are a considerable number of hostels and group homes which are, in one sense or another, an NHS responsibility. In fact, the NHS has necessarily had to take the initiative in many parts of the country in providing residential accommodation for hospital residents who were ready for discharge but for whom no local authority accommodation was available. Some of these hospital units have been functioning as long-stay hostels for many years. Others consist of recently acquired large old houses. These have been bought or leased by the NHS specifically for the use of mentally handicapped people. Sometimes they function as 'pre-discharge hostels', in which case the residents are still on the books of the hospital and are officially counted as patients (this is an important consideration when it comes to considering the entitlement to supplementary benefits and other allowances); in other cases they are officially discharged from the hospital but are still receiving supportive services from hospital staff — e.g. hospital-based social workers, community psychiatric nurses and occasional visits from psychiatrists or psychologists where needed. The residents are then registered with a local general practitioner and are encouraged to use the normal range of local services available to the general public, as well as any special services that they need.

One of the problems resulting from the restricted range of housing accommodation arises from the fact that very few leave these hostels for group homes or other accommodation. From the point of view of the residents themselves this is as it should be, since the hostel is their home. On the other hand, it is less satisfactory for people in hospital who are waiting for a local authority hostel place. This dilemma underlines the need for a much wider range of housing units for handicapped people. Some will be needed as training units, where people will live in homely and domestic settings but where residents are being systematically trained for more independent living e.g. by learning to use local shops, budget, cook and serve meals, and generally learn all the skills necessary for daily living before moving on to accommodation where they will live more independently and with less support. Other people will be living in accommodation that is for all practical purposes their home, where fewer training demands will be made, even though they will be expected to contribute to the running of the household.

Even though the range of accommodation is severely limited at the moment, it should be possible even within a single hostel to arrange for a person to go on living in the same home but with the support given being gradually diminished as his needs change (Tyne, personal communication). This calls for a much more flexibly structured service which need not be based on units with specialized functions.

The information available suggests that people living in local authority hostels have relatively few disabilities and handicaps. A DHSS survey of sixty-eight units containing some 3,691 residents carried out by Myfanwy Morgan in 1970 showed that 97 per cent were able to feed themselves, 82 per cent were able to wash and dress themselves, 11 per cent were singly or doubly incontinent and 4 per cent were doubly incontinent. These figures were largely confirmed by a comparable survey carried out in 1976 by the Office of Population Censuses and Surveys on behalf of the Jay Committee. This also showed that only 12 per cent were reported as having behaviour problems (e.g. being aggressive, destructive or over-active) and that more than two-thirds were allowed out of the hostel grounds on their own and without supervision.

Rather less is known about the characteristics of people living in hospital-type hostel accommodation. Much of this accommodation has been established for many years with the result that the residents have become very settled and in some cases quite elderly. Even the newer type of Health Service accommodation probably caters for more severely handicapped people who have nevertheless responded well to intensive training and rehabilitation regimes in hospital and who therefore no longer need to remain there.

The Trent and Wessex Regional Health Authority is developing innovative schemes in an effort to provide residential accommodation in the community for all adults who need it. In parts of Wessex, for example, a deliberate attempt has been made to cater, within each locally based hospital participating in the 'Wessex experiment', for a wide range of mentally handicapped people, including the more severely handicapped. This is in marked contrast to most local authority provision where, as we have seen, residents are on the whole very competent. The evidence available so far suggests that it is possible to run a small hostel-type hospital which includes a proportion of severely handicapped people, including those who are incontinent or non-ambulant. People with severe behaviour disorders, however, are more problematic since they may disturb other residents and make it difficult for staff to maintain the homely and domestic atmosphere which should characterize such units.

The Sheffield Development Project, on the other hand, tries to provide a range of different units, some run by local authorities for the more independent adults, some run by the NHS for people with different degrees of handicap. Both the Wessex and Trent schemes are being carefully evaluated by independent research teams.

Homes for living and learning

The discussion so far, in common with much of the public debate, has been on buildings rather than what is to go on inside them. In fact, we have little information about the kind of life lived by hostel residents, how they themselves perceive it and react to it or about the attitudes of staff who work in the homes or of those who are responsible for the service. The main exception is the CMH publication *Looking at Life* (Tyne 1978) which provides valuable information on the quality of life experienced by people in a variety of accommodation, ranging from hospital wards through hostels to boarding houses. There is very little by way of official guidance from central government or from the main professional bodies about the principles of providing residential care for mentally handicapped people, the kind of practices which are thought desirable or undesirable or anything approaching a coherent philosophy of care. It is hardly surprising, therefore to find enormous variations in the way residential homes are organized and run not only between one local authority and another but also within the same authority.

This finding applies, of course to virtually all mental handicap services. Many studies of hospitals repeatedly conclude that it is impossible to make generalizations about hospitals, since the quality of care varies so much from one ward to another, even when the two wards contain residents with very similar disabilities and needs. Similarly, one Social Education Centre may be fifteen years out of date in its methods compared to another Centre a few miles away, although both are within the same Social Services Department and have clients with very similar disabilities. Residential homes are no exception to this general principle; indeed, they probably illustrate more than any other sector the extent to which mental handicap services are isolated from one another as well as from other services. In the absence of any guidelines from central or local government, each unit becomes not merely autonomous but isolated.

Guidelines are particularly needed on questions of maintaining a balance between regarding the hostel as the home of the people who live in it or as a place where everything is done to equip them with new skills and abilities to enable them to live with greater independence outside the hostel. Although these issues are often polarized, there is no reason why elements of both models should not be able to work side by side.

In his book *Half-way Houses*, Robert Apte (1965) distinguishes between what he calls the 'permanent model' and the 'transitional model' of hostels. On the permanent model, no assumptions are made about the resident's ability to move to more independent accommodation and relatively little is done to train people to live more self-sufficiently. Indeed, the regime of some hostels seems almost designed to reinforce dependence. For example, there are hostels where residents are not allowed to make their beds, prepare a simple snack or even a cup of tea and take little or no part in the actual running of the hostel on the grounds that domestic and other staff are specifically employed for this purpose, and that their livelihoods cannot be threatened. Such a regime cannot actively prepare people to move out, whether to group homes or to other accommodation.

The transitional model, on the other hand, places much more emphasis on active training and preparation for community living. An active regime of training in activities for daily living is introduced, concentrating on purchase and preparation of meals, budgeting, shopping, saving, the intricacies of hire purchase agreements, use of post office, supplementary benefits and so on. Where residents are attending Social Education Centres, hostels tend to concentrate on the activities for daily living aspects of training, particularly home care and budgeting. Some of these hostels provide comprehensive assessments of their residents on the Progress Assessment Charts or similar scales and set specific goals for each resident, sometimes making use of systematic rewards.

Almost the only information about the organization and function of hostels comes from the CMH survey of residential provision carried out during 1975 to 1976 (Tyne 1977). Visits were made to 45 hostels, 18 group homes, 20 hospitals and hospital units, 4 village communities and also to a number of voluntary homes and private boarding houses. Using Apte's distinction, Tyne reported that nearly all of the hostels were operating the 'permanent model' of care. The transitional model was only being applied in one out of nearly 50 hostels visited, characterized by Tyne as consisting of a 'rather bleak and unrelenting environment'. A few hostels, while claiming to operate along transitional principles, were nevertheless doing relatively little to prepare their residents for more independent living. But some were genuinely trying to provide a homely and domestic living environment while at the same time systematically fostering the skills of their residents.

Conflicts sometimes arose in these cases between staff on the one hand who wanted their residents' evenings to be full of bright purposeful educational activities, and those who said 'well after all, it is their home, and if they want to slump in front of the TV all evening just like most people in our society do, then is it for us to stop them?'. There is an inherent tension of which many staff were aware, between the need to set goals for residents and to encourage progress towards those goals, and the need to provide an accepting and intimate 'home'. Although staff were often aware of the dilemmas, it appeared that they seldom had an opportunity to explore solutions to them in any depth, to talk through the problems at length, to see a range of alternative solutions. Staff were seldom aware of other hostels, and tended to arrive at highly individualistic solutions in their own setting.' (Tyne 1977:52)

Tyne's survey suggests that staff were not only aware of the dilemma of needing to choose between providing a living and a learning environment and of the difficulties of reconciling the two, but would have warmly welcomed guidance and leadership on these questions from those responsible for the service. They had a strong sense of their own isolation and, while welcoming some aspects of the freedom and autonomy that they were given, also regretted the absence of any clear-cut policy on the functions and management of the hostels.

The structure of Social Service Departments at the present time does not always make it easy for such guidance to be made available. Quite frequently a single officer is in charge of all residential services provided by an SSD (he may sometimes be responsible for day services as well). These officers pay quite frequent visits to the hostels but often lack any detailed knowledge of the needs of mentally handicapped people. In general, management seems to see the role of hostels as that of providing a permanent home, partly because there is simply nowhere else for the residents to go and partly because this is to some extent the tradition of residential homes in the community — at least for adults. On the other hand, some of the hostel staff were aware of the limitations of providing nothing more than a home and would have liked the chance to stretch the abilities of their residents a little further, even if there was then nowhere else for them to live. This applies particularly to the need to help residents to develop their skills in the area of self care and activities for daily living, as well as helping them to take advantage of ordinary community recreational, sport and leisure facilities. The most able residents were able to take advantage of these facilities with relatively little help, but this was by no means true of all. The OPCS survey referred to above suggested that a third of the residents were not allowed out without supervision.

In the absence of specific, technical guidance on methods of training and rehabilitation, however, it still seems useful to look for guidance to some of the general principles and practices of residential care which are now being discussed in local authority circles. The most recent of these is the document issued by the Personal Social Services Council *Residential care reviewed* (PSSC 1977). This is a liberal and humanitarian document, basing its principles on the privacy and individuality of each resident. Although it is concerned with residents of all ages, whether disabled or not, it nevertheless suggests that each residential home should draw up a statement of its aims and that these should be publicly discussed with residents and with all levels of staff. Furthermore, the document suggests that each resident is entitled to have an individual programme of activities which is designed to meet his individual needs. These suggestions are particularly welcome in the field of mental handicap, where the developmental and rehabilitative needs of residents can be systematically assessed. At the very least, it seems important to provide each hostel with an opportunity to work out its aims and the principles by which these aims are to be realized. Similar suggestions have been made by the NDG for other services, such as Social Education Centres and hospitals. On the other hand, hostel wardens have sometimes exercised too much autonomy in rejecting residents who might not 'fit in'. A balance has to be struck between implementing a policy and maintaining autonomy. It is, of course, important that a distinction should be made between general aims as statements of intent and specific objectives which identify the performance which is to be evaluated and the person who is responsible for seeing that something is done. The work of Albert Kushlick and his colleagues on the Wessex Health Care Evaluation Research Team has resulted in a set of very precise procedural guidelines on the day-to-day management of residential facilities for mentally handicapped people. These are concerned with a large range of specific detailed 'performances'. Even more detailed guidelines have been produced in North America in the context of what are generally called 'programme audits' or accreditation exercises. Facilities are inspected by specially trained teams who evaluate the performance of a residential or community facility, using very detailed procedures which are sent to the institution concerned in advance. It was intended at one time to link accreditation with funding, but this has proved impracticable. These accreditation exercises do, however, have the advantage of pinpointing a very large number of very specific practices within any given facility and provide a framework within which staff can discuss both their general aims and ways in which these aims can be realized in the day-to-day activities of the facility.

These methods have been developed by two separate organizations. The Accreditation Council for Services for Mentally Retarded and other Developmentally Disabled Persons has produced 'Standards for services for developmentally disabled individuals' (1978), together with a detailed survey questionnaire, as well as a more recent document 'Standards for community agencies serving persons with mental retardation and other developmental disabilities' again with a detailed questionnaire. In addition, the National Institute for Mental Retardation based at York University, Toronto, has been developing a Programme Analysis of Service Systems (PASS) (Wolfensberger and Glenn 1975). This is based on principles of normalization and also provides for a detailed and quantitative analysis for both residential and community facilities. These systems are being increasingly developed in North America and have latterly been the subject of a comprehensive evaluation in three Australian States (Berry, Andrews and Elkins 1977). (The NDG is currently examining these systems).

But these policies are needed not only for the individual hostels themselves but for the total system of residential provision of which hostels are only one element. Tyne's survey, as well as other evidence, suggests that local authorities have not in general developed a coherent strategy of residential services in the community, or made any attempt to relate these to the needs of people currently in hospital. Such a strategy must inevitably plan for a much wider range of residential accommodation than hostels alone.

We will conclude this chapter, therefore, by briefly listing some examples of this range of alternatives.

Group homes

A group home consists of an ordinary or only slightly adapted house with no more than ten residents. Sometimes a group home may include one or two members of staff living in or close by. In some instances pairs of council houses are used, residents living in one, with a warden living next door. Some are visited at frequent intervals by social workers or community nurses, whereas others are visited only from time to time or 'on demand'. Residents of group homes may be ex-hospital residents or may come direct from the community; such homes have been sponsored by both health and local authorities.

Although group homes for the mentally ill have been developing over a number of years, their counterparts for the mentally handicapped are only just beginning. Only thirty-five 'unstaffed homes' were recorded by DHSS for 1976; the Centre on Environment for the Handicapped estimate that the total number of mentally handicapped people currently living in ordinary homes is between 400 and 500.

Of the group homes visited by Tyne in the course of his survey, most contained former hospital residents who had gone through various formal rehabilitation and social training programmes, particularly in the six months before leaving hospital. Many of them continue to receive some form of supervision from hospital staff, though this was often in the course of being 'handed over' to Social Service staff. Understandably, no two homes were alike. Some were successful, despite very severe financial, practical and relationship problems; others were in danger of disintegrating at the first crisis. These difficulties are discussed by Tyne and also by Race and Race (1976) describing the 'Cherries' project in Slough. An example of a successful innovative scheme is the group home shared by students and mentally handicapped young people in Cardiff (Mansell 1977).

A number of parents' societies have also been investigating whether it would be possible for a family to leave their house to their handicapped son or daughter, provided that he or she can live in it as a member of a group home. Alternatively, the house might be made over to the Social Services Department with the same proviso. There are very considerable legal as well as practical problems in this scheme, but there are signs that these might be overcome; the idea certainly seems worth exploring.

Parents are also beginning to consider the use of housing associations to provide accommodation for handicapped people; grants are available under certain circumstances for schemes of this kind. Here again, this seems a promising development although few specific examples have been reported so far. Parents have also been buying or adapting property and either running it themselves or transferring responsibility to Social Service Departments. More joint schemes are now being developed, particularly with the development of joint financing. It is now possible for joint financing to be given in the form of grants to voluntary organizations; this should result in projects in which voluntary societies and the statutory agencies develop a working partnership to provide residential accommodation.

Villages and other residential communities

There are a number of residential communities in different parts of

the country, run by various organizations. The Camphill communities, run along Rudolf Steiner lines, are the best known of these;
others include various CARE (Cottage and Rural Enterprises)
communities, those run by the Home Farm Trust, the Peter
Bedford Trust and the L'Arche communities. Most of these are
rural but an increasing number are now also being set up in urban
areas. Some of these communities are fairly selective, taking only
people who can contribute productively to the life of the community; others, like Ravenswood in Berkshire, offer permanent
care.

Private homes

A number of private homes, including nursing homes, are available
and widely used by Social Service Departments. DHSS figures
indicate that in England as a whole some 32 per cent of all hospital
provision was met by private or voluntary organizations in 1975;
among the London boroughs the figure was 47 per cent.

Very little is known about the quality of care given in these
homes. Some of them are undoubtedly poor, and give a quality of
service which is considerably inferior to that available even in
hospitals. They are not always adequately inspected or supervised.
Above all, they are often miles away from the communities which
they serve so that people can be separated by more than 100 miles
from their families.

Boarding houses and lodgings

There has been considerable concern in the last few years about the
number of people discharged from psychiatric hospitals of all kinds
who are living a very poor quality of life in boarding houses. Many
of these are in seaside towns where there is little or no provision for
mentally handicapped people for work or training during the day
but others are also in the main conurbations. Considerable disquiet
has been expressed in the Press and by parents' organizations about
mentally handicapped people being 'exploited by landladies' and
living in poor and dirty conditions with several people sleeping in
one room and paying extortionate rents.

It is undoubtedly true that a number of people who no longer
need the services of a hospital have been discharged into the
community and are now living in lodgings and boarding houses of
various kinds. The quality of supervision available to such ex-
patients varies considerably from one area to another. Many
hospitals only discharge people if they are sure that there is

somewhere satisfactory for them to go and that there is adequate supervision to meet their needs in the community. Others have been less careful. It is impossible to say how many of these 'ex-hospital patients' are mentally ill and how many are mentally handicapped. Furthermore, many landladies undoubtedly provide a homely and domestic environment and act as foster parents in all but name.

Parts of North Wales have for many years been developing a guardianship scheme in which landladies are specifically recruited, trained and finally supported in looking after mentally handicapped people. They are not discharged to such accommodation until the authorities are satisfied that it is appropriate, and that the residents themselves can be occupied during the day either through work or through attending Day Centres. In general, however, very little is known about such provision and people discharged from hospital tend to be unrecorded unless they are actually receiving a service of some kind. It certainly seems reasonable to suggest that no one should be discharged from a mental handicap hospital without ensuring that there is somewhere adequate for them to live and that there is work or occupation for them during the day.

Community hospitals

The 1971 White Paper outlined the policy of providing small, locally based hospitals catering for 'not more than 200 mentally handicapped people from that particular community'. In fact, very few such hospitals have been developed, partly because of the deteriorating financial situation, partly because of difficulty in finding appropriate sites and partly also, perhaps, because not enough thought had been given to the organization and planning of such hospitals, how they were going to relate to the local districts and above all what the residents in these new hospitals were going to do during the day.

There have, however, been a number of interesting developments along these lines, particularly in Sheffield, Peterborough and in parts of the Wessex region. The Sheffield Development Plan envisages a wide range of residential facilities within the community, including two ninety-six-bedded small, locally based hospitals, in addition to a number of twenty-four-bedded hostels. The local authority was to provide for less severely handicapped people, the hospital units for those with more severe handicaps. Although every attempt has been made to provide a homely and domestic environment, with twenty-four-bedded units divided into family units of eight, the total conception of the building has still been criticized as too institutional by the Centre on Environment for the

Handicapped and by the Campaign for the Mentally Handicapped. Furthermore, attitudes have changed considerably since 1971 so that people are now questioning whether hospital facilities are needed at all and asking whether it would not be possible for the more severely handicapped people to live in groups of eight, but more widely scattered in ordinary domestic housing.

The Peterborough scheme (the Gloucester Centre) also involves a small locally based hospital catering for local people both on an in-patient and an out-patient basis and acting as a community resource for mentally handicapped people, whether they are resident in the hospital or not.

There would probably be general agreement that mentally handicapped people who need to go into hospital or into any form of long-term residential care should not be sent to a large, distant and isolated hospital with generally poor access by public transport. On the other hand, people are now increasingly questioning whether such units really need to be hospitals at all, whether they need to be adjacent to a District General Hospital and whether they should be primarily run by doctors and nurses. What is needed is a base for mental handicap services in a small community; this should certainly provide some residential accommodation, both long term and short term and should act as a kind of specialist resource centre not only for mentally handicapped people but for staff and families as well. Centres of this kind have been established for children, as at the Honeylands Centre in Exeter, but similar facilities are needed for adults as well. The emphasis should be on active treatment and rehabilitation based on the assessed needs of the individual. But most mentally handicapped people simply need somewhere to live which they can truly call their home.

Conclusions

This chapter has argued for the need for a whole range of residential accommodation for mentally handicapped children and adults and for enlarging the range of options between hospital, hostel or nothing to a wider range of facilities, including hostels, group homes and varying types of supported accommodation. Each community needs to develop a coherent strategy of residential care so as to make the best possible use of a broader range of provision.

If we can develop a coherent housing policy we shall be able to effect a real reduction in the number of people who are now inappropriately placed in our larger hospitals. We turn to the needs of these 50,000 people in the following chapter.

9

HOSPITALS

Introduction

Mental handicap hospitals are seldom out of the news. Unfortunately, the publicity that they receive is often unfavourable, concentrating on committees of enquiry, legal actions brought against staff, stories of poor conditions, overcrowding and poor staff morale. Rather less attention is paid to the more positive and progressive aspects of the work of the hospitals, the extent to which attitudes and facilities have changed in the past ten years or the enormous difficulties and restrictions under which staff are working. As a result, the general public, as well as families of mentally handicapped people and staff working outside hospital services, often have a far from accurate picture of the work that their colleagues in the hospital service are trying to do.

It is very difficult, nevertheless, to provide anything like a comprehensive or accurate account of the work of the hospital service. In the first place, there are enormous variations both between and within hospitals. Despite the very substantial improvements which have undoubtedly taken place in the country as a whole, it remains a sad fact that there are some hospitals which are still providing services and a quality of life which are hopelessly out-of-date and in which time seems to have stood still. There are other hospitals where reasonable improvements have been made, but where certain wards and living units are still run along rigid and authoritarian lines, in contrast to neighbouring wards which are progressive and liberal in their approach. There are islands of excellence even in hospitals that are otherwise old-fashioned, just as there are backwaters even in a hospital that is generally progressive. There is probably no such thing as a 'good' or 'bad' hospital.

Most hospitals have been adopting a much more 'open door' policy not only towards their residents but towards the general public, so that it is relatively easy for people in the local community, including families, to make up their own minds about their nearest hospital. Many hospitals have now appointed voluntary services organizers or have designated a senior member of the hospital staff to be responsible for fostering community relationships. Moreover, it is not all a one-way traffic; hospital residents themselves are increasingly taking part in voluntary work in the community. The facilities of the hospitals, such as gymnasia, swimming pools and recreation facilities are also occasionally being used by the general public. This 'open door' policy should lead to better understanding and community involvement so that the walls can be broken down and the hospital come to be seen as part of the community rather than as outside it. The basic task is one of communication.

The heritage of the hospital

People living and working in mental handicap hospitals are having to pay a very heavy price for the decisions of earlier generations, who produced buildings and policies which have now largely outlived their usefulness and are in some cases a gross anachronism. Many of our larger hospitals were created in the last quarter of the nineteenth century at a time when the general public, together with most of the professional opinion of the day, believed that it was necessary to segregate mentally handicapped people permanently from the rest of society. Such policies were based on a number of complex and interrelated beliefs. There was, for example, a real anxiety that the level of national intelligence would deteriorate with changing fertility patterns; it was feared that people of below average intelligence would continue to have more children at the very time when those of above average intelligence were beginning to limit their families. New ideas from biology and genetics, later allied to the use of the newly developed intelligence test movement, were invoked to conjure up the danger of a national degeneracy, brought about by a relatively small number of people of 'inferior stock'. Influential case histories were published purporting to demonstrate the pervasive effects of poor genetic endowment on subsequent generations (Jones 1960).

The advent of universal education as well as the rapid advance of industrial technology towards the end of the nineteenth century and in the first decades of the twentieth century inevitably brought to light a large number of individuals who were unable to cope with the demands of education, of work, or of society as a whole. Furthermore, the early use of selection and ability testing during the first world war again pointed to the existence of a substantial minority of individuals who were unable to cope not merely with the demands of intelligence tests, but with the kind of training and learning situations demanded by military service.

A variety of converging influences therefore led to the creation of 'colonies' specifically for mentally handicapped people. Many of them were placed in isolated settings, far removed from centres of population; very little was provided by way of occupational activities, so that most people had to stay on the wards all day. There was little or no contact between the sexes. People were generally admitted under compulsory orders and were not therefore free to leave. Both they and the staff who worked with them were largely forgotten by society. Such colonies gradually became an accepted feature of our services. They increased in number, new 'villas' were erected, each catering for thirty to sixty people, though there was still nothing like enough occupation and activity during the day. These colonies were administered by locally appointed managers and were basically a public assistance responsibility. Many had no more than a visiting doctor; the day-to-day management was left largely to nursing staff. Nevertheless, despite this generally bleak and isolated situation, a number of hospitals were beginning to develop progressive and enlightened policies; then as now some hospitals were years ahead of their time.

These colonies became part of the new National Health Service in July 1948 and were henceforward known as hospitals. Control therefore passed from the local authorities to the NHS; hospital management committees were appointed as managers of the hospital and were in effect responsible to the former Regional Hospital Boards and through them to the Ministry of Health and particularly to its Board of Control. This Board not only carried out regular inspections of all hospitals but also scrutinized all the compulsory admission orders. Although the Board of Control may in retrospect be criticized for failing to raise standards and for operating somewhat narrow criteria of a good hospital service, they nevertheless represented a channel through which the hospital service could express some degree of accountability. Their functions came to an end with the 1959 Mental Health Act and were later partly taken over by the Hospital Advisory Service set up by Richard Crossman following the report of the committee of enquiry into Ely Hospital. In 1976 the Development Team for the Mentally Handicapped replaced the HAS with further modifications of role (DTMH 1978).

A number of people now regret the decision to absorb these colonies into the NHS in 1948. It is argued that the NHS has failed to meet the needs of mentally handicapped people in hospitals and has failed to secure for the mentally handicapped in general a fair share of the resources of the NHS. In its evidence to the Royal Commission on the NHS, MIND argues that,

> despite recent improvements, mental handicap hospitals have relatively fewer doctors and fewer qualified nurses and, despite recent increases, have less money spent on them in proportion to the numbers of patients, than any other branch of the hospital service. Access by mentally handicapped people to other medical specialisms and general hospital facilities is severely limited ... (MIND 1977:15).

The first chapter of the National Development Group's Report (1978) to the Secretary of State on mental handicap hospitals puts it in the following terms:

> The decision to absorb mental handicap colonies or institutions into the NHS in 1948 was not followed up with sufficient vigour. The service was badly neglected from the beginning; it was never given the staff or the resources for the treatment or training which research findings had shown to be feasible. Staff shortages made it difficult to provide more than basic physical care; specialist treatment was often not available, e.g. medical and nursing staff, psychologists, speech and physiotherapy, services for the visually handicapped. Those with multiple handicaps did not receive the health services they needed; staff were unable to get access to specialists working in community health services. There were, of course, a number of areas where these difficulties were successfully overcome but most staff would, we believe, agree with the view that the NHS has not done its job by the mentally handicapped.

It is interesting to speculate on the possible development of these hospitals if the decision had not been taken to include them within the NHS in 1948. Presumably, they would have developed as some form of local authority service and might even have been incorporated into the by now reorganized Social Service Departments recommended by the Seebohm Committee in 1968. Even if they had been administered by the former Medical Officers of Health within the pre-1970 local government framework, they might still have become a social service responsibility under Seebohm.

A number of organizations have argued for transferring some or all of the responsibilities of mental handicap hospitals from the NHS to Social Service Departments. Their argument is that the main task of working with mentally handicapped people is fundamentally developmental, educational and social. Mental handicap is no longer seen as primarily a medical problem, though the health needs of mentally handicapped people are not in doubt. MIND argues that,

> as the basic definition of mental handicap is retarded or incomplete intellectual development, it would seem that for most mentally handicapped people the basic responsibility for meeting their needs should rest with the training, educational and social services. Provided that their social and educational needs are dealt with in this way, the medical contribution could be better focused on meeting strictly medical needs and in the important task of applying research screening techniques and preventive measures to reduce the incidence of mental handicap in its most severe form (MIND 1977).

It is also widely accepted that many mentally handicapped people have additional psychiatric disorders, including mental illness, and that psychiatrists should certainly be available to provide and co-ordinate appropriate psychiatric treatment.

The possibility that at least parts of existing mental handicap hospitals might be transferred to Social Service Departments was considered and rejected by the then Social Services Secretary, Barbara Castle, in an important policy speech on mental handicap made to the NSMHC in February 1975. The suggestion was rejected because Social Service Departments were still very new, and also because of the recency of two traumatic reorganizations — of the NHS and of local government boundaries. Such a transfer of responsibility necessarily also implies a massive transfer of finance. Even a small transfer of responsibility, involving only the occupational, industrial therapy and social education sectors of the hospital on an agency basis calls for large numbers of additional staff from existing local authority Departments at a time when only 30 per cent of ATC staff are appropriately qualified, and when day services are themselves trying to develop the range of their work (see Chapter 7).

In the long term, however, a radical reorientation of the work of the mental handicap hospital towards a social services model is not unthinkable. Quite apart from the training and rehabilitative functions, it has also been argued that the basic task of hospital staff is concerned with the provision of residential care. Very few residents are receiving active medical or technical nursing treatment of a kind which only a hospital, by its very nature, can provide. Apart from the minority of residents who have psychiatric disorders, or who undoubtedly need active medical and nursing treatment, the majority of residents are primarily receiving residential care, as well as training and rehabilitation to enable as many as possible to live in the community or in 'as near normal a setting as possible'. In both senses, therefore, what we now know as a hospital might, in the long term, come to be regarded as a residential and training establishment for those people who, for whatever reason, are unable to use facilities in the community.

The aims of the mental handicap hospital

There is much uncertainty at the present time about the functions and aims of mental handicap hospitals. Whatever may happen in the future as a result of changes in Government policy, the recommendations of the Royal Commission on the Health Service, of the Jay Committee and of the NDG's Hospital Report, we cannot escape from the fact that there are some 50,000 people living this year in hospitals for the mentally handicapped. Some are living in grossly unsatisfactory conditions; some are not receiving the specialist services which they undoubtedly need and about 40 per cent are recorded as taking no part in the training and rehabilitative activities of the hospital.

Essentially, the problem of the mental handicap hospital is always the problem of numbers. First, the hospitals are grossly overcrowded. There are still wards of over 50 adults and over 30 children, despite a five-year plan, launched in October 1969, to eliminate wards of this size. Even wards of 30 adults and 20 children are far too large to afford either comfort or privacy for residents, or to offer them conditions which even approximate to those that they would find in local authority residential care. When people cannot get away from one another, when there is nowhere to go to be private and alone, tensions are bound to build up and violence and aggression are more likely. Overcrowding applies not only to the wards and living units but also to the training areas. People are sitting together in cramped conditions, with little opportunity for the creation of small groups or individual work.

Second, there is the problem of the people who 'do not need to be in hospital'. A number of surveys have been carried out, all showing that a significant proportion of people now in hospital do not need the facilities of the hospital, and could leave immediately if there was somewhere in the community for them to go. Estimates vary from one survey to another, but conservative estimates place the numbers at between a quarter and a third (McKeown and Teruel 1971; Browne *et al.* 1971). Some hospital staff have even taken the view that only 10 per cent of those now in hospital actually need the services of a hospital, as opposed to some other form of residential care (Sykes 1977). But because alternative forms of residential care are not available, many thousands of hospital residents are inevitably going to spend the rest of their lives in mental handicap hospitals. Community facilities are developing very slowly and although, as we saw in Chapter 8, hospitals are themselves taking the initiative in finding alternative accommodation for those residents who are able to leave hospital, the numbers who are leaving represent a mere trickle. In fact, the reduction in the number of hospital residents every year is of the order of only 2 per cent.

The 1971 White Paper, representing official Government policy, planned for a reduction in the number of hospital beds to 29,000 by 1991.

But even if more people could be discharged into the community, all the signs suggest that hospital beds are more than ever needed for short-stay care. More and more people are being admitted to hospital for a period of a few weeks, mainly to provide relief for their families, but also, in some cases, to carry out a specific programme of assessment or treatment for the sake of the individual himself. But short-term care, although providing a very useful service, hardly relieves the overcrowding of the hospital which is essential to the provision of a better service. Short-term care should also be provided both by community agencies and by voluntary organizations; the hospital should not have to take almost the entire burden, as it does at the present time. NDG Pamphlet 4 *Short-term residential care* (May 1977) makes some suggestions on how short-term care facilities can be more strategically planned.

Discussions about 'those who no longer need hospital care' tend to be simplistic. 42 per cent of residents living in mental handicap hospitals have lived in the same hospitals for over twenty years; some 80 per cent for more than five years and a further 15 per cent for periods of one to five years. These figures show quite clearly that the mental handicap hospital is the home of most of those who live in it. If this can be accepted, then it follows that much more must be done to turn the hospital into a home for those people who are likely to live in it for some time to come, if not for the rest of their lives. At the same time, hospitals are trying to develop their training and rehabilitation facilities so that as many people as possible can live outside the hospital in some form of sheltered or adapted accommodation, whether this is provided by the Health Service itself, by local authorities, voluntary organizations, housing associations or by the residents themselves, living independently with some social work support.

We can therefore consider the tasks of the hospital under a number of headings:

(i) Providing a home;
(ii) Providing opportunities for training and rehabilitation to more independent community living;
(iii) Providing specialist services for all who need them;
(iv) Providing specialist resources for the surrounding community.

These aims correspond to those identified by the National Development Group in their recent report on the hospital service and are discussed in considerable detail in the body of that report (NDG 1978). This chapter will therefore be limited to a brief discussion of some of the more important issues.

The hospital as a home

Substantial improvements in living conditions have been made over the past ten years. Although these vary greatly between and within hospitals, there is no doubt that standards as a whole have risen greatly.

A major impetus to change was given by the 1969 Minimum Standards Exercise. These minimum standards were expressed in terms of size of living units, the provision of personal clothing and locker space for each resident and specific staffing ratios for medical, nursing and domestic staff. Earmarked funds were made available to bring about these and other improvements, including better food.

Progress in implementing these minimum standards has been uneven, to say the least. The DHSS regularly publishes in its annual statistical returns the performance of each hospital in reaching these standards. Although the overall rate of progress is encouraging, only 15 out of the 71 hospitals with more than 200 beds have been successful in reaching all of them. The recruitment of domestic staff seems to have been a particular problem. Thus, of the 71 hospitals with over 200 beds, 12 gave insufficient night or day space and 5 gave too little of either to their residents. Nine hospitals provided no personal clothing or a cupboard to store them in; 13 hospitals still had dormitories of more than 20 beds for children or 30 for adults; 15 had insufficient nursing and domestic staff; 18 were below standard for nurses and 49 for ward orderlies and domestic staff; 3 hospitals were below standard for medical staff.

These minimum standards represented only a crude and unsatisfactory beginning to providing a better quality of life. Clearly, many other features could have been included.

It would be wrong, however, to underestimate the amount of progress that has been made. Many hospitals have gone a long way towards providing a more homely and domestic environment. A great deal is being done to divide up the large ward into smaller units, and to do everything possible to allow residents to express their individuality and to retain some degree of privacy. Cubicalization of various kinds has been introduced in most hospitals; more residents sleep on divan beds, with individual counterpanes; they have their own cupboard or bedside locker and their own personal clothing. Much has also been done to divide up the traditional barrack-like day room with chairs arranged around the walls or lined up in rows in front of the television set. The eating arrangements have also become very much more domestic; it is not at all uncommon to see individually laid tables, with tablecloths, cutlery, condiments and sauces. A plated meal service, however, is an almost inevitable result of centralized catering, although some hospitals are trying to provide an individual service, with cafeteria facilities offering choice at lunch-time, and meals served from serving dishes at other times.

The washing and toileting facilities are still unbelievably primitive in many wards, affording no dignity or privacy as well as being grossly inadequate for people with whom incontinence may be a problem. It seems unbelievable that hospital villas could have been built or retained with only one or two toilets for thirty or even forty residents.

The provision of personal clothing has had a major impact not only on the residents themselves but also on casual visitors to the hospital. It is relatively rare now to find groups of residents shuffling about in ill-fitting, standard issue institutional clothing, already ruined by the centralized laundry. The purchase of personal clothing has been considerably helped by the increased entitlements of residents, and also by the introduction of domestic washing machines on the wards and living units. Nursing staff have often gone out with residents to help them to choose their own clothes in local shops, and have relied less than in the past on hospital shops or on bulk purchase of personalized clothing. The problems of laundry and storage have by no means been overcome but the sheer transformation in the appearance of residents over the past few years has made a major psychological difference both on the residents and on outsiders. Clothes can make all the difference to attitudes.

Attempts have also been made to provide a more homely and domestic environment in a variety of other ways. For example, breaking up a large dormitory into smaller units encourages friendships and small groups of people spending time together. A wider range of leisure and recreational activities is now provided on most living units, so that residents are not faced, as they used to be, with a choice between watching television and doing nothing. Most hospitals also provide a very wide range of evening activities, including Bingo, discos, evening classes — both inside and outside the hospital — clubs, outings and so on. Every attempt is made to provide as much choice as possible for each resident; those who would rather stay at home and watch television are free to do so but other activities are also available.

Being able to choose is what distinguishes home from an institution. This is why attempts are now being made to provide a much wider range of choice for residents. This alone justifies a reduction in the size of living units. There is little scope for choice when you are living together with thirty or fifty people; the demands of the institution are bound to come first. Smaller living units provide a greater range of opportunities for choice. In general, groupings of twelve adults and eight children are now regarded as desirable; these are being planned in the new locally based hospital units (described in Chapter 8) but even in the older traditional hospitals attempts are being made to break down the size of living units and to create smaller groupings of residents.

Equally important is the delegation of decision making to staff of these units. It is now widely agreed that staff should have as much freedom and flexibility as possible to run units in their own way, free from interference from those above but nevertheless still within the framework of the hospital policy agreed by all. Research by King, Raynes and Tizard (1971) investigated the style of management and organization of a wide range of residential units for handicapped children. Broadly speaking, a higher standard of care was provided by staff who were left free to make crucial day-to-day decisions — e.g. about times of getting up and going to bed, week-end and evening activities, questions concerned with meal-times, clothing, the organization of recreational activities etc. How much decision making can be delegated obviously depends on the size of the organization and ways in which individual units fit into the overall programme, but the basic principle of maximum delegation and devolution of decision making is an important one.

The early work of King, Raynes and Tizard (1971) has been essentially confirmed in later work by Zigler and his associates (for a brief summary see Zigler and Balla (1977)) and also by Raynes and her associates in later studies of twenty-one residencies in different institutions for the retarded in the USA (Pratt, Raynes and Roses 1977). Raynes and her colleagues devised two indices of the quality of care — the Revised Resident Management Practices Scale and the Index of Informative Speech. They also developed an index of perceived participation in decision making, derived from question-naires given to all direct care workers in each building. They con-cluded that 'the more workers feel themselves involved in decisions affecting their work, the better the quality of care provided for residents on both measures of care, and the higher the staff's morale'.

It is now becoming increasingly clear that direct care staff develop resident-orientated as opposed to institution-orientated care in direct proportion to the extent that they themselves are given responsibility for decision making. The more hierarchical the structure, the more institutional the system. Rather more surprising is the finding that size of institution is not as relevant as one might have supposed. A small hostel or living unit can be run along rigidly institutional lines, just as a larger living unit can, by good management, be very resident orientated. The levels of disability of the residents is also not as crucial as one might have supposed. Although it is true that the more severely retarded residents receive an inferior quality of care, this is not necessarily inevitable. The Zigler studies also showed that levels of expenditure, as measured by cost per resident per day, levels of staffing as measured by number of aides and professional staff per resident, were not related to the quality of care for residents. 'Apparently, simply increasing expenditure on personnel will not necessarily guarantee better care for the retarded. Rather, it is how these personnel are utilized in the settings in which they are found' (Zigler and Balla 1977:271).

The main finding that emerges from a wide range of research studies and of visits from the Development Team for the Mentally Handicapped (1978) is one of enormous variability both between and within hospitals. Even when allowances have been made, such factors as the disabilities of residents, size of unit and staffing levels, and variations in the quality of care are still very striking. This underlines the need for an overall policy of residential care to be agreed and implemented by all levels of staff.

The hospital as a learning environment

The need for an agreed policy is just as great in the field of training and rehabilitation as it is in the field of residential care. Hospitals have done a great deal to develop their training and rehabilitation activities over the past ten years but the approach has been rather piecemeal and haphazard. Training units have been set up within most hospitals, and some have adopted advanced and progressive practices for fostering the abilities of residents. However, these are not always well co-ordinated with the activities of other training units, nor with the staff of the living units. Although a wide range of activities is provided, these are not necessarily part of an overall treatment programme, based on systematic assessment of the needs of the individual. It is one thing to provide activities, quite another to relate these to the assessed needs of individuals. No matter how successful the work of an individual training department, failure to co-ordinate training with other departments deprives the resident of opportunities to use in one environment skills that he has learned in another. There is considerable research evidence to indicate that failure to generalize experiences across settings is one of the specific difficulties that mentally handicapped people have in learning new tasks.

Foundations for any training programme lie in the process of assessment of individual needs. Fortunately, assessment is no longer seen as a specialized task which can only be carried out by highly trained but exceedingly rare psychologists. A variety of fairly simple and straightforward methods are now becoming available which allow direct care staff to systematize their knowledge and observations of the people with whom they are working. These methods have been briefly summarized in earlier chapters. Even a quick and somewhat superficial assessment, such as the one-page Wessex case-register form, is a useful start and can provide a foundation for more careful and wide-ranging assessment procedures.

It is now widely agreed that assessment must always lead to a programme of action. Assessment for assessment's sake is a waste of time. From an accountability point of view, it is also increasingly accepted that each residential facility should have a stated programme of objectives which are related to the needs of the individual resident. This programme should be regularly reviewed, should be publicly available to all staff who come in contact with the resident and should as far as possible be fully discussed both with the resident and with his family.

Programmes of training will obviously vary with the needs of the individual but the over-all aims are generally concerned with helping each person to live more independently. The more severely or profoundly handicapped may need to be taught basic self-care skills, concerned with feeding, dressing, toilet training, as well as fundamental communication skills such as eye contact, listening, play and communication. Signing systems and alternative methods of communication are now increasingly being taught to mentally handicapped people, both in schools and in residential settings (see Kiernan 1977).

At a higher level, programmes of social education have been developed for many years. These involve systematic training in various areas of independent living, including understanding money, budgeting, shopping, use of public facilities such as shops, post offices, sports and recreation centres etc. Activities for daily living (ADL) are also being systematically taught; these include basic survival skills such as preparing a snack or cooking a more elaborate meal, bed-making, domestic skills involved in simple repairs, keeping a house clean, gardening, keeping pets etc.

The resident's training programme must also aim to help him to make systematic and step-by-step progress towards more independent living. Most hospitals now try to do this by providing training in settings that gradually approximate more and more to those found in the community. Many, for example, now have 'training flats' equipped with the ordinary range of household furniture and fittings, in which small groups of three or four residents can live together and be given gradually increasing degrees of responsibility to manage their own lives.

Hospitals have also acquired houses both inside and outside the hospital grounds which were formerly lived in by hospital staff but are now used as training units. Larger hospitals require a range of accommodation in order to provide a graduated series of steps towards greater independence. Hospital residents who have been prepared to live in group homes, for example, clearly need to be left almost entirely to their own devices in order to give them the experience of living independently, even though they know that staff support is available in case of difficulty. Those who are not yet ready for this degree of independence spend part of the day in training flats but return to their living units at night.

In addition to the more 'obvious' social education programmes, hospital staff are increasingly turning their attention to the rather more intangible social skills which can make all the difference between community acceptance and rejection. People who have lived in hospitals for many years tend to carry some of the hallmarks of institutionalization, even when they have become quite competent and independent. For example, they may talk too loudly in public, stare at people on public transport, talk too freely to strangers and draw attention to themselves in a variety of ways. Social skills are just as important as the actual 'mechanics' of using public facilities.

Methods of social skills training are now being developed, particularly in mental illness and psychiatric units; they are even more relevant in units for the mentally handicapped. For example, various role-play and rehearsal techniques are now used, identifying small points where a resident may have 'gone wrong', and encouraging discussion on how others would have coped with the same situation. Films and even videotapes are sometimes used for this purpose.

The more such training is provided in or near real-life situations, the more it is likely to be not only learned but used. However, it is no use simply sending people in the community to cope as best they can, even if only for a single day; effective training clearly depends on knowing exactly what a trainee can do, and estimating how much help is required to help him to reach the next stage of his development. Staff therefore should provide as much help as is necessary, but then gradually reduce the amount of help by small steps, leaving the trainee to cope on his own, though within reach of support. For example, many residents are able to use an automatic washing machine on the living unit, but may be completely lost in the local launderette. Similarly, a resident who may be able to make sensible purchases of clothes from a hospital shop may become confused or disturbed in a large chain store. Staff will therefore need to accompany the resident initially, but gradually leave him to do more and more for himself.

Needless to say, no two people will react in the same way to identical training situations. This is why training programmes must be based on the assessed needs of individuals. It is always difficult to strike a balance between doing too much and too little.

Training for work
Training for independent living includes training for work. If more people are going to be rehabilitated from hospital to the community, active programmes of preparation for work will need to begin in hospital. Although the Social Education Centres will be able to provide further training for some, they cannot necessarily be expected to cater for all the people who no longer need to be in hospital.

The number of mentally handicapped people who can work or be trained to work is much greater than people generally believe. Research carried out in the 1950s showed that even severely handicapped people could be trained to work at quite complicated tasks, provided they were given time to learn, and taught by systematic principles of training. These principles were set out in a number of books, films and publications and were widely adopted both in hospitals and in Adult Training Centres. As a result of these programmes, some hospital residents were helped to obtain jobs in the community, either on their own or in enclave systems — i.e. small groups working under the supervision of a member of staff specially appointed for the purpose (Clarke and Clarke 1974; Elliott and Whelan 1975).

Some of the early enthusiasm for work training and rehabilitation was lost as a result of the difficulties of discharging people to employment, as well as the difficulty of finding work in hospitals. Although most hospitals were developing their training facilities in 'industrial therapy' or 'work therapy' units, the work actually available in those units was often not related to the needs of residents or to work opportunities available in the community. Many of them were forced to rely on contract work or any other work that they could obtain to keep people occupied. Much of the work was therefore dull, repetitive and merely diversionary. Furthermore, the need to fulfill contracts and deadlines, while giving the outward appearance of industrial conditions, often led to the interests of the contractor being given priority over the training needs of residents. It was not uncommon, for example, to see staff busily at work themselves, assembling, packing and storing materials, while trainees had little or nothing to do.

The organization, management and staffing of the industrial training units was often unsatisfactory. There was little or no evidence of assessment of skills, strengths and weaknesses, with the result that only general activities were provided, based on a rough estimate of suitability for the group as a whole. Under these circumstances it was difficult to find work to stretch the abilities of the most able on the one hand or training opportunities for people with severe handicaps on the other.

Most frustrating of all was the absence of community facilities for those people who were ready to leave hospital, who were well trained and probably able to get and keep a job but who had to remain in hospital because there was nowhere for them to live and no community provision suitable for their needs.

Nevertheless, a number of hospitals have begun to provide work experiences and training as part of a graded and systematic programme leading to rehabilitation into the community or, where this is not possible, to meaningful and useful work within the hospital. The motivation to provide training programmes was particularly great in those hospitals which still contained a substantial number of more able residents who stood a good chance of being successfully rehabilitated. Accordingly, hospital staff intensified their efforts to provide a co-ordinated programme of work preparation, social education and further education.

Forging effective links with community agencies is likely to increase the range of work opportunities for hospital residents. Only about a thousand people living in hospitals go out to open employment every day, returning to the hospital at night, but the percentages vary greatly from one part of the country to another.

Similar variations are reflected in the number of people making use of local Social Education Centres — the total numbers were only around 600 in 1975. It is therefore essential for hospital staff to make contacts with a wide range of organizations and agencies concerned with employment in the community and, moreover, to work together with the Social Education Centre in an effort to develop an integrated and co-ordinated policy of rehabilitation to open or at least sheltered employment.

The basis of all the suggestions made here and, in much more detail in the NDG's (1978) Hospital Report, involve a systematic and properly planned programme to develop the skills and abilities of each individual resident. The goal of the programme may be quite limited, e.g. holding a spoon for feeding or a hammer for nailing; on the other hand it may involve not only getting a job but keeping it.

The hospital as a base for specialist services

Whatever its long-term future, hospitals need to provide specialist services for those who need them. These specialist services involve not only residential care for those who, for the time being, cannot live anywhere else, but also specialized and active treatment of the many disabilities and handicaps that are found in mentally handicapped people, especially those in hospital.

Paradoxically, hospitals have not found it easy to mobilize the full resources of the National Health Service, so that people in mental handicap hospitals have often been unable to get access to specialized treatment facilities which were available to other mentally handicapped people living in the community.

Reasons for this are far from clear. Hospital patients have access to the ordinary out-patient facilities of the District General Hospital and are often given preferential treatment on waiting lists; consultants and other specialists visit hospitals and run out-patient clinics there; furthermore, the whole range of aids and appliances are just as available to mentally handicapped people in hospital as to the rest of the community.

In practice, however, the health needs of hospital residents are not satisfactorily met. A recent survey by Maureen Oswin (1977) of 200 severely and multiply handicapped children living in hospitals reflected a depressing picture of unmet medical and paramedical needs.

33 of the children in the study were *known* to be blind; and it was suspected that approximately 50% of the 200 children might

have some hearing losses; but the majority of the children had not had their handicaps fully assessed, and the staff were so unsure of the extent of the children's sensory handicaps that no accurate figures for partial sight or deafness could be obtained. Fewer than 5 of the 200 children had been issued with glasses. Only one child wore a hearing aid. There was confusion about how to help deaf children to communicate. Only one of the children was receiving any intensive specialist educational help for her sensory handicaps.

There was also a reluctance on the part of some orthopaedic consultants to treat physically disabled children who were also mentally handicapped. This discrimination meant that these children were at risk of developing gross and crippling deformities. She also states in her main report that 'the children's general health needs were neglected: e.g. some of the children suffered from chronic conditions such as catarrh, tooth decay, skin disorders, intestinal upsets, runny ears, sore eyes' (Oswin 1978).

These problems arise to some extent as a result of the isolation of the hospital from the rest of the NHS and community services and partly from the lack of knowledge on the part of staff on means of getting access to these services. Studies carried out by the Development Team suggest that it is not so much a question of services not being available as not being demanded. This applies particularly to the whole range of aids and appliances which are supplied under the NHS. These include wheelchairs, walking aids, hearing aids, spectacles and more specialized equipment. Staff are not given the opportunities to become familiar with the developments that are taking place in the rehabilitation of multiply handicapped people outside the hospital service — e.g. by visiting Special Schools and specialist rehabilitation Centres, exhibitions on aids for the disabled and so on.

Residents with physical and sensory impairments should, therefore, as a matter of routine be seen by specialists in the relevant disciplines and provided with the full range of treatment which is appropriate to their needs. This calls, for example, for paediatricians, and specialists in physical and orthopaedic medicine, otologists and opthalmologists. Regular screening should be provided to detect visual and hearing impairments at the earlier stages, as well as specialized assessment of visual and auditory functions in people in whom these capacities are impaired or in doubt. A large number of people in hospital have undetected hearing or visual impairments, and are often thought to be too severely handicapped to be 'testable', although new methods of assessing sensory function in 'unco-operative' people have been available for a number of years in specialist centres.

The shortage of speech therapists and physiotherapists is particularly serious. The number of whole-time equivalents employed in mental handicap hospitals is around 20 speech therapists and 80 physiotherapists. Although these numbers are obviously completely inadequate to cope with the demand for their services, it would be unrealistic to expect a significant increase in the number of such specialists who are prepared to work full time in mental handicap hospitals. Nevertheless, a number of area therapists have been able to provide for part-time services within the hospitals and have discussed with nursing staff the most appropriate ways in which highly specialized and scarce resources can be best deployed. For example, a speech therapist can provide an excellent service by helping living unit staff to carry out basic assessments of speech, language and communication functions and helping them to arrive at a simple programme of activities which are relevant to the needs of individuals and small groups. In other words, they act as specialist consultants and advisers, rather than limiting their role to a one-to-one clinical service. Much the same can be said of physiotherapy: there are obviously specialized treatments which only physiotherapists can carry out but they can work most effectively through other staff by suggesting simple activities and exercises, postures which help to make the best use of residual motor skills, appropriate feeding positions etc.

In addition to needs arising from motor, sensory and communication handicaps, hospital residents also have need for specialist psychiatric help. This applies in particular to those people who are suffering from some form of psychiatric disorder in addition to, or complicated by, their mental handicap. For example, a number of people may have a superimposed psychotic disorder, including a schizophrenic or depressive illness; others show various forms of organically determined disorders which require skilled investigation and specialized treatment. Psychiatric services are also needed for the elderly mentally handicapped person and for those who are referred through the Courts.

But in 1976 there were only about 140 consultant psychiatrists working in mental handicap. Many of them spend a good deal of their time working in the community, providing psychiatric services and advice in out-patient clinics, Social Education Centres and Special Schools, and are active in community teams, whether based in the hospital or in the community. So far as their work within the hospital is concerned, psychiatrists are increasingly inclined to concentrate on those residents who actively require psychiatric help, but opinion within the profession varies. There are still some who see the psychiatrist as the clinical director of a large and complex organization, with final responsibility for decision making in virtually all aspects of the life of the hospital. Although there are now few medical superintendents left, consultants still carry the final medical responsibility for admission, treatment and discharge. In some cases, however, much of the day-to-day responsibility is delegated to training departments and to senior nursing staff. The precise legal position of the mental handicap consultant is badly in need of clarification.

In summary, then, the task of the mental handicap hospital is to provide specialist services to all its residents who need them. Some of these services can at the present time only be given within the mental handicap hospital, while others will in future be more satisfactorily provided in various community settings. In the meantime, it is the task of the hospital to mobilize community health and other specialist resources and help residents to gain access to these, either by going out to the services or by bringing the services into the hospital.

The hospital as a community resource

Hospitals are increasingly providing services not only for those people who live in them but for the community of which they form a part. It is increasingly common for hospital staff, working both singly and in teams, to provide an active service to a variety of community agencies.

Although consultants have done this for some years, they are now being joined by community nurses, psychologists, social workers and other specialists. A number of hospitals have been reorganized in such a way that teams are responsible for a particular geographical area; in some cases hospital residents who originate from a particular area have been grouped together in certain living units which are also the responsibility of the same clinical teams. These teams take complete responsibility for any admissions that become necessary, including short-term admissions, and try to get to know not only mentally handicapped people living in the community, but also their families and the staff who work with them. One of their aims is to prevent emergency or crisis admissions and to try to work together with local staff in order to prevent such crises and to develop plans for meeting them.

Such teams have been doing useful preventitive and follow-up work in the mental illness service for some years and are only slowly being developed in the mental handicap service. This is partly due to the shortage of staff, partly to the much slower turn-over of hospital residents and partly to the fact that mental handicap nurses have only recently been able to take advantage of training opportunities in the field of community psychiatric nursing. Such teams essentially try to provide a specialist mental handicap service for the health district in which the hospitals are situated and, wherever possible, to surrounding health districts as well. This is much easier in those cases where a mental handicap hospital serves a defined geographical or administrative area than in those numerous cases where a hospital has to provide a service for a very wide area. This is particularly the case around London. Even though many of the existing residents may have originated from distant areas, attempts are now being made to restrict future admissions to a much narrower geographical area. The hospital then builds up a working relationship with community agencies within that area and assumes a primary responsibility for it. This does not, however, solve the problem of the 'stateless' resident — i.e. people who have for all practical purposes lost all contact with the areas from which they were originally admitted.

Where the staff of the mental handicap hospital provide a service for the health district in which it is situated, they act as mental handicap specialists and work closely with their colleagues in the existing health, local authority and voluntary services. They help to staff the kind of Child Development Centres suggested by the Court Committee on Child Health Services; they provide specialist support to staff of ESNS schools, Social Education Centres, sheltered workshops and other community agencies working with mentally handicapped people. They also provide a source of specialist support for families, often on a domiciliary basis.

There is some evidence that by working in this way the demand for long-term admissions for hospital care is significantly reduced. A community-orientated hospital service is also likely to be able to provide better follow-up and supportive services for those people who have been discharged from hospital. For example, staff of local authority hostels are more likely to accept more severely handicapped people if they know that they can call on a specialist resource team to advise them on programmes of self-care training, behaviour modification and so on. Similarly, families who are given such support are more likely to be able to keep their son or daughter at home or to consider helping him to return to the family. Peripatetic teams of this kind, working closely not only with families but with staff of community agencies, are likely to be much more in evidence in future. Such teams might be based on the mental handicap hospital, if it is near enough, but could equally be based in community facilities (Development Team 1978).

The essential feature of proposals such as these is the idea of the hospital as a community resource, rather than as a final resort. The hospital will in future be seen as an integral component of community services. This calls for a major reappraisal of the functions of the hospital. Although many of its staff will inevitably need to spend most of their time working with those people who are resident in hospital, others will be appointed specifically to provide a comprehensive, locally based service. Some psychiatrists, psychologists, social workers and specialist therapists are already being appointed on this basis, dividing their time between working with hospital residents and working with people in the community. Although this calls for higher numbers of staff, the investment is likely to be cost effective in the long run, since it is likely to prevent unnecessary admission to hospital and is also likely to provide a more effective service for people who have been discharged from hospital.

The hospital can also provide services for people living in the community on a daily basis. Some hospitals, for example, have provision for 'day patients' who cannot, for various reasons, use community facilities. This applies particularly to the more severely handicapped adults who cannot obtain a place in the Social Education Centres; such people attend the hospital training facilities on a daily basis, and also make use of the social and recreational facilities of the hospital at other times.

Despite these trends, a number of the larger mental handicap hospitals are still isolated, both geographically and professionally, from the surrounding community. Some would like to provide a community service but are so short of staff and resources that their first priority must go to their own residents. This represents something of a vicious circle, since they are unlikely to be able to discharge people from hospital unless they are in an active and dynamic relationship with community services.

Leaving hospital

The 1971 White Paper planned to reduce the number of mental handicap hospital beds from just under 60,000 to about 27,000 over the twenty-year period 1971-1991. Although there has been an encouraging fall in the number of children's places, it seems unlikely that the number of hospital places will be reduced to 27,000 by 1991.

There is no doubt that a significant number of adults now resident in hospital have no need of hospital facilities. The most recent estimates by the Development Team, based on information of the abilities of some 7,000 residents provided by hospital staff themselves, indicates that just under a quarter could be discharged to a home or to a residential hostel immediately without any special facilities necessary for management, apart from those normally provided in a local authority hostel. Some of this group may also be able to live in group homes. They are rated as competent in all areas of self help, and are ambulant, continent, free of behaviour problems and not disruptive in any way. A further 10 per cent have only mild behaviour problems which could be corrected with a short period of treatment and self-help training; this group should be suitable for discharge home or to a hostel after a period of pre-discharge training.

Extrapolating these figures to the country as a whole, some 16,000 residents in English hospitals alone could leave hospital if alternative residential accommodation was available. We have described some of the alternative types of living accommodation which are now beginning to be provided, and have stressed that the Health service is itself taking some initiatives in providing such accommodation, rather than placing the entire responsibility on local authority Social Service Departments.

Although 16,000 seems a large number, the problem is much more manageable if considered in terms of population units of 100,000 people — say the population of a medium-sized town. Considered in these terms, the numbers involved are only around thirty-five. However, a more radical policy of discharging hospital residents would also need to consider the more severely handi-capped residents who, although not now suitable for discharge, might be trained to live more independently in various forms of sheltered accommodation. The total number of hospital residents, including the most severely handicapped, would involve something over 100 people per 100,000 population. Even this number is manageable, given the availability of funds and favourable community attitudes.

It seems more realistic to approach the problem by concentrating initially on those people who are ready to leave hospital now. Most of them could probably be accommodated by making use of a range of alternative living accommodation, along the lines described in Chapter 8. Local authorities have, not surprisingly, given priority to mentally handicapped people still living in the community, rather than to those who are now living in hospital. However, the balance is being redressed to some extent by Health authorities taking the initiative in trying to provide accommodation for hospital residents. Both groups clearly are entitled to their share of community residential accommodation, but the needs of those now living in hospital are often forgotten or given a low priority.

Closer and more effective collaboration between hospital and local authority staff is likely to make some impact on this problem. Ending the isolation of the mental handicap hospital by the use of community teams and by working for much closer collaboration between hospital and local authority staff should make it possible to make effective plans for the needs of individual residents. Now that hospitals are relating more organically to given geographical areas and to the staffs of local services, it should be easier to draw up plans to carry out joint assessments of the abilities and disabilities of each individual and to record a written plan to meet those needs. This has not generally happened in the past; many hospitals had not effectively come into contact with their local authority counterparts or had simply sent lists of people who were 'ready for discharge'. Local authorities without appropriate facilities tended to argue that many of these people were 'not suitable for our facilities'.

One of the administrative problems already mentioned is the problem of the 'stateless resident'. These are people who have lost all contact with the place from which they were originally admitted, perhaps twenty years ago. The local authority refuses to accept responsibility to provide services for such people; furthermore, the people themselves may not necessarily want to return. For all practical purposes, they are citizens of the local community. That community is not, however, under the present system, given any resources to provide services for them. This problem is particularly acute in parts of the Home Counties. For example, Epsom and St. Albans are surrounded by mental illness and mental handicap hospitals, full of people who have lived in these hospitals for many years and who have lost all contact with their point of origin. Local communities will have to be given the resources to provide services for these people, if they are not to remain in hospital for the rest of their lives. The Government is now considering how this administrative and organizational problem can be resolved.

Even where a local authority does accept responsibility for a resident, it is not necessarily able to find the resources to do so. Rehabilitating hospital residents is not necessarily a high priority at local level, particularly in places where community attitudes are not favourable. All local authorities are under such severe financial constraints at the present time that they are not likely to provide services for people being discharged from hospital without very special forms of help. Joint financing represents one possibility, but there are others.

Whatever the administrative arrangements, many hospitals are now trying to provide active community experiences for all their residents, particularly the most able. Intensive training is being provided in activities for daily living, not only within the hospital but also outside. Residents are being encouraged to make use of the whole range of community facilities, including further education, sports, recreation and leisure facilities, as well as providing them with experience of shopping, eating in restaurants, going to football matches and other public entertainments.

Conclusions

Although hospital buildings constitute an unfortunate legacy from the past, active attempts are now being made on all sides to provide a more homely environment and a better standard of residential care, as well as systematic and active programmes of training and rehabilitation. The hospital is also increasingly being seen as part of the community, rather than outside it; it is being used as a specialist resource not only for those inside it but for people in the community.

Nevertheless, we have to face the fact that many thousands of people are now living in hospitals who have no need of the facilities of those hospitals. Although the immediate task is to improve the quality of life of hospital residents and the conditions of staff who work with them, we need in the long term to ask some fundamental questions about the future of the hospital service, and the extent to which the National Health Service should contribute to the needs of mentally handicapped people in more effective partnership with community agencies.

10
TRAINING STAFF

Introduction

This is a good moment to consider fundamental changes in staff training. The Warnock report has made important suggestions for ways in which staff of the education service can become more skilled in working with handicapped children and young people, though their recommendations are just as relevant for staff of all disciplines, whether they are working with adults or children and whether they are employed by the education, health, social service or the voluntary agencies. Similarly, the Jay Committee is making important suggestions for the future development and training needs of staff working in nursing and residential care, while the Central Council for Training in Social Work is considering a report on the training of instructors in Adult Training (Social Education) Centres.

The problems encountered in staff training for work with the handicapped are only part of the much wider problem of staff training in other fields. But such problems are given higher priority by other professions; we need the same sense of urgency in helping our own practitioners to keep abreast of modern knowledge. For example, no physician or surgeon could afford to be ten years behind in his treatment of acutely ill patients, nor could an engineer building motorways or bridges afford to ignore recent developments in technology. Indeed, many of the advances in mental handicap are partly of a technological nature rather than a growth of new and fundamental knowledge about the nature of mental handicap itself. The two are obviously linked: for example, it was the development of powerful electron microscopes that led to the identification of the chromosome structures specific to Down's Syndrome and provided a better understanding of the biology of this condition. Further technical advances have led to amniocentesis and antenatal screening methods; similarly many of the advances in prescriptive methods of teaching are technological in character and need to be learned as techniques, even though they can only be effectively used if they are informed by a knowledge of the goals of education as a whole.

We have now reached a point where there is a wide general awareness of the existence of these advances in technology but not enough knowledge of their nature. There is a yawning gap between what is known and what is done.

This gap is bigger in some areas of knowledge than others; for example, the previous chapter showed that much has been done to improve the environment and living conditions of our long-stay hospitals, although such changes used to be resisted on the grounds that people would not appreciate them or would abuse them — a version of the old 'coals in the bath' argument, once used when universal education and later universal suffrage were being suggested in the nineteenth and early twentieth centuries, and still sometimes heard today in relation to equal pay and equal rights for women. But although there is now more agreement that mentally handicapped people not only deserve but can also appreciate the same standards and quality of life as other people, the technology of teaching and the application of systematic methods of training and rehabilitation have not yet fully penetrated into the day-to-day professional skills of many practitioners, nor is their importance fully realized by administrators and those who provide resources.

Obstacles

What are the obstacles standing in the way of the aim of more effective staff training?

(1) Single discipline training: we largely train our staff in separate professional compartments, and give them little chance to experience the work of colleagues in other disciplines, despite paying lip-service to notions of multidisciplinary teamwork.

(2) Initial courses of professional training are often too short to provide more than a superficial overview of mental handicap; in any case their content is quickly overtaken by developments in service delivery and research. Furthermore, mental handicap may be only a very small element of initial training courses which are designed to equip their students for work with a much wider range of clients.

(3) There are few opportunities for further training for people who are only going to be working with mentally handicapped people for short periods and in a limited way. If handicapped people are going to live increasingly in the community and to use the

ordinary services and resources of the community, staff working in these services should obviously have some basic knowledge about recent developments and should have opportunities to think about their attitudes to handicapped people.

(4) There are no national and few local strategies for helping staff who are working wholly or largely with mentally handicapped people to attend advanced courses of training leading to awards such as diplomas and higher degrees.

(5) We are also short of bridges between research workers and practitioners, and do not even have a clear idea of what such bridges might look like, and what kind of two-way traffic might flow across them. There is certainly considerable dissatisfaction on both sides with the lack of effective partnership between research workers and practitioners.

(6) Quite apart from programmes of staff training as such, few practitioners are given opportunities to familiarize themselves with the work of colleagues in their own discipline or in related fields. The isolation of field staff from one another is a major obstacle to progress; for example, there is little cross-visiting between teachers in schools, training centres or hospitals, far less a coherent programme of staff exchanges even within the same authority.

(7) Staff who do attend refresher and retraining courses often complain that they have little opportunity to put into practice what they have learned. Similarly, there is no mechanism by which those who provide such courses can evaluate the extent to which course members apply their knowledge on returning to their own work settings, nor do they have the resources to continue to provide tutorial support to their students once they have left.

(8) Any national or local strategy for staff development will have to tackle the problem of where the trainers are going to come from. Experienced practitioners do not always have the skills to teach their colleagues or organize training programmes.

Need for a national plan

What is needed now is a national plan for staff development for all staff working in services for mentally handicapped people. The general aims of such a plan might include:

(i) To provide opportunities, for all staff working in the service, to attend a range of refresher courses to update their skills and knowledge;

(ii) To learn about the work of other agencies and professionals

and if possible to work in other service settings for brief
periods;
(iii) To provide continuing opportunities for staff to meet at
local level to discuss ways of sharing and increasing their
professional skills and to develop locally based research.

How can such aims be realized?

First, by a framework for staff training developed initially at
national level, preferably by a special college set up for the
purpose. Such a national training college would not replace existing
statutory training bodies such as the General Nursing Council or
the Central Council for Education and Training in Social Work.
There will always be a need for such bodies to be concerned with
basic initial training as well as with longer post-qualifying or post-
experience courses for staff within particular professions. But
organizations such as the GNC or CCETSW could usefully be
complemented by a body with special responsibilities for stimulating further advanced training for those working with the handicapped.

The main function of a national college would be to develop a
national strategy for post-experience training of people working in
services for the handicapped, whether already formally qualified or
not; such courses might be organized along in-service lines at first,
and would not initially lead to any of the existing recognized
awards. Eventually, however, a modular or course-unit pattern
might be developed leading to a special qualification in mental
handicap which could be awarded after the successful completion of
a specific number of study units. Such awards would need to be
validated by a national body and recognized by employers as
carrying a special qualification.

A Special Education Staff College

The Warnock Committee has proposed that a Special Education
Staff College should be established at national level. They suggest
that such a College might co-ordinate and develop high-level
conferences and advanced courses for senior groups of advisers,
administrators and teachers, and also act as a national resource
centre collecting and disseminating information about new research
and development. It should also collaborate with the proposed
Special Education Research Group and the Schools Council section
on special education.

But this proposal might well be broadened to include staff
working outside the education service, and cater for advanced

courses for people working in health, local government or voluntary agencies.

A number of functions might be suggested for such a national staff training college. These include:

(1) The development of a series of outline curricula covering certain core components which would need to be known by staff of all disciplines. These would be fairly basic, and might include material on the nature and prevalence of mental handicap, recent advances in understanding the nature of handicap and organization of services and suggestions made for improvements both in service organization and delivery.

(2) Providing advanced courses of varying levels of duration for senior staff who are themselves being given positions of responsibility in training staff at local level. It is essential to ensure that people being given increased staff training responsibilities in the area of handicap should themselves undergo intensive refresher courses and be able to discuss recent developments in an atmosphere of constructive criticism and debate.

(3) The college might also initially carry out limited validating functions for courses being developed at regional levels and act as a source of informal advice and consultation to groups of staff developing training courses at local levels. Such validating functions need not be permanent, and might eventually be handed over to other national or local bodies, but it seems important to develop at least some initial mechanism for dialogue on the content and organization of courses, in order to avoid fragmentation and unacceptable degrees of variation in quality from one part of the country to another.

(4) Such a staff college must also be able to respond to a wide range of requests for information and materials from staff at all levels of the service and also from parents and relatives. It should have a comprehensive library and should issue frequent specialized reading lists on specific topics; reading lists might be needed for specialists with time to read in depth but short lists should also be made available to busy practitioners who want to update their reading but need help in knowing where to begin. In addition, an invaluable service for all levels of staff can be provided by short news-sheets such as the *Highlights* series produced by the National Childrens Bureau; these contain a condensed summary of current research knowledge in a particular area, and a short guide to further reading. These *Highlights* are printed on one or two sides of paper and distributed in bulk to large numbers of staff. They can be read in ten

minutes but can then be used as a basis for more detailed study
and for discussion with colleagues in workshops or on local
courses.
(5) The Staff College might, in addition to its national functions,
also provide a local staff development service. This would help
to keep its feet on the ground and provide its staff with experience of the problems of developing training programmes at
grass roots level.
(6) Some of the staff might be mobile and provide some form of
tutorial support for staff who are meeting difficulties in implementing training programmes at local level; they should also
be available to help in the launching of regional counterparts
to the national college.

These are merely tentative suggestions for some of the functions
of such a college; they are offered here because the proposal for a
staff college made by the Warnock Committee is essential to a
national staff training strategy but perhaps merits expansion in a
number of respects.

One problem might be identified before leaving this subject. It
seems likely that a national staff college of the kind proposed by
the Warnock Committee would attempt to provide for the needs of
staff dealing with an even wider group of clients than those
currently included within special education. Indeed, as already
indicated, it would be unfortunate if such a college confined its
activities to staff employed by the education service or to those
working only with handicapped children and young people up to
the age of 21 or 25. There is therefore a risk that the 'special needs'
of staff working with the mentally handicapped might become
submerged. Although this danger might be avoided by careful
planning and by setting up specialist sub-groups for particular
needs, there are those who will argue for a national staff college to
launch and validate advanced post-experience training specifically
for people working in the field of mental handicap.

Local counterparts

No national plan, however well designed, can hope to succeed
without a small core of key training personnel responsible for
meeting the needs of staff at local level.

Key workers

One partially relevant precedent for such appointments can be

found in the Training Project Officers (TPOs) who were established in each Health Region after 1969 in order to spearhead local
initiatives for the training of nursing staff in mental handicap
hospitals; these appointments followed hard on the series of
inquiries into mental handicap hospitals which revealed an urgent
need for staff to update their knowledge. TPOs were appointed in
each of the fifteen Health Regions; their work was co-ordinated
from the King's Fund, an independent agency with a special
interest in mental handicap but with considerable experience in staff
development programmes both inside and outside mental handicap
services. Unfortunately, the scheme came to an end in most Regions
with the 1974 reorganization of the NHS which devolved responsibility for nurse training to Area Health Authorities. A useful
report on the TPO scheme has been prepared by Pantall (1974).

The parallel with TPOs should not be extended too far; what is
needed now is a programme which is not limited to a single
profession, however numerous, but which is deliberately designed
from the outset to meet the needs of staff from all disciplines,
within the NHS, in local government and in voluntary agencies.

It is difficult to see how such an organizational framework could
be created on the basis of the existing training agencies, all of
whom seem to have responsibilities which are limited to specific
departments; for example the Training Officers of Social Service
Departments deal only with their own employees, just as LEA
Teachers' Centres cater largely for teachers. The main professional
organizations are mainly concerned with the interests of their own
members, and provide courses on specific topics relevant to mental
handicap from time to time. For example, Training Officers in
Social Service Departments organize a large number of courses but
mental handicap has not so far been one of the more prominent
training topics in Social Service Departments, nor is this surprising
since this is only one of a large number of client groups with whom
social workers have to deal. Similarly, Teachers' Centres act as an
in-service training agency for all teachers, though a number have
appointed curriculum development officers specifically for special
education, and in some cases even for specific groups within special
education, such as the mentally handicapped.

Using adult education resources

Training Officers will nevertheless need to be based on an existing
agency, and to use its resources to the full, even though they might
be organizing courses and programmes for a much wider range of
staff than normally make use of that agency.

But if such training staff are also to fulfill the broader in-service functions being outlined here, they will need to be given the support and resources to provide training courses for staff outside the school system; amongst those who might be included are staff of Adult Training (Social Education) Centres, residential and field social workers, Further Education staff and others working in a variety of NHS settings — including nurses in mental handicap hospitals, health visitors, community nurses, speech, physio- and occupational therapists, psychologists, medical staff such as community physicians, general practitioners, clinical medical officers etc. Although it is unusual for Teachers' Centres to provide in-service training for staff who are not working in the Education Service, there is no reason in principle why they should not do so; the obstacles are partly administrative (no precedent for crossing boundaries in this way) and financial (such posts and training courses would have to be funded with help from outside funds, with the education service acting on an agency basis).

The publication of the Warnock Report, and the inevitable period of consultation which must follow, provides a valuable starting point for planning to meet the training needs of the whole range of staff working with handicapped people. It could be argued that staff training is a function of adult education and should therefore be seen as the responsibility of the education service. This does not mean that the education service should accept the entire responsibility or that it should usurp the functions of existing training agencies or personnel. The education service clearly lacks the detailed knowledge of the many developments that have taken place in fields other than their own, and would need to work in partnership with existing organizations. The suggestion here is that the adult education service might take the *initiative* in local discussions designed to provide a framework within which staff working in the mental handicap service can seek to update their knowledge and skills. Training courses of various kinds might in future be based on Colleges of Adult Education, or in the new style Institutes of Higher Education which are replacing some of the more narrowly based Colleges of Education which specialized in the training of teachers.

A start might be made by following up the suggestions made in the Warnock Report that training initiatives might spring from the regional conferences on special education. They stress that certain staff training courses might be provided jointly by two or more services — e.g. education, social services and health. The role of Joint Consultative Committees at Area level is also mentioned as a possible springboard for action.

One of the tasks of the new style regional training officers would be to liaise with training officers with specific responsibilities for staff working for one of the existing agencies; for example, with the Nurse Training Officers both at Area and Regional levels, and with Training Officers working for Local Education Authorities and Social Service Departments. These officers would still need to provide a range of training courses for staff working for their particular agencies, particularly where developments in practice relate largely to their own professions. For example, certain advances in education, medicine or social work may only be of immediate interest to members of those professions, especially where workshop or practical training needs to be given in addition to theoretical work. Nevertheless, it is important to devise a procedure at local level to ensure that as much in-service training as possible is given on a multidisciplinary basis, so that staff from different professions can discuss new developments in research and practice that are relevant to the work of all. The Training Officer will therefore need to fulfill a delicate co-ordinating function in ensuring that courses that are relevant to more than one discipline are co-ordinated either by him, working through the Adult Education Service, or on an agency basis by one of the other training departments. For example, courses on working with families of mentally handicapped people might be attended by nurses (particularly community nurses), social workers, teachers, ATC staff, as well as by parents. At the present time such courses are likely to be mounted quite independently by each of the agencies. The training officer would therefore need to try to co-ordinate efforts that are too often fragmented and help to ensure that staff employed by different agencies could join together for in-service training courses as often as possible. He would also need to liaise with the relevant parent and voluntary organizations: parents of handicapped people, and on occasion handicapped people themselves, are joining in with professional staff to take part in discussions of new developments and consider ways in which local services and collaboration can be improved in the light of our growing knowledge of good practice and advances in knowledge and research.

Where are the trainers coming from?

Very little attention has been given so far to the problem of the people who are going to be asked to provide the training and refresher courses. Even if the Government provides the funds for a significant increase in the number of lecturers and other training staff that will be needed, whether in Colleges of Adult Education or elsewhere, it will be difficult to ensure that staff filling these new posts will be suited to the job. Simply to be an able practitioner is not enough; people concerned with staff training need a wide-ranging knowledge of the field as a whole, and must be able to relate their own personal and professional interests to developments in related professions. They must also be reasonably well read and informed about work outside their own field. Such people will not be easy to find, and there will be pressure to fill such posts with staff whose posts have become redundant as a result of the traumatic reorganization undergone by colleges of education and other local authority institutions of higher education in recent years.

One of the most urgent priorities, therefore, lies in the provision of intensive induction courses for all those who are likely to be given new responsibilities for staff training programmes.

How can this be done? In the long term, people who are themselves going to be responsible for staff development should have the opportunity to attend courses specially designed for them: the Special Education Staff College seems well suited for this purpose, provided it accepts training functions which are not limited to those concerned with children and young adults but is prepared to extend its remit to include those outside the education service proper. In the shorter term, higher level courses for staff trainers might be provided on a regional basis, using such regional machinery as already exists for LEAs.

A start might be made by selecting a regional centre of excellence which will provide a resource centre and a training base for staff development. This might be an existing College, Polytechnic or University already providing courses in mental handicap, Teacher's Centre or a specialist training agency such as the British Institute for Mental Handicap or Castle Priory College. Selecting the right agency and the right people to provide the foundations is critical to the success of the whole enterprise.

Putting training to work

One of the biggest problems in any programme of staff training lies in ensuring that those who go on training courses have opportunities to put into practice what they have learned. It is a perennial complaint among newly qualified staff, as well as experienced staff who go on refresher courses, that efforts to apply their new-found knowledge and skills are frustrated in one way or another. There are many reasons for this, not all of them remediable. Senior staff may be unduly cautious and conservative or may be opposed in principle to the kind of changes which new staff want to see; such changes may be seen as contrary to the policy of the agency, and require much more consultation and discussion than is apparent at first sight. New staff are easily discouraged by such attitudes from senior staff and tend to feel resentful that their ideas are being blocked; they may come to dismiss what they have learned and those who have taught them as 'out of touch' and 'unrealistic' and eventually share the views of their seniors that the system they know works reasonably well and may be the best one after all.

Although no one can assume that everything new and innovative is good, and everything else is old-fashioned and reactionary, some means will have to be found to bridge the gulf which is often found between training agencies and the places where the training is supposed to be applied.

Various proposals to this end are beginning to be made, but these are mainly for new recruits to the professions who are in their probationary year — e.g. in teaching, though even here teachers often complain of feeling isolated and unsupported in the face of such comments from their seniors as 'you'd better forget about all that stuff they taught you in college and learn what it's really all about'. Such comments are a form of initiation ceremony or *rite de passage*, and are sometimes taken more literally than is intended, though all too often they reflect the real situation all too clearly.

Staff going on courses or on secondment after some years of experience in an agency may find it even more difficult to change their way of working; they will have built up a certain routine of working to which both they and their immediate colleagues have become accustomed; it may be inconvenient to change this, even though they are convinced of the advantages of doing so. For example, a nurse may have gone on a short course on methods of training people to feed themselves, and become quite proficient in using prompting, fading and reward methods of training. But introducing these methods to the ward where she works will have consequences for other nurses who may have established an 'efficient' and 'quicker' routine of feeding the children themselves.

Staff training is not, therefore, merely a matter of providing opportunities for staff to update their knowledge and skills but of preparing them for the difficulties of applying what they have learned when they return to their place of work. Some training courses now try to provide active preparation for this — for example, they not only discuss the problems the student will have and consider how they might be tackled, but arrange opportunities to act out or 'role play' possible ways of handling these situations. Such 'simulations' may seem artificial but they can be made quite realistic in the hands of experienced group leaders. Furthermore, giving the students the chance to play the role of the sceptical superior back at work may help them to gain some perspective on how the senior or line manager feels about students coming off a course full of new ideas and techniques which may be quite threatening to his self-image as a leader.

One example can be taken from a training project carried out by Tom Foxen and Judith McBrien at the Hester Adrian Research Centre in which groups of five senior psychologists and special education advisers from different parts of the country receive an intensive one-week course in behavioural methods of teaching multiply handicapped children. Part of the course takes place in a special school, with the head teacher and staff acting as instructors; in some of the sessions they play the part of sceptical or even hostile teachers to prepare them for the reception they might receive when they go back to their own LEAs to introduce what they have learned to the ESNS schools for which they are responsible.

Another strategy for providing support to students is illustrated in the position of the study supervisor for the new Certificate in Social Service, now being developed by the Central Council for Education and Training in Social Work. The study supervisor may be based either on the college or on the agency but his essential task is to help the student to relate his college-based learning to the demands of the agency and of his own work setting. The study supervisor should be able to move freely between college and agency; ideally, the agency should undertake to provide opportunities for the student to make use of his training, at least on an experimental basis, while the college will need to provide enough practical support as well as discussion on the difficulties of implementation he is likely to encounter.

This kind of link could be usefully developed for other forms of in-service training. For example, teachers in special schools or classes commonly attend various forms of in-service training, ranging from a short course of evening lectures to a combination of these with block periods of one or more weeks when they are away from school attending advanced workshop-type courses. The more practical the training, the more necessary it becomes for them to be able to try out their developing skills in their own classrooms. For example, a teacher workshop may develop specific methods of teaching language or self-care skill. Teachers should be able to experiment with such methods in a systematic way in their own classrooms and then report the results to their colleagues on the workshop. In this way they can compare notes, data and experiences and learn at first hand about the difficulties of application and evaluation. They can also confront the tutor with these problems and discuss them with him and with fellow members of the group.

Some teacher workshops operate on a modified case conference model; a member discusses a specific teaching programme for a particular child, bringing full details of the child's abilities, assessment charts and all other relevant information, supplemented by tape recordings or even video recordings where appropriate. The rest of the group discuss the teaching objectives, task analysis, methods of presenting the task and the general strategy as well as the specific tactics for helping the child to achieve the objective. Suggestions are then made for the teacher to try out in the interval before the next workshop, when he reports back to the group on the effectiveness or otherwise of the suggestions that have been made. The group may then modify their suggestions in the light of the child's response to the programme and the teacher's difficulties in implementing them.

Such forms of in-service training clearly demand a commitment not only from those attending the course but also from the head-teacher and other staff members. There must be some form of undertaking that the teacher will be given support and facilities to undertake the necessary school-based assignments, and some practical recognition of the principle that teachers on in-service courses are in one sense in the student role, even though they may be fully qualified and highly experienced.

Students on initial professional training courses as well as those on in-service courses have problems relating college-based teaching to the practical demands of their field placements. Course tutors and field placement supervisors increasingly try to work together to provide a framework within which a consistent approach to theory and practice can be developed. For example, great care is taken in selecting field work supervisors who are not only well qualified and experienced practitioners but are reasonably well read and up to date in their knowledge of developments in their field and can discuss such developments with their students in an informed and critical manner. Such a combination of qualities is not found in every field work supervisor; course tutors are sometimes accused of being excessively selective in their choice of people whom they consider to be suitable to supervise their students, thereby limiting the range of placement options available. These are already limited by the extent to which tutors believe the agency as a whole is adequate in service delivery and staffing generally. Clearly students should have experience of a wide range of service agencies, including those that provide a less than satisfactory standard of service and supervision; on the other hand, college tutors will also wish to ensure that they see examples of the best practice and are supervised by people who are in full sympathy with the aims of the course.

Pyramid training

One consequence of adopting a national and local strategy to staff training is that some attempt might be made to develop a systematic approach in which staff who go on courses would be given opportunities not only to use their knowledge when they return to their place of work but then be helped to pass on their skills to other people in the locality.

This approach is sometimes known as pyramid training and can take a number of forms. Essentially, a small team is selected to attend a particular course, on the understanding that they will set up similar training courses on returning to their own area. It is sensible to allow them some time to become familiar with the new methods themselves by using them in their own work setting, but there is a clear obligation to set up a training course for others in their localities, and for facilities to be made available to them to do so.

People coming on these courses at local level would in their turn have an obligation to pass on their knowledge to new groups. In this way, a systematic training strategy is introduced, which might start at regional level but quickly spreads down the pyramid and results in courses at local level. Eventually, staff of every agency would have opportunities to be trained by a team who had themselves been trained by others; at least they would be likely to be working in an agency with someone who had been on a team.

There are clear advantages in setting up a regional team consisting of people who are themselves fully trained and able to design and deliver a series of courses on a wide variety of topics. Nevertheless, some topics may be quite specialized and may call for only one training team in each region, with local counterparts taking up their work as required. Similarly, decisions will need to be made on the extent to which such training teams should be multidisciplinary or single discipline; here again, some of the procedures may be specialized — e.g. some forms of medical treatment, or technical developments in speech or physiotherapy; hopefully, such specialized refresher courses will also be provided by the relevant professional associations, but this cannot be assumed.

As far as behavioural methods of teaching are concerned, there are strong advantages in forming multidisciplinary teams, including teachers, nursing staff and SEC instructors. Such a team may need to consist of at least two people from each discipline while they are being trained, so that they can then split into teams of two when they themselves become a training team at local level. One person cannot be expected to undertake the responsibility of providing training courses on his own; a team of two is the absolute minimum, and three are much more efficient, allowing more flexibility in the organization of courses, so that the team members are less frequently called away from their main work.

Another approach to training can be illustrated by the travelling training team. The former Institute of Mental Subnormality (now the British Institute for Mental Handicap) developed a small behaviour modification training team which tried to respond to requests from agencies all over the country to set up short two- or three-day training workshops. Although such training teams will obviously try to run workshops along as realistic and practical lines as possible, a great deal of support is necessary from hospital staff if visiting teams are to have any long-term impact. A training team based in the agency will need to build on the foundations laid by the visiting team, in order to ensure that such a visit is really a launching pad for new developments rather than just another short-term measure which leads nowhere. It is hardly surprising that staff feel frustrated when prospects for skill development are dangled in front of them without their really being able to grasp them.

It is always worth asking 'What will happen when the circus leaves town?' The training strategy being outlined here would make it possible to develop training teams at regional and finally at local level. Such teams would soon be known to local staff and should be easily accessible for further support and advice. They are more likely to be seen as local resource than a more distant team, however effective its visit may have been.

One of the aims of a local training scheme should be to make available a mobile task force of skilled and experienced people who would be able to provide a series of short training courses not merely at some convenient site but within schools, residential homes, SECs, hospital wards and living units and other places where mentally handicapped people live and work. Their work would not overlap with other advisors or managers whose job it was to help staff to develop a better service but would be limited to specific training functions which were requested by the agency itself. For example, staff of a residential home may request help in improving their methods of training residents in self-care or communication skills; staff of an SEC may seek guidance on methods of assessing competence in motor skills. It should not be necessary for staff of a unit to depend on a national course hundreds of miles away for such support; some means will need to be found of making expert help available locally, and then ensuring that staff receive any further guidance they need to help them to implement the advice given.

The provision of continued tutorial support to people who have attended national or regional courses is particularly important where relatively new and unfamiliar methods of teaching are being developed. Such staff may initially need considerable help from tutorial staff in applying what they have learned; even though tutorial support will not solve some of the organizational or personality problems which may be standing in the way of implementation, it can do much to increase staff confidence in mastering the skills that have been taught and relating them to their own work setting. Ideally, such tutorial support should come from a regional or even local level — e.g. from the Training Officers or from senior staff who are committed to helping staff to implement what they have learned. Although these problems are likely to affect only the first group of staff returning from training, the success of a training pyramid depends entirely on ensuring that the first steps on the ladder are secure.

The essence of these suggestions is that each locality needs to build up a task force of staff who are themselves recently trained to a known standard of proficiency. They depend on one or more centres at national or regional level who will provide the initial training courses — i.e. the apex of the pyramid.

At the present time only one or two institutions have extensive experience in providing courses for staff of all levels and disciplines. Castle Priory College, a staff training college run by the Spastics Society, provides courses for all staff who wish to come, whether or not their work is connected with the physically handicapped; the British Institute for Mental Handicap at Kidderminster provides both short and longer training courses, and also has branches in most parts of the country, with honorary tutors who organize conferences and short training courses for staff in their areas. But neither Castle Priory nor BIMH has a formal training commitment to individual authorities or agencies, though the tuition fees and expenses of staff members are usually paid by their employers. Since they do not have the resources to provide tutorial support to people once they have attended the courses, there is no means of knowing whether people attending have applied what they have learned on returning to their places of work or whether their employers have shown the slightest interest in helping them to do so.

It might be argued that we can no longer afford the luxury of failing to make use of the skills of people who have been on advanced courses at a specialized institute. The kind of national strategy with local counterparts suggested here might provide a useful framework for future development, but a start will have to be made at national level — perhaps by means of the Staff College suggested by Warnock, or in the case of mental handicap services, by asking one or both of the two existing institutes to modify its work along these lines. Needless to say, special resources in the form of additional tutorial staff and links with academic and professional bodies would be necessary but this should not prove difficult.

Interim suggestions

Although some of the suggestions made in this chapter call for a national training strategy and for well-planned regional and local developments, a good deal can be done now to lay the foundations or to build on work already begun.

For example, the isolation of staff might be tackled by organizing a systematic programme of cross-visiting for staff in various services — e.g. schools, SECs, residential homes, hospitals, employment services, further education colleges. Each staff member should be able to spend at least a full day every two months in another agency, either similar to his own, or working in related fields. For example, a teacher working in a day school for ESNS children should in time visit several other similar schools, as well as schools for children with other handicaps; in addition, he should see one or more hospital schools, a Social Education Centre, residential homes, an FE college, an Employment Rehabilitation Centre or Young Persons Work Preparation Course, to name but a few. The list of agencies will need to be drawn up locally by people with a wide knowledge of all available facilities.

Such visits might be followed up by carefully arranged systems of staff exchange for short or longer periods, so that staff can not only visit, but have opportunities of working, in a different setting.

These initiatives need to be organized with care, preferably by someone specifically appointed for the purpose. He would need to be given a co-ordinating role which would enable him to work across and between health and local authority boundaries and to co-ordinate his work with officers who already have training responsibilities for their own employees. Such an appointment is necessary because no one now has the responsibility or authority to implement a co-ordinated policy for staff development at local

level. The study supervisor described earlier might initially undertake some of these functions but he would need to work to a policy
clearly identified and agreed by all the agencies involved. This will
not be an easy task but should yield high returns if it can lessen the
isolation of staff and thereby lead to better morale and improved
communications.

Changing staff behaviour in the work setting

These suggestions reflect a new emphasis in our approach to
questions concerned with staff development. We used to think of
training as something that was provided in universities and colleges
either before people enter a profession or at some period after they
have started work. Initial and post-experience training of this kind
will always be needed, and none of the suggestions made here are
intended as substitutes for this. But we need to think of other
approaches as well because knowledge is expanding so fast that
even people trained quite recently are rapidly becoming out of date
with developments. Even those whose full-time job consists of
training others are finding it hard to keep up with the wide range of
advances in their own field.

We therefore need to think of staff development as a continuous
process which is intimately related to their day-to-day work. It is
not even a matter of 'in-service training' taking the form of weekly
lectures or workshops, important though these are. It is more a
question of setting standards of staff performance, of helping staff
to become skilled in carrying them out and of providing them with
the resources to do so. Seen in this light, training is not something
special but an integral component of one's day-to-day work.

Such an approach can only be developed if there are agreed
guidelines on what constitutes good professional practice. These
have not been available so far but a number of attempts are now
being made to draw up standards by which the quality of a service
can be measured. Some of these apply to all agencies and settings,
others relate more specifically to specific agencies such as those
concerned with residential care, training and rehabilitation or
domiciliary services. Others apply largely to planners and management.

Drawing up detailed guidelines of good professional practice is a
formidable task because we have very little information about what
staff actually do in their day-to-day work, how far they feel this
corresponds to their own idea of good practice and the extent to
which they feel change is necessary. In the absence of such detailed
studies, we have to fall back on consensus views and try to prepare

guidelines for general discussion and consultation. There is then a danger that such guidelines produced at a national or even professional level are seen as an attempt to impose uniformity from above or dismissed as 'out of touch with reality'.

Despite these problems, it can be argued that the mental handicap services have suffered exceptionally badly from the absence of national guidelines and that perhaps we have gone too far in the direction of local and professional autonomy. We largely lack any yardsticks against which we can measure the quality of a service in general and the performance of staff in particular. Such guidelines are particularly necessary at a time when mental handicap services are largely administered within 'generic' health and local authority services, for whom mental handicap is only one of many responsibilities and who cannot be expected to have detailed knowledge of what constitutes a good service.

The publication of the elements of such guidelines has begun. The NDG pamphlets on day services (1977b) and the more detailed report on hospital services (1978) are a case in point; they are not only intended for the staff of these services but also for those at a planning and managerial level outside the mental handicap service itself — e.g. officers and members of Area Health Authorities and Social Services Departments, Community Health Councils, voluntary groups, Joint Consultative Committees and planning teams at every level.

Another example of an attempt to produce a 'standards' document relating to hospitals for the mentally ill as well as the mentally handicapped has been published by a working party set up by the Secretary of State for Wales (Welsh Office 1978). Reference has already been made in Chapter 9 to the much more elaborate and sophisticated 'accreditation' instruments developed in North America, including the Program Analysis of Service Systems (PASS) (Wolfensberger and Glenn 1975) and the Standards for Services for Developmentally Disabled Individuals produced by the Accreditation Council for Services for Mentally Retarded and other Developmentally Disabled Persons (ACMRDD 1978).

In addition to the Welsh Office and NDG documents, the most thoroughgoing British attempt to provide detailed service and operational guidelines arises from the work of the Health Care Evaluation Research Team in the context of the 'Wessex experiment'. As part of their evidence to the Committee of Inquiry into Nursing and Care (the Jay Committee), Kushlick and his colleagues (Kushlick, Felce, Palmer and Smith 1976) outlined a series of what they termed 'packages', each of which specified in detail the exact nature of a wide range of performances considered necessary to a service for mentally handicapped people. They need to identify a given individual or group of individuals responsible for carrying them out, the settings and conditions under which the performances are carried out and the methods to be used to maintain or change the performance of the person concerned — e.g. monitoring. More recently, they have been developing detailed procedural checklists, initially aimed at procedures for the day-to-day running of a residential home.

Another example of a package can be taken from the work of the Mental Handicap in Wales Applied Research Unit who developed 'room management' procedures originally for students in special needs units of SECs but which have been extended to similar units elsewhere as well as to hospital living units. The basic procedures involve measures to ensure that students are 'engaged' in an activity and are suitably rewarded for doing so (e.g. Porterfield 1978). Preliminary results suggest that such approaches, far from stifling individual initiative and ingenuity, provide ample opportunity for guidelines to be applied flexibly and imaginatively to suit the needs of the individual (Blunden, Director of the Mental Handicap Section, Wales Applied Research Unit (1978) personal communication).

Finally, the NDG is currently engaged in the task of looking at existing guidelines which have been developed to enable people at local and national level to evaluate the quality of the services they are delivering. This may result in some national guidelines being developed for local use, as for national agencies such as the Development Team or some other form of national or regional advisory service.

Detailed guidelines and standards thus fulfill at least two purposes. First, they provide a series of detailed objective statements which enable the day-to-day quality of the service to be monitored, both by the staff themselves and by the managers, whether these are 'generic' or not. Second, they provide a means of instituting and maintaining good professional practice in the setting in which people work. The key to staff training does not therefore lie solely in sending a few people away to take advanced diplomas and courses, though these do have their place. It lies in teaching staff to use and maintain relevant skills in their own place of work. This in turn calls for senior staff who are not merely competent practitioners but also skilled in the techniques of adult education. For example, they will need to be familiar with a wide range of techniques of helping colleagues to change their behaviour, including simulation techniques, such as role play and job rehearsal and they will need to be aware of the emotional and social incentives relevant to the needs of individual staff members. It is clearly not enough to lay down specific guidelines, however good they may be, and to expect staff to follow them. Managers and seniors will therefore need to be among the first to receive skilled help in techniques of communication and adult education.

This point applies even more strongly to the training required by the Special Education Advisory and Support Service proposed by the Warnock Committee. It is not enough simply to take skilled teachers out of their classrooms and to designate them as advisers; there is no reason to suppose that the two skills are necessarily found together in the same person. Training in styles and strategies of working with other adults is essential.

Blunden (personal communication) points out that such a practical on-the-job training need not be incompatible with the creation of a 'profession', and that much of the training of architects and engineers takes place in this way. He emphasizes that the basic requirements of such a system would be:

(i) an agreed set of basic procedures appropriate to each establishment with respect to such aspects of treatment as standards of care and training;
(ii) trainers who would be skilled in helping managers to introduce such procedures to a facility;
(iii) an organization whose task it would be to draw up the standards and to monitor the extent to which they were achieved in any given establishment.

Clearly, we need to think through our methods of staff training from first principles and to develop innovative approaches.

Conclusions

The key to a better service for mentally handicapped people undoubtedly lies in staff training. Proposals for better services, central or even local government priority for the mentally handicapped, new buildings or the injection of additional resources call for staff who are not only highly trained but are provided with opportunities to update their skills as new knowledge becomes available.

This seems self-evident enough but we are still having to pay the price of our earlier neglect of staff training and retraining. A considerable number of people working in full-time mental handicap services either lack appropriate training for the work or were trained a long time ago. Many others who have part-time responsibilities for working with mentally handicapped people as part of a generic service have received little or no training in any aspect of mental handicap and may have completely outmoded ideas and attitudes. All staff, whether full-time or part-time practitioners, badly need opportunities to become aware of the rapid changes that are taking place in this field and to participate as far as possible in innovations that are now taking place in many parts of the country.

This chapter makes a number of suggestions for ways in which all staff can be provided with a wider range of training and retraining opportunities.

It goes beyond the proposal made in the Warnock Report for a Special Education Staff College and suggests that a national staff training plan is needed not only for people working in the education service but for all staff, whether employed by the National Health Service, local government or the voluntary agencies. Such a national plan would need to be complemented by a locally planned strategy for staff development, possibly administered by the Adult Education service and co-ordinated by a Training Officer specially appointed for the purpose and responsible for training programmes for all staff working with a particular client group. These plans would probably need to be developed for staff working with a wide range of disabled people, but the special training needs of staff working with the mentally handicapped must not be submerged in too generic a programme.

A national plan would also need to tackle the problem of how to build better bridges between research workers and practitioners. It is not merely a matter of research workers 'disseminating' their results but of working alongside practitioners to develop some of the implications of their own findings. It is not enough simply to write reports and to hope that practitioners will read them. Efforts will also need to be made to help staff to put new ideas and methods in practice and to develop a research attitude to their day-to-day work.

REFERENCES

Accreditation Council for Services for Mentally Retarded and Other Developmentally Disabled Persons (1978) *Standards for Services for Developmentally Disabled Individuals*. Chicago: Joint Commission on Accreditation of Hospitals.

Anderson, E. (1973) *The Disabled Schoolchild. A Study of Integration in Primary Schools*. London: Methuen.

Apte, R. (1967) The Local Authority Hostel as a Transitional Institution. In Freeman, H. and Farndale, J. (eds) *New Aspects of the Mental Health Services*. Oxford: Pergamon.

Baranyay, E. (1976) *A Lifetime of Learning*. London: National Society for Mentally Handicapped Children.

Bayley, M. (1973) *Mental Handicap and Community Care*. London: Routledge and Kegan Paul.

Begab, M. (1977) Closing Address. In Mittler, P. (ed.) *Research to Practice in Mental Retardation*. Baltimore, Maryland: University Park Press.

Belmont, J. (1971) Medical-Behavioural Research in Mental Retardation. In Ellis, N. (ed.) *International Review of Research in Mental Retardation* (vol.5) New York: Academic Press.

Berry, P., Andrews, R. and Elkins, J. (1977) *An Evaluative Study of Educational, Vocational and Residential Programs for the Moderately to Severely Mentally Handicapped in Three States*. Brisbane, Queensland: Schonell Educational Research Centre.

Bijou, S. (1966) A Functional Analysis of Retarded Development. In Ellis, N. (ed.) *International Review of Research in Mental Retardation* (vol.1). New York: Academic Press.

Birch, H.G., Richardson, S.A., Baird, D., Horobin, G. and Illsley, R. (1970) *Mental Subnormality in the Community*. Baltimore, Maryland: Williams and Wilkins.

Bland, G. (1979) Hospital Schools for the Mentally Handicapped. In Craft, M. (ed.) *Tredgold's Mental Deficiency* (12th edn.). London: Bailliere and Tindall (in press).

British Psychological Society (1963) Report of the Working Party on Subnormality. *Bulletin British Psychological Society* 16:53-72.

_____ (1966) *Children Admitted to Hospitals for the Mentally Subnormal*. London: BPS.

Bronfenbrenner, U. (1974) *Is Early Intervention Effective?* (vol.2). Washington, DC: US Department of Health, Education and Welfare.

Browne, R.A., Gunzburg, H.C., Johnston, H., MacColl, K., Oliver, B. and Thomas, A. (1971) The Needs of Patients in Subnormality Hospitals if Discharged to Community Care. *British Journal of Mental Subnormality* 17:1-18.

Carr, J. (1970) Mental and Motor Development in Young Mongol Children. *Journal of Mental Deficiency Research* 14:205-20.

_____ (1975) *Young Children with Down's Syndrome*. London: Butterworth.

Castell, J.H.F. and Mittler, P. (1965) Intelligence of Patients in Subnormality Hospitals: a Survey of Admissions in 1961. *British Journal of Psychiatry* 111:219-25.

Cheseldine, S. and McConkey, R. (1979) Parental Speech to Young Down's Syndrome Children: an Intervention Study. *American Journal of Mental Deficiency* (in press).

Clark, D. (1974) Psychological Assessment in Mental Subnormality. In Clarke, A.M. and Clarke, A.D.B. (eds) *Mental Deficiency: the Changing Outlook* (3rd edn.). London: Methuen.

Clarke, M., Riach, J. and Cheyne, W. (1977) *Handicapped Children and Pre-School Education*. Glasgow: University of Strathclyde, Department of Psychology.

Clarke, A.D.B. (1978) Predicting Human Development: Problems, Evidence, Implications. *Bulletin British Psychological Society* 31: 250-8.

Clarke, A.M. and Clarke, A.D.B. (1974) (eds) *Mental Deficiency: the Changing Outlook* (3rd edn.). London: Methuen.

_____ (1974) Biosocial Factors. In Clarke, A.M. and Clarke, A.D.B. (eds) *Mental Deficiency: the Changing Outlook* (3rd edn.). London: Methuen.

_____ (eds) (1976) *Early Experience: Myth and Evidence*. London: Open Books.

Cobb, H.V. (1972) *The Forecast of Fulfilment*. New York: Columbia University Press.

Cooper, V. (1978) Training for Employment. In Wynn Jones, A. (ed.) *What About the Retarded Adult?* Taunton: NSMHC (SW Region).

Cope, C. and Anderson, E. (1977) *Special Units in Ordinary Schools: An Exploratory Study of Special Provision for Disabled Children*. Windsor: NFER.

Cowie, V.A. (1970) *A Study of the Early Development of Mongols*. Oxford: Pergamon.

Craft, M. and Craft, A. (1978) *Sex and the Mentally Handicapped*. London: Routledge and Kegan Paul.

Cunningham, C.C. (1973) The Application of Educational Technology to Mental Retardation. In Clarke, A.D.B. and Clarke, A.M. (eds) *Mental Retardation and Behavioural Research*. Edinburgh: Churchill Livingstone.

_____ (1974) The Relevance of Normal Educational Theory and Practice to the Mentally Handicapped. In Tizard, J. (ed.) *Mental Retardation: Concepts of Education and Research*. London: Butterworth.

_____ (1975) Parents as Educators and Therapists. In Kiernan, C.C. and Woodford, P. (eds) *Behaviour Modification with the Severely Retarded*. Amsterdam: Associated Scientific Publishers.

Cunningham, C.C. and Jeffree, D.M. (1971) *Working with Parents: Report of a Workshop for Parents of Preschool Mentally Handicapped Children*. Manchester: National Society for Mentally Handicapped Children and Hester Adrian Research Centre, University of Manchester.

Cunningham, C.C. and Sloper, P. (1978) *Helping Your Handicapped Baby*. London: Souvenir Press.

Davie, R., Butler, N. and Goldstein, H. (1972) *From Birth to Seven*. London: Longmans.

Department of Education and Science (1975) *Educating Mentally Handicapped Children*. Education pamphlet 60. London: HMSO.

_____ (1978) *Special Educational Needs*. Report of the Committee of Enquiry into the Education of Handicapped Children and Young People (Chairman: Mrs. M. Warnock). Cmnd. 7212. London: HMSO.

Department of Health and Social Security (1971) *Better Services for the Mentally Handicapped*. Cmnd. 4683. London: HMSO.

_____ (1972) *Census of Mentally Handicapped Patients in England and Wales at the end of 1970*. London: HMSO.

_____ (1974) *A Decade of Progress: A History of the Training Council For Teachers of the Mentally Handicapped*. London: HMSO.

_____ (1975) *Census of Residential Accommodation 1970*. (M. Morgan). London: HMSO.

_____ (1976) *Fit For the Future:* Report of the Committee on Child Health Services. (Chairman: Professor S.D.M. Court) Cmnd. 6684. London: HMSO.

_____ (1976a) *Priorities in the Health and Personal Social Services in England: A Consultative Document*. London: HMSO.

_____ (1976b) *Prevention and Health: Everybody's Business*. London: HMSO.

_____ (1977) *The Way Forward: Priorities in the Health and Personal Social Services*. London: HMSO.

_____ (1977a) *Adult Training Centres for the Mentally Handicapped and Day Centres for the Mentally Ill*. London: HMSO.

_____ (1978) *Facilities and Services of Mental Illness and Mental Handicap Hospitals in England, 1975*. London: HMSO.

Development Team for the Mentally Handicapped (1978) *First Annual Report 1976-1977*. London: HMSO.

Douglas, J.W.B. (1964) *The Home and the School*. London: McGibbon and Kee.

Duncan, S.B. (1978) Problems of Prenatal Screening Programme for Down's Syndrome in Older Women. *Journal of Biosocial Science* 10: 141-6.

Early, R. (1975) A Secondary-Aged School for the Educationally Subnormal. *Teaching and Training* 13:22-4; 48-55.

224 *People not Patients*

Elliott, J. and Whelan, E. (eds) (1975) *Employment of Mentally Handicapped People.* King's Fund Paper 8. London: King's Fund.

Fogelman, K.R. (ed.) (1976) *Britain's Sixteen Year Olds.* London: National Childrens Bureau.

Friedlander, B.Z. (1970) Receptive Language Development in Infancy: Issues and Problems. *Merrill Palmer Quarterly of Behaviour Development* 16:7-51.

Fryers, T. (1978) Epidemiology in Severe Mental Handicap 1961-1977. In Fryers, T. and Whelan, E. (eds) *Mental Handicap Research Forum.* Manchester: NW Regional Health Authority.

_____ (1978a) Severe Handicap: The Dynamics of Prevalence Epidemiology in an English City 1961-1977. Unpublished Ph.D. thesis, University of Manchester.

Gillham, B. (1978) *The First Words Language Programme: A Basic Language Programme for Mentally Handicapped Children.* London: George Allen & Unwin.

Grant, G. (1971) Some Management Problems of Providing Work for the Mentally Disordered, with Particular Reference to Mental Handicap. Unpublished M.Sc. thesis, University of Manchester.

Greengross, W. (1976) *Entitled to Love.* London: Mallanby Press.

Grossman, H. (1973) *A Manual on Terminology and Classification in Mental Retardation.* Series 2. Washington, DC: American Association on Mental Deficiency.

Gunzburg, H.C. (1975) *Progress Assessment Charts* (12th edn.). Stratford: Social Education Publications.

_____ (1975a) Institutionalised people in the community. *Research Exchange and Practice* 1:36-50.

Hargrove, A. (1965) *Serving the Mentally Handicapped.* London: National Association for Mental Health (MIND).

Huckman, D. (1978) Practical Aspects of Placing Mentally Handicapped Persons in Employment. In Wynn Jones, A. (ed.) *What About the Retarded Adult?* Taunton: NSMHC (SW Region).

Hughes, J.M. (1975) The Educational Needs of the Mentally Handicapped. *Educational Research* 17:228-33.

Jackson, S. and Struthers, M. (1975) *A Survey of Scottish Adult Training Centres.* Glasgow: Scottish Society for the Mentally Handicapped.

Jamieson, M., Partlett, M. and Pocklington, K. (1977) *Towards Integration: A Study of Blind and Partially Sighted Children in Ordinary Schools.* Windsor: NFER.

Jeffree, D. and McConkey, R. (1976) *Let Me Speak.* London: Souvenir Press.

Jeffree, D., McConkey, R. and Hewson, S. (1977) *Let Me Play.* London: Souvenir Press.

Jones, K. (1960) *Mental Health and Social Policy 1845-1959.* London: Routledge and Kegan Paul.

Kedney, R. and Whelan, E. (eds) (1976) *The Education of Mentally Handicapped Young Adults.* Bolton: Bolton College of Education (Technical).

Kellett, B. (1976) An Initial Survey of the Language of ESNS Children in

Manchester: the Results of a Teachers' Workshop. In Berry, P. (ed.) *Language and Communication in the Mentally Handicapped*. London: Arnold.

Kiernan, C.C. (1977) Alternatives to Speech: a Review of Research on Manual and Other Forms of Communication with the Mentally Handicapped and Other Non-communicating Populations. *British Journal of Mental Subnormality* 23:6-28.

Kiernan, C.C. and Jones, M.C. (1978) *The Behaviour Assessment Battery*. Windsor: NFER.

Kiernan, C.C., Jordan, R. and Saunders, C. (1979) *Starting Off: Establishing Play and Communication in the Handicapped Child*. London: Souvenir Press.

King, R.D., Raynes, N.V. and Tizard, J. (1971) *Patterns of Residential Care: Sociological Studies in Institutions for Handicapped Children*. London: Routledge and Kegan Paul.

King's Fund Centre (1975) *Adult Education for Mentally Handicapped People*. London: King's Fund.

Kushlick, A. (1975) Improving the Services for the Mentally Handicapped. In Kiernan, C.C. and Woodford, P. (eds) *Behaviour Modification with the Severely Retarded*. London: Associated Scientific Publishers.

Kushlick, A. and Blunden, R. (1974) The Epidemiology of Mental Subnormality. In Clarke, A.M. and Clarke, A.D.B. (eds) *Mental Deficiency: the Changing Outlook* (3rd edn.). London: Methuen.

Kushlick, A., Blunden, R., Horner, D. and Smith, J. (1975) Goal-Setting. Unit 9 of *Handicapped Person in the Community*. Milton Keynes: Open University Press.

Kushlick, A., Felce, D., Palmer, J. and Smith, J. (1976) *Evidence to Committee of Enquiry into Nursing and Care*. Report 129. Winchester: Health Care Evaluation Research Team.

Leeming, K., Swann, W., Coupe, J. and Mittler, P. (1979) *Teaching Language and Communication to the Mentally Handicapped*. Curriculum Bulletin 8. London: Schools Council/Evans/Methuen (in press).

Lewis, E.D. (1929) *Report of an Investigation into the Incidence of Mental Deficiency in Six Areas, 1925-1927*. In Report of the Mental Deficiency Committee, Part IV. London: HMSO.

Lowman, P. (1975) Permanent Employment in Industry for the Mentally Handicapped Person. In Elliott, J. and Whelan, E. (eds) *Employment of Mentally Handicapped People*. London: Kings Fund.

McAllister, M. (1974) Further Education for Mentally Handicapped Adults: Provision at Cranage Hall and Mary Dendy Hospitals. In Mittler, P. and Gittins, S. (eds) *The Educational Needs of Mentally Handicapped Adults*. Middleton: National Society for Mentally Handicapped Children. (NW Region).

McConkey, R. and Jeffree, D. (1975) Preschool Mentally Handicapped Children. *British Journal of Educational Psychology* 45:307-11.

McKeown, T. and Teruel, J.R. (1971) An Assessment of the Feasibility of Discharge of Patients in Hospitals for the Subnormal. *British Journal of Preventive and Social Medicine* 24:116-19.

McMaster, J. (1973) *Towards an Educational Theory for the Mentally Handicapped*. London: Arnold.

Manpower Services Commission (1977) *Young People and Work* (the Holland Report). London: MSC.

_____ (1978) *Developing Employment and Training Services for Disabled People: An MSC Programme*. London: MSC.

Mansell, J. (1977) Unpublished paper from Students Union. University College, Cardiff.

Marshall, A. (1967) *The Abilities and Attainments of Children Leaving Junior Training Centres*. London: National Association Mental Health.

MIND (1977) *Evidence on Mental Handicap to the Royal Commission on the National Health Service with Regard to Services for Mentally Handicapped People*. London: MIND.

Ministry of Health (1968) *Model of Good Practice for Adult Training Centres*. London: HMSO.

Mittler, P. (ed.) (1973) *Assessment for Learning in the Mentally Handicapped*. Edinburgh: Churchill Livingstone.

_____ (ed.) (1977) *Research to Practice in Mental Retardation* (vol.3: Biomedical Aspects). Baltimore, Maryland: University Park Press.

_____ (1978) Needs of the Under Fives: Comments on Warnock. *Special Education: Forward Trends* 5:12-13.

Mittler, P. and Ward, J. (1970) The Use of the Illinois Test of Psycholinguistic Abilities on English Four Year Old Children; a Normative and Factorial Study. *British Journal of Educational Psychology* 40:43-53.

Mittler, P,. and Gittins, S.G. (1974) (eds) *The Education of Mentally Handicapped Adults*. Manchester: NSMHC.

Mittler, P. and Simon, G. (1978) Building Support for the Mentally Handicapped and their Families. *Health and Social Service Journal* 88: 541-2.

National Development Group for the Mentally Handicapped (1976) *Mental Handicap: Planning Together*. Pamphlet 1. London: DHSS.

_____ (1977) *Mentally Handicapped Children: A Plan for Action*. Pamphlet 2. London: DHSS.

_____ (1977a) *Helping Mentally Handicapped School Leavers*. Pamphlet 3. London: DHSS.

_____ (1977b) *Day Services for Mentally Handicapped Adults*. Pamphlet 5. London: DHSS.

_____ (1978) *Helping Mentally Handicapped People in Hospital*. London: DHSS.

National Society for Mentally Handicapped Children (1977) *STAMINA: Minimum Standards for ESNS schools, ATCs and Residential Homes*. London: NSMHC.

Newson, J., Newson, E. and Barnes, P. (1973) Child-Rearing Practices. In Butcher, H.J. and Pont, H.B. (eds) *Educational Research in Britain* (vol.3). London: University of London Press.

Nesbitt, M. (1976) The Final Years in the Special School. In Kedney, R. and Whelan, E. (1976).

Office of Health Economics (1978) *Mental Handicap: Ways Forward*. London: OHE.

Office of Population Censuses and Surveys (1976) Live births: Age of

Mother. *Population Trends* 4:40.

Office of Population Censuses and Surveys (1979) Nurses and Residential Social Workers Caring for the Mentally Handicapped. Report prepared for the Committee of Enquiry into Nursing and Care of the Mentally Handicapped (Chairman: Mrs. P. Jay). London: HMSO.

Oswin, M. (1977). In MIND (1977).

—— (1978) *Children Living in Long Stay Hospitals.* London: Spastics International Medical Publications and Heinemann.

Pantall, J. (1974) *Training Project for Hospitals for the Mentally Handicapped.* Business School, University of Manchester.

Perkins, E., Taylor, P.D. and Capie, A. (1976) *Helping the Retarded: A Systematic Behavioural Approach.* Kidderminster: Institute of Mental Subnormality.

Personal Social Services Council (1977) *Residential Care Reviewed.* London: PSSC.

Pierse, A. (1973) A Bold Experiment at Bromley. *Special Education* 62: 12-14.

Porterfield, J. (1978) Profoundly Handicapped Adults Can Do Much More: Report of a Research Study. *Teaching and Training* 16:3-10.

Pratt, M.W., Raynes, N.V. and Roses, S. (1977) Organisational Characteristics and their Relationship to the Quality of Care. In Mittler, P. (ed.) *Research to Practice in Mental Retardation* (vol.1). Baltimore, Maryland: University Park Press.

Preddy, D. and Mittler, P. (1979) Characteristics of Children in Special Schools and Hospital Schools for the Mentally Handicapped in North West England. Final Report to Department of Education and Science (in preparation).

Pugh, G. and Russell, P. (1977) *Shared Care: Support Services for Families with Mentally Handicapped Children.* London: National Childrens Bureau.

Race, D.G. and Race, D.M. (1976) Investigation into the Effects of Different Caring Environments on the Social Competence of Mentally Handicapped Adults. Progress Report 2. Department of Applied Statistics, University of Reading.

Reiter, S. and Whelan, E. (1975) Vocational Counselling of Mentally Retarded Young Adults. *British Journal of Guidance and Counselling* 3: 93-106.

Roberts, J.A.F. (1952) The Genetics of Mental Deficiency. *Eugenics Review* 44:71-83.

Rondal, J. (1977) Maternal Speech in Normal and Down's Syndrome Children. In Mittler, P. (ed.) *Research to Practice in Mental Retardation.* Baltimore, Maryland: University Park Press.

Rothschild Report, The (1971) *A Framework for Government Research and Development.* Cmnd. 4814. London: HMSO.

Russell Report, The (1973) *Adult Education — A Plan for Development.* London: HMSO.

Sanders, L. (1974) The First Three Years. In Mittler, P. and Gittens, S.G. (eds) *The Educational Needs of Mentally Handicapped Adults.* Manchester: NSMHC (NW Region).

Shearer, M.S. and Shearer, D. (1972) The Portage Project: A Model For

Early Childhood Education. *Exceptional Children* 39:210-17.

Smith, J., Glossop, G., Hall, J. and Kushlick, A. (1977) A Report on the First Six Months of a Home Teaching Service for Pre-school Handi- capped Children. (The Wessex Portage Project). Winchester: Health Care Evaluation Research Team.

Solly, K. (1975) *A Philosophy of Leisure in Relation to the Retarded*. London: NSMHC.

Spain, B. and Wigley, G. (eds) (1975) *Right from the Start: a Service for Preschool Handicapped Children*. London: NSMHC.

Stedman, D. (1977) Important Considerations in the Review and Evalua-- tion of Educational Intervention Programs. In Mittler, P. (ed.) *Research to Practice in Mental Retardation* (vol.1). Baltimore, Maryland: University Park Press.

Stein, Z. and Susser, M. (1963) The Social Distribution of Mental Retarda- tion. *American Journal of Mental Deficiency* 67:811-21.

Stevens, M. (1976) *The Educational and Social Needs of Children with Severe Handicap* (2nd edn.). London: Edward Arnold.

_____ (1978) *Observe — then Teach* (2nd edn.). London: Edward Arnold.

Stuart, F. (1975) *Recreation for the Retarded: a Handbook for Leaders*. London: NSMHC.

Swann, W. and Mittler, P. (1976) A Survey of Language Abilities in ESNS Children. *Special Education: Forward Trends* 3:24-7.

Sykes, P. (1977). In MIND (1977).

Thomas, D., Firth, H. and Kendall, A. (1978) *ENCOR — A Way Ahead*. London: Campaign for the Mentally Handicapped.

Tizard, B. (1975) *Early Childhood Education: A Review and Discussion of Current Research in Britain*. Windsor: NFER.

Tizard, J. (1964) *Community Services for the Mentally Handicapped*. Oxford: Oxford University Press.

Tuckey, L., Parfitt, J. and Tuckey, B. (1973) *Handicapped School Leavers: Their Further Education, Training and Employment*. London: National Childrens Bureau; Windsor: NFER.

Tyne, A. (1977) *Residential Provision for Adults who are Mentally Handicapped*. London: Campaign for the Mentally Handicapped.

_____ (1978) *Looking at Life in a Hospital, Hostel, Home or Unit*. London: Campaign for the Mentally Handicapped.

Verbraak, P. (1975) A New Prevalence Figure for Mental Retardation in the Netherlands. In Primrose, D. (ed.) *Proceedings of Third Congress of the International Association for the Scientific Study of Mental Deficiency*. Warsaw: Polish Medical Publishers.

Vernon, P.E. (ed.) (1957) *Secondary School Selection*. London: British Psychological Society.

Wedge, P. and Prosser, H. (1973) *Born to Fail?* London: National Childrens Bureau.

Welsh Office (1978) *Standards of Care for Mentally Ill and Mentally Handicapped Patients in Hospital*. A Report of a Working Party to the Secretary of State for Wales. Cardiff: Welsh Office.

Whelan, E. and Speake, B. (1977) *Adult Training Centres in England and Wales: Report of the First National Survey*. Manchester: National

Association of Teachers of the Mentally Handicapped and Hester Adrian Research Centre, University of Manchester.

Williams, P. and Gruber, E. (1967) *Response to Special Schooling*. London: Longmans.

Wolfensberger, W. and Glenn, L. (1975) *Program Analysis of Service Systems* (3rd edn.). Handbook. Toronto: National Institute on Mental Retardation.

World Health Organisation (1968) *Organisation of Services for the Mentally Retarded*. Technical Report Series 392. Geneva: WHO.

Wynne Griffiths, G. (1973) The Prevention of Down's Syndrome (Mongolism). *Health Trends* 5:59-60.

Zigler, E. and Balla, D. (1977) The Social Policy Implications of a Research Program on the Effects of Institutionalisation on Retarded Persons. In Mittler, P. (ed.) *Research to Practice in Mental Retardation* (vol.1). Baltimore, Maryland: University Park Press.

INDEX

AAMD classification, 33-7
accountability, 4-7
accreditation, 5, 169-70
Accreditation Council for Services for the Mentally Retarded, 5, 170
acquired mental handicap, 54
adaptive behaviour scales, 34-6
adolescent assessment unit, 121
adult education, 117-20
adult experiences, the need for, 106-8
Adult Literacy programmes, 139
Adult Training Centres
  change of name to Social Education Centres, 128
  first national survey of, 128
  and Further Education staff, 118
  and Government policy, 127-8
  isolation of staff in, 125-6
  'model of good practice' for, 128, 141, 145
  number of places in, 15-17, 125, 127
  and school leavers, 111, 114
  and staff training, 126-7
  and training for work, 107-8
  See also Social Education Centres
Adult Training Centres in England and Wales, 128
advocacy, 3
'alternative living units', 163
American Association on Mental Deficiency, 33
amniocentesis, 58-9
Anderson, E., 99
Andrews, R., 170
antenatal services, 54
Apte, R., 166
Area Health Authorites, 13, 17
assessment
  of adolescents, 121
  comprehensive, 61-2

assessment, cont.,
  by parents, 11, 67
  of school leavers, 111, 113-15
  by teachers, 92
assessment charts, 73, 150
assessment scale, an, 82-3
Australia, 170
Austria, 59

Balla, D., 184, 185
Baranyay, E., 117
Barnes, P., 48
Bayley, M., 43
BBC, the, 139
Begab, M., 30
Behaviour Assessment Battery, 73
behaviour modification, 150
behaviourist approach to mental handicap, 37-8
Belmont, J., 81
Bernstein, B., 46
Berry, P., 170
Better Services for the Mentally Handicapped (White Paper 1971)
  community hospitals, 173
  principles, 8-9
  service targets, 6, 127, 154, 195
  severe mental handicap, 48-50
  suggested revision of, 52
Bijou, S., 37-8
Birch, H.G., 47
Bland, G., 81
Blunden, R., 60, 218, 219
boarding houses, 172-3
Board of Control, Ministry of Health, 177
British Institute for Mental Handicap, 208, 213, 214
British Psychological Society, 32
Bronfenbrenner, U., 47

Browne, R.A., 180
Butler, N., 55, 223

Campaign for the Mentally
     Handicapped, 99, 167, 174
Camphill communities, 172
Capie, A., 150
Careers Officers, 114
Carr, J., 47, 60
Castle, Barbara, 179
Castle Priory College, 208, 214
Castell, J.H.F., 32
Central Council for Education and
     Training in Social Work, 86, 126,
     199, 202
Centre of Environment for the
     Handicapped, 171, 173
Certificate in Social Service, 126, 140,
     210
Chartered Institute of Public Finance
     and Accountancy, 7
'Cherries' project, the, 171
Cheyne, W., 70
Child Development Centres, 63, 194
children, development of, 67-8
children, in ESNS schools,
     abilities and disabilities of, 82-3
     clinical characteristics of, 80-2
     numbers of, 79-80
civil rights, 2-3
Clark, D., 23n, 29
Clarke, A.D.B., 26, 90, 150, 188
Clarke, A.M., 26, 32, 90, 150, 188
Clarke, M., 70
classification systems, 30-8
Cobb, H.V., 113
Committee of Inquiry into Nursing and
     Care, 217
community care, 159-65
Community Health Councils, 13
community hospitals, 173-4
Community Mental Handicap Teams,
     63
comprehensive assessment, 61-2
continuing education, 103-5
Cooper, V., 148
Cope, C., 99
Cottage and Rural Enterprises, 172
Court Report on Child Health Services,
     the, 55, 59, 63, 194
Cowie, V.A., 52
Craft, A., 107
Craft, M., 107
creative activities, 95-6

crisis periods, 156-8
criteria, for defining mental handicap,
     intellectual abilities, 22-30
     social competence, 20-2
Crossman, Richard, 4, 177
Cunningham, C.C., 11, 61, 73, 79, 87,
     89

Davie, R., 45, 54
Day Committee, 50
*Day Services for Mentally Handicapped
     Adults*, 128, 141
Department of Education and Science
     curriculum, 89
     design of schools, 84
     responsibility of for mentally
          handicapped, 76
     school leaving age, 115
     special classes for ESNS children, 99
     teacher training, 87
Department of the Environment, 162
Department of Health and Social
     Security
     planning guidelines, 157
     priorities of, 17
     statistics of, 7, 172, 182
     terminology, 31
'developmental disability', 31
Development Team for the Mentally
     Handicapped
     District Handicap Teams, 63
     severely handicapped, 50
     hospital services, 185, 191, 195
     purpose of, 4
Diploma in the Training of Mentally
     Handicapped Adults, 126, 140
Disabled Living Foundation, 120
Disablement Resettlements Officer, 121
Distar, 95
District Handicap Teams, 62-5
Douglas, J.W.B., 21
Down's Syndrome
     clinical characteristics of, 80-1
     numbers with, 41, 52-4
     screening for, 58-9
     and social class, 47
Duncan, S.B., 59

Early, R., 117
early education, *see under* education
early help, 57-8
early identification, 60-1
early services, 62-8

education, of the mentally handicapped,
aims of, 75-6
and adults, 117-20
continuing, 103-5
early forms of, 68-73
preschool, 64-5
problems of, 77-9
in schools, *see under* Educationally
Subnormal Mild/Severe Schools
See also Adult Training centres,
Social Education Centres
Education Act (1976), 3, 97
Educationally Subnormal-Mild Schools,
24-5
Educationally Subnormal-Severe
Schools
children in, *see* children in ESNS
schools
curriculum of, 88-90
and integration, 96-100
numbers, design and organization of,
83-5
nursery units in, 71
and reading, 119
teachers in, 85-8
teaching methods in, 91-4
Elkins, J., 170
Elliott, J., 188
Ely Hospital, Committee of Enquiry, 4,
117
employment, 107, 134-5, 147-8
encephalitis, 54
ENCOR, 163

*Facilities and Services of Mental Illness
and Mental Handicap Hospitals in
England and Wales*, 7
families
adjustment of to handicapped child,
64
and crisis periods, 156-8
and housing, 153-6
involvement of, 11-12
and school leavers, 110
and Social Education Centres, 145-6
family planning, 54
Felce, D., 217
First Words Learning Programme, 95
Firth, H., 163
Fogelman, K.R., 46
fostering, 155
Foxen, T., 210
*Framework for Government Research
and Development, A*, x

France, 59
Friedlander, B.Z., 95
Fryers, T., 42
further education, 117-20, 139-41

Gateway Clubs, 120
General Nursing Council, 202
genetic counselling, 54, 59
German measles, 54, 59
Gittins, S.G., 117
'glass wall' problem, the, 96
Glenn, L., 217
Gloucester Centre, the, 174
Goal, 95
Goldstein, H., 45, 55
Grant, G., 108
Greengross, W., 107
Grossman, H., 34, 36
group homes, 170-1
Gruber, E., 25
Gunzburg, H.C., 82, 109, 150

Half-way Houses, 166
Hargrove, A., 20
Health Care Evaluation Research Team,
73, 217
Health Care Planning Teams, 13
Hester Adrian Research Centre, ix, 73,
210
Hewson, S., 73
Highlights, 203
Holland Report, the, 122
Home Farm Trust, 172
home teaching, 72-3
Honeylands Unit, 65, 155
Hospital Advisory Service, 4, 177
hospital residents, 14-15, 16, 50-1
hospital schools, 81-2
hospitals
aims of, 190-95
as a community resource, 193-5
discharging from, 195-8
historical background of, 176-80
as homes, 182-5
as learning environments, 185-90
numbers in, 180-1
and specialist services, 190-3
tasks of, 181-2
and training for work, 188-90
hostels
alternatives to, 170-4
characteristics of people in, 165
guidelines for, 166-70
numbers and type of, 162-4

housing
    for the family, 153-6
    for the individual, 152-3
    local attitudes to, 159-60
Housing Act (1977), 162
Housing Association grants, 162
Huckman, D., 148
Hughes, J.M., 82, 84

incapacities associated with mental
        handicap, 49 tab.
incidental learning, 90
Index of Informative Speech, 185
'industrial therapy units', 189
infant mortality rates, 42, 53
in-service training, 100, 210
integration, at school age, 96-100
intelligence tests, 22-30
International Classification of Diseases,
        36-7
Inventory of Vocational Interests, 108
IQ, 22-30, 32, 112-13

Jackson, S., 128
Jamieson, M., 99
Jay Committee, the,
        hostels, 51, 165
        hospitals, 180
        staff training, 199, 217
Jeffree, D.M., 71, 73, 95
Jim's People, 95
Job Creation Scheme, 136
Joint Care Planning Teams, 12, 13, 17,
        113
Joint Consultative Committees, 12, 13,
        113, 206
joint financing, 13-14, 128, 146, 154
joint services, planning, 12-15
Jones, K., 176
Jones, M.C., 73
Jordan R., 73
Junior Training Centres, 79, 85, 112

Kedney, R., 117
Kellett, B., 88, 138
Kendall, A., 163
Kiernan, C.C., 73, 94
King, R.D., 184
King's Fund Centre, 117, 205
Kushlick, A., 6, 60, 169, 217

language abilities, of the mentally
        handicapped, 71, 82, 83, 106, 138

language and communication teaching,
        94-5
L'Arche communities, 172
learning difficulties, 25
Leeming, K., 48, 71, 78, 83, 89, 94, 95
Let Me Play, 73
Let Me Speak, 73
Let's Go, 139
Lewis, E.D., 53
local authorities
        ATCs, 127
        education, 98, 117
        hospital residents, 196-7
        NHS, 12-13, 52
        residential accommodation, 154,
            162-3
        Special Care Units, 157
local community organizations, 160-1
lodgings, 172-3
Looking at Life, 160, 166
Lowman, P., 136-7, 148

McAllister, M., 118
McBrien, J., 210
McConkey, R., 71, 73, 95
McKeown, T., 180
McMaster, J., 87
Manpower Services Commission, 121,
        122, 148
Mansell, J., 171
Marshall, A., 106, 112
maternal malnutrition, 54
meningitis, 54
'mental deficiency', 30
Mental Deficiency Acts, 32
mental handicap
        attitudes to, 19, 159-60
        certification of, 19
        definition of, 19-20
        and discrimination, 3
        and environment, 53-5
        mild, *see under* mild mental handicap
        prevalence of, 52-5
        severe, *see under* severe mental
            handicap
Mental Handicap in England and Wales
        Applied Research Unit, 218
Mental Health Act (1959), 23, 31-3, 177
mental illness, 1, 159
'mental retardation', 30, 33-4
'mental subnormality', 30-1
mild mental handicap
        prevalence of, 43-5
        and social disadvantage, 45-7

MIND, 178-9
'mini-learning experiment', 92
minimum standards, 6, 182
Ministry of Health, 177
misdiagnosis, 22
Mittler, P., 23, 32, 47, 48, 54, 63, 71, 83, 96, 106, 114, 117
mongolism, *see* Down's Syndrome
Morgan, M., 51, 165
multiple handicap, 81

'Named Person', 64, 114
National Association of Mental Health, 85-6
National Association of Teachers of the Mentally Handicapped, 128, 140
National Child Development Study, 45, 46
National Children's Bureau, 104, 203
National Development Group for the Mentally Handicapped
    description of, ix-x
    examination of evaluation systems, 170
    national guidelines, 218
    pamphlets on
        ATCs/SECs, 105, 141-51
        day services, 128, 141, 217
        school leavers, 113
    proposals for
        Community Mental Handicap Teams, 63
        integration of severely handicapped, 85
    report on hospitals, 178, 181, 182, 217
National Foundation for Educational Research, 99
national guidelines, 217, 218
National Health Service
    joint planning, 12-13, 52
    hospitals, 177-8, 190-1
    residential accommodation, 163-4
National Institute for Mental Retardation, 170
National Society for Mentally Handicapped Children, 4, 14, 141, 148, 162
Nesbitt, M., 107, 115, 116
Newson, E., 48
Newson, J., 48
non-accidental injury, 43
North America, 5, 31, 77, 169
numbers, of mentally handicapped, 52-5
nursery schools, 70

Oaklands School, Isleworth, 117
Office of Health Economics, 41
Office of Population Censuses and Surveys, 50, 51, 165
ordinary services, 9-11
Oswin, M., 190-1

'packages', 217-18
Palmer, J., 217
Pantall, J., 205
parental involvement, 47, 71, 72, 139
Parental Involvement Project, 71, 73
parents' needs, 65-7
parents' societies, 171
Parent Workshops, 73
Parfitt, J., 104
Park Lane Further Education College, Leeds, 118
Pathway Experiment, 148
Peabody Language Development Kit, 95
Partlett, M., 99
peripatetic teaching, 72
peripatetic hospital services, 194
Perkins, E., 150
Personal Social Services Council, 4, 169
Peter Bedford Trust, 172
phenylektonuria, 58
physical handicap, 20
Pierse, A., 99
Plans and provisions for residential and day places 1969-91, 16 tab.
play, 95
playgroups, 69-70
Pocklington, K., 99
Porterfield, J., 218
Pratt, M.W., 184
Preddy, D., 114
'pre-discharge hostels', 164
preschool children, 47, 64-5
Preschool Play Groups Association, 70
primary prevention, 58-9
principles, 8-9, 100-2
Priorities for Health and Personal Social Services in England, 17, 127
private homes, 172
professional attitudes to mental handicap, viii
professional practice, standards of, 216
Programme Analysis of Service Systems, 170, 217
'programme audits', 169
Progress Assessment Charts, 82, 150
Progress Evaluation Indices, 150

Prosser, H., 46
psychiatrists, 192-3
public attitudes to mental handicap, viii, 1-2, 159-60
Pugh, G., 65, 155
pyramid training, 212-15

Race, D.G., 171
Race, D.M., 171
Ravenswood, 172
Raynes, N.V., 184
rehabilitation, 188-90
Reiter, S., 108
Report of the Royal Commission on the Law Relating to Mental Illness and Mental Deficiency, 31
residential accommodation, 154-74
Residential Care Reviewed, 4-5, 169
Revised Resident Management Practices Scale, 185
Revised Stanford Binet test, 29
reward training, 93
rhesus incompatibility, 54, 59
Riach, J., 70
risk registers, 54
Robers, J.A.F., 47
Rondal, J., 48
Roses, S., 184
Rothschild Report, the, x
Royal College of Psychiatrists, 31
Royal Commission on the Health Service, 180
Royal Medico-Psychological Association, *see* Royal College of Psychiatrists
rubella, *see* German Measles
Russell, P., 65, 155
Russell Report on Adult Education, the, 104

Sanders, L., 118
Saunders, C., 73
school leavers
    abilities of, 111-13
    and adult experiences, 106-8
    and changes in environment, 108-9
    crisis periods for, 156-7
    educational needs of, 105-6
    existing and proposed services for, 110-22
    families of, 110-12
    and severity of handicap, 122-3
school leaving age, 116
school records, 81

Schools Council survey of language abilities, 47, 70, 83
Scott Report, the, 86
Seebohm Report, the, 126, 178
self-fulfilling prophecy, 21
self-help groups, 69
senior schools, 116-17
'sense training', 90
service agencies, 211
services, *see* ordinary *and* special services
service targets, 6
severe mental handicap
    prevalence of, 41-3
    and school leavers, 122-3, 157
    and social class, 47-8
    specific abilities and disabilities of those with, 48-52
severe subnormality, defined, 31
sexuality, 107
Shearer, D., 72
Shearer, M.S., 72
Sheffield Development Project, 165, 173
sheltered employment, 121-2, 134
Short-term Residential Care, 181
sign languages, 94, 138
Simon, G., 63
Sloper, P., 61, 73
Smith, J., 73, 217
smoking, in pregnancy, 54
social class
    and educational achievement, 46
    and language codes, 48
    and prevalency of mental handicap, 43
    and reproductive complications, 55
    and use of services, 59
social competence, 20-2
Social Education Centres
    and admission and assessment, 144-5
    and advanced work, 146-9
    basic information on, 128-35
    and the community, 142-3
    and families, 143-4
    and hospitals, 190
    isolation of, 134, 147
    and social education, 137-41
    and special care, 145-6
    students in
        abilities and disabilities of, 131-4
        age of, 129-30
        prospects for, 134-5
    and training methods, 149-51
    and work training, 135-7

Social Service Departments, 126, 136, 168, 178-9
Social Service Training officers, 205
social skills training, 187-8
Society for Mentally Handicapped Children, 61
Solly, K., 120
Spain, B., 60
Spastics Society, 14, 61, 214
Speake, B., 44, 128, 132-5, 136
Special Care Units, 84-5, 112, 127-8, 146, 157
Special Education Advisory and Support Service, 219
Special Education Research Group, 202
Special Education Staff College, 202-4
special schools, 70-2, 115-16
special services, 9-10
specialist services, 190-3
sports, 119-20
staff training
  and adult education resources, 205-7
  college for, 202-4, 208
  as a continuous process, 216-19
  at local level, 204-7
  a national plan for, 201-2
  obstacles to, 200-1
  put into practice, 208-12
  'pyramid' method, 212-15
  and the trainers, 207-8
  and travelling teams, 213
STAMINA documents, 4
standard deviation units, 32
'Standards for community agencies serving persons with mental retardation and other developmental disabilities', 170
'Standards for Services for Developmentally Disabled Individuals', 170, 217
'stateless resident', 197
statutory agencies, 161-2
Stedman, D., 47
Stein, Z., 45
Stevens, M., 86, 87, 95
Struthers, M., 128
Stuart, F., 120
subnormality, defined, 31
Susser, M., 45
Swann, W., 48, 71, 83, 106
Sykes, P., 180
systematic teaching, 138-9, 150

targets for 1991, 15-17
Taylor, P.D., 150
Teachers' Centres, 88, 205, 206
teachers, in ESNS schools, 85-8
teacher training, 87, 88, 99
teaching methods, 91-5
terminology, 30-1
Teruel, J.R., 180
Thomas, D., 163
Tizard, B., 47, 53
Tizard, J., 184
Terman Merrill test, *see* Revised Stanford Binet test
Toy Library movement, 69
training, residents in hospital, 185-8
training staff, *see* staff training
Training Council for Teachers of the Mentally Handicapped, 86, 126
Training Project Officers, 205
Tuckey, B., 104
Tuckey, L., 104
Tyne, A., 51, 160, 163, 164, 166, 167-8, 171

underexpectation, 107-8
'under-functioning', 76
United Nations Declaration of the Rights of Disabled People, 2
USA, 77

'verbal reasoning tests', 24
Verbraak, P., 42
Vernon, P.E., 24
villages, 171-2
voluntary organizations, 160-1

Ward, J., 47
Warnock Committee Report, the
  ATCs, 140
  further education, 117
  integration in education, 98-9
  preschool education, 47, 64, 69, 70, 72
  school education, 77-8
  school leavers, 113, 114, 116
  staff training, 199, 202, 206, 219
  teacher training, 87, 88, 99
Way Forward, The, 17, 127, 156
Wechsler Intelligence Scales, 29
Wedge, P., 46
Welsh Office, 217
Wessex experiment, the, 165, 186, 217
Wessex Health Care Evaluation Research Team, 169, 217

Westhill College, Birmingham, 87
Whelan, E., 44, 108, 117, 128, 132-5, 136, 188
When the Bough Bends, 65
White Paper 1971, *see* Better Services for the Mentally Handicapped
Wigley, G., 60

Williams, P., 25
Wolfensberger, W., 170, 217
World Health Organization, 36, 44
Wynne Griffiths, G., 54

Young People and Work, 122

Zigler, E., 184, 185

eople not pe